THE CATHOLIC UNIVERSITY OF AMERICA
CANON LAW STUDIES
No. 210

Constitutions for Diocesan Courts

A HISTORICAL SYNOPSIS AND COMMENTARY

BY

William E. Vaughan, J.C.L.
Priest of the Diocese of Salt Lake

A DISSERTATION

Submitted to the Faculty of the School of Canon Law of the Catholic University of America in Partial Fulfillment of the Requirements for the Degree of Doctor of Canon Law

THE CATHOLIC UNIVERSITY OF AMERICA PRESS
WASHINGTON, D. C.
1944

Nihil Obstat:
LUDOVICUS MOTRY, S.T.D., J.C.D.,
Censor Deputatus.

Imprimatur:
✠ DUBANUS G. HUNT, D.D., LL.D.,
Episcopus Lacus Salsi.

In urbe Lacus Salsi, Utah, 5 maii, 1944.

Printed by
THE MESSENGER PRESS
Carthagena, Ohio

To

My Father and Mother

TABLE OF CONTENTS

FOREWORD ix

CHAPTER I

HISTORICAL INTRODUCTION 1

CHAPTER II

THE NATURE, VALUE AND SOURCES OF A CONSTITUTION FOR DIOCESAN COURTS 7

CHAPTER III

THE ORGANIZATION OF THE COURT 19

Article 1. The Introductory Rules 19
Article 2. The Officers of the Court Roster 22
Article 3. Rules for the Roster 43
Article 4. Rules of the *Turnus* 46

CHAPTER IV

REGULATIONS ON EQUIPMENT, TIME, PLACE, CONDUCT AND REPORTS 48

Article 1. Equipment of the Diocesan Court 48
Article 2. Regulations on Time 53
Article 3. Regulations on Place 55
Article 4. Regulations on Conduct in Court 55
Article 5. Annual Reports 56

CHAPTER V

THE PARTIES, THEIR PROCURATORS AND THEIR ADVOCATES 57

CHAPTER VI

JUDICIAL PROCEDURE 61

ARTICLE 1. THE PRELIMINARY RECEPTION OF CAUSES 61

A. The Pre-*Libellus* Consultation 61
B. From the Reception of the *Libellus* to the First Session 67

ARTICLE 2. THE ACTS 70
ARTICLE 3. SESSIONS AND DECREES 75
ARTICLE 4. THE SESSION FOR CONSIDERING THE *Libellus* 77
ARTICLE 5. THE SESSION FOR THE JOINDER OF ISSUE 82
ARTICLE 6. JUDICIAL EXAMINATIONS IN GENERAL 84
ARTICLE 7. THE SESSION FOR THE JUDICIAL EXAMINATION OF THE PARTIES 88
ARTICLE 8. THE SESSION FOR THE JUDICIAL EXAMINATION OF WITNESSES 89
ARTICLE 8. THE SESSION FOR THE JUDICIAL EXAMINATION OF EXPERTS 91
ARTICLE 10. COMMISSIONS 94
ARTICLE 11. THE SESSION FOR CONSIDERING DOCUMENTS, PRESUMPTIONS AND INDICATIONS 102
ARTICLE 12. PUBLICATION OF THE ACTS; *Conclusio in Causa;* THE DISCUSSION 105
ARTICLE 13. THE SESSION FOR THE SENTENCE 108

CHAPTER VII

APPEALS 112

CHAPTER VIII

UNUSUAL CAUSES 117

ARTICLE 1. CRIMINAL CAUSES 117
ARTICLE 2. ROMAN CAUSES 121

CHAPTER IX

INFORMAL CASES 123

ARTICLE 1. GENERAL RULES 123
ARTICLE 2. THE ADMINISTRATIVE PROCEDURE OF LACK OF FORM CASES 126
ARTICLE 3. THE SUMMARY PROCEDURE OF CANON 1990 129
ARTICLE 4. PAULINE PRIVILEGE CASES 133
ARTICLE 5. CASES INVOLVING PROOF OF DEATH 135

CHAPTER X

JUDICIAL EXPENSES 139

APPENDIX

TENTATIVE CONSTITUTION 143

CONCLUSIONS 178

BIBLIOGRAPHY 179

ABBREVIATIONS 185

ALPHABETICAL INDEX 187

BIOGRAPHICAL NOTE 199

CANON LAW STUDIES 201

FOREWORD

HOLY Mother Church, with consummate wisdom, has ever directed the energy of her millions of beloved children by universal legislation. But mindful of the wonderful diversity among them she has also at all times encouraged local legislation for its inspirational and practical guidance. The bishop to her is a divinely constituted legislator directing the activities of his diocese. In the field of procedure may be found an excellent example of this cooperation. Many universal laws direct procedure in formal trials. But local conditions and circumstances require regulations, and this becomes the responsibility of the bishop. A constitution for the diocesan court is then nothing more than the ordinary's authoritative directions for the judicial department of his diocese.

The aim of this dissertation on the constitution for the diocesan court is naturally not legislation itself but suggestions and background for legislation. Briefly it considers what the universal lawmaker leaves to the disposition of the local legislator in procedural work. Naturally the scope is vast because the term "constitution" in this work includes not only fundamental law but also detailed rules of court and norms for even minor activities. The suggestions given can be neither exhaustive nor undisputed.

The early pages give a short history of this legislation. This is followed by a consideration of the full purpose and the timeliness of constitutions for local courts. The greater portion of the work deals with possible material for laws. Finally there is presented a tentative set of rules to assist, more by outline than by detail, in the formation of individual diocesan constitutions.

The model of the tentative rules and possibly the main source of the material for the suggestions is the constitution or *normae* of the Sacred Roman Rota. Parallel law and general principles of procedure furnish many more suggestions, as do writers in particular fields. Because the work is primarily for American courts, authors cognizant of conditions in America are quoted where possible. Finally a limited survey of customs in representative dioceses, large and small, revealed important trends. Universal legislation is repeated on occasions especially where this is necessary to present an orderly continuity.

The writer takes this occasion to express his gratitude and appreciation to the Most Reverend Duane G. Hunt, Bishop of Salt Lake, and to the Most Reverend James E. Kearney, former Bishop of Salt Lake and now the Ordinary of Rochester, for their assistance and encouragement, to individual priests of the Archdioceses of New York, Boston, Chicago, Montreal and Quebec and of the Dioceses of Cleveland, Rochester, Kansas City and Salt Lake for much helpful cooperation, to the Faculty of the School of Canon Law of The Catholic University of America for considerate guidance and to many friends for their constant encouragement in the preparation of this dissertation.

CHAPTER I

HISTORICAL INTRODUCTION

1. The ecclesiastical court made a quiet beginning in apostolic times[1] and gradually developed under both internal and external pressure through the early Christian centuries. At the time of its recognition by the empire solemnities and formalities however were few and strictly practical. The decree of recognition by Emperor Constantine, a miniature constitution in itself, laid an extended framework for uninterrupted growth of judicial procedure that parallels the advance of procedure in civil courts.[2] The accumulated and sifted regulations of the next thousand years are preserved in the *Corpus Iuris Canonici.*[3] The Council of Trent instituted a reform in diocesan courts by withdrawing all matrimonial and criminal causes from the deacons, archdeacons and other persons inferior to the bishop,[4] but the subsequent two hundred years witnessed an infiltration of laxity and even corruption.[5] The advent of Pope Benedict XIV marked the beginning of two centuries of

1. Mt. XVIII, 15-16; I Cor. VI, 1-3; Tit. III, 2-9; *Didascalia,* II, 22-23 — Funk, *Didascalia et Constitutiones Apostolorum* (2 Vols. Paderborn, 1905) I, pp. 84-114.
2. 35th Title, *De Episcopali Iudicio et de Diversis Negotiis,* of the *Constitutio Sirmondiana I, Theodosiani Libri XVI* (ed. Mommsen-Meyer, 3 vols., Berolini, 1905), II, 142-152.
3. Cf. especially the second part of the Decretals of Gratian; the second book of the Decretals of Pope Gregory IX and the second books of the Liber Sextus of Pope Boniface VIII and of the Clementine.
4. *Conc. Trident.,* sess. XXIV, *de ref. matrim.,* c. 20.
5. Cf. Benedictus XIV, ep. encycl., *"Matrimonii,"* 11 apr. 1741, *Introductio — Codicis Iuris Canonici Fontes cura Emi. Petri Card. Gasparri Editi* (9 vols. Romae [postea Civitate Vaticana]: Typis Polyglottis Vaticanis, 1923-39. Vols. VII-IX *ed. cura et studio Emi. Iustiniani Card. Seredi*), n. 307; (hereafter this work will be cited *Fontes.*); Benedictus XIV, ep. encycl., *"Quamvis Paternae,"* 26 aug. 1741, ¶ 1 — *Fontes,* n. 315; Benedictus XIV, const., *"Dei miseratione,"* 3 nov. 1741, ¶¶1-3 — *Fontes,* n. 318.

distinctly diocesan court legislation that has gradually made of the diocesan court an instrument of outstanding efficiency. This great canonist himself issued a most important document of reform, the Benedictine Constitution, *Dei miseratione*, in 1741. The instruction of the Sacred Congregation of the Council of 1840[6] and two similar works issued in 1883, one by the Holy Office and the other by the Sacred Congregation for the Propagation of the Faith,[7] concentrated on procedure in marriage causes while three other great instructions published by the congregations in 1878 (by the Sacred Congregation for the Propagation of the Faith), 1880 (by the Sacred Congregation of Bishops and Regulars) and 1883 (by the Sacred Congregation for the Propagation of the Faith) set forth rules on procedure in criminal causes.[8] This constant zeal of the Holy See for efficiency and perfection in judicial procedure culminated in the reform of the Roman tribunals under Pope Pius X and in the extension of many improvements of this reform to the diocesan courts in the Code of 1918. The solicitude of the supreme authority in the Church that the high standard set by the Code be observed throughout the world has not lessened in recent years but continues to be manifest especially in such masterful instructions as those of 1923, of 1931 and of 1936.[9]

2. Throughout the centuries there has been a background of local legislation on judicial procedure, most of which naturally has not been preserved. The limited sphere of the authority of such legislation prevented its widespread dissemination and consequent

6. S.C.C., instr., *"Cum moneat glossa,"* 22 aug. 1840 — *Fontes*, n. 4069.
7. S.C.S. Off., instr. (*ad ep. Rituum Orient.*), a. 1883 — *Fontes*, n. 1076; S.C. de Prop. Fide, instr., *"Causae matrimoniales,"* a. 1883 — *Fontes*, n. 4901.
8. S.C. de Prop. Fide, instr., *"Quamvis,"* 20 iul. 1878; S.C. Ep. et Reg., instr., 11 iun. 1880 — *Fontes*, n. 2005; S.C. Prop. Fide, instr., a. 1883 — *Fontes*, n. 4900.
9. S.C. Sacr., instr., 7 maii 1923 — *Acta Apostolicae Sedis*, Comment-Officiale (Romae, 1909- —), XV (1923), 389. (Henceforth this publication will be cited *AAS* and the Instruction of May 7, 1923 will be referred to as *Instructio a.* 1923); S.C. Sacr., instr., 9 iun. 1931 — *AAS*, XXIII (1931), 457 (henceforth cited *Instructio a.* 1931); S.C. Sacr., instr., 15 aug. 1936 — *AAS*, XXVIII (1936), 313 (henceforth cited *Instructio a.* 1936).

acknowledgment so that even Cardinal Gasparri's footnotes of the Code trace universally accepted legislation back only to the first appearance of explicitly enacted worldwide law. Many individual institutes however made their beginnings in diocesan courts, as specialized historical research on these subjects reveals. Thus the office of the present day *officialis* is a result of experiments in the local ecclesiastical courts of France.[10] Also through the centuries instructions by ordinaries to their delegates and representatives have set forth local legislation, which were, so to speak, the beginnings of diocesan constitutions.[11]

3. However it seems that no complete instruction or constitution by local ecclesiastical authorities on judicial procedure, in the sense considered in this dissertation, was written, or at least preserved, until the monumental Austrian Instruction of 1855.[12] Drawn up and promulgated for his archdiocese by the greatest ecclesiastical power of Austria during the second half of the nineteenth century and the Father of the Austrian Concordat of August 18, 1855, Joseph Cardinal Rauscher (1797-1875), Prince-Archbishop of Vienna, this masterful local constitution was approved by the Holy See *"in forma ordinaria"* for all Austria and subsequently exercised great influence on local courts throughout the world and on universal legislation. The Third Council of Baltimore

10. "Les officiaux sont une resultate necessaire de l'evolution des institutions diocesaines... a partie de XIe siecle... L'official a ete surtout une institution francaise." — Edouard Fournier, *Les Origines du Vicaire General,* (Paris: Auguste Picard, 1922), pp. 63, 62, 70; cf. also Bassibey, *Le Mariage devant les Tribuneaux Ecclesiastiques,* (Paris: Librairie Religieuse H. Oudin, 1899), nn. 4, 28.
11. Thus Bishop Pierre d'Orgemont (1384-1393) of Paris gave an instruction to his vicars general for the period of his visitation to Rome and the paragraph *"In judicio"* contains his detailed delegations and rules for procedure in judicial affairs — preserved in a pamphlet by Edouard Fournier entitled *Le Vicaire General au Moyen-age,* (Paris: Chez L'Auteur, 1923), pp. 10-15.
12. *Instructio Austriaca Josephi Cardinalis Rauscher,* 4 maii 1855 — *Analecta Iuris Pontificii,* Romae, (1855-1868; Paris, 1869-1891), II (1857), 2546-2565 (henceforth referred to as the Austrian Instruction).

recommended it to the bishops of America[13] and its influence is discernible in the instructions of the Sacred Congregation for the Propagation of the Faith of 1878 on criminal procedure[14] and of 1883 on procedure in matrimonial causes, which begins with a verbal quotation of ¶¶ 95 and 96 of Cardinal Rauscher's work.[15] The instruction of 1878 incorporates especially the Cardinal's employment of collegiate commissions for gathering evidence, possibly one of the forerunners of the present obligatory collegiate tribunal for certain criminal causes.[16] The Austrian Constitution is noted for its instruction on the evaluation of testimony and in this especially it had a marked influence on the reform of the Tribunals of the Holy See.[17] The Sacred Roman Rota on several occasions has quoted Cardinal Rauscher *verbatim* in giving reasons for its interpretations of testimony[18] and it is said that from this work "a good deal of the jurisprudence of the S. Roman Rota has been deduced."[19] The influence of the Austrian Constitution continues through the legislation of the Code and is seen again in the Instruction of 1936.[20]

While most of this celebrated work of a local legislation is now universal law, nevertheless it contains some material that continues as local legislation and therefore may be a source of suggestions for diocesan court constitutions. For instance, ¶¶ 133-138 deal with attempted reconciliations; ¶¶ 141-142 with preliminary investigation of causes and ¶ 214 with the delegation of a commission for gather-

13. *Acta et Decreta Plenarii Baltimorensis Tertii A.D. MDCCCLXXXIV*, (Baltimore: John Murphy & Co., 1886), nn. 304-305; Smith, *Elements of Ecclesiastical Law*, Vol. II, *Ecclesiastical Trials*, (5. ed., New York: Benziger Bros., 1892), p. 375.
14. Compare ¶¶ 97-99 of the Austrian Instruction with the early paragraphs of the Instruction, *"Quamvis,"* of July 20, 1878.
15. S.C. Prop. Fide, instr., *"Causae matrimoniales,"* a. 1883 — *Fontes*, n. 4901.
16. C. 1576 § 1.
17. Doheny, *Canonical Procedure in Matrimonial Cases*, (Milwaukee: Bruce Publishing Co., 1938), pp. 213 and 221 (hereafter cited *Canonical Procedure.*)
18. Thus *S. Romanae Rotae Decisiones*, (Romae: Typis Vaticanis, 1912-—), IV (1912), p. 42 quotes ¶ 148 and p. 243 quotes ¶ 150.
19. Doheny, *Canonical Procedure*, p. 213.
20. For example, Art. 117 of this Instruction.

ing information in remote sections. It is true that much material of this Instruction (notably ¶¶ 1-94) does not belong in a local constitution and also that it lacks many elements desirable in a full constitution for diocesan courts, nevertheless it may be considered the first widely known work of this kind by a local legislator and a milestone in the history of ecclesiastical judicial procedure.

4. The years immediately subsequent to the promulgation of the Code of 1918 are not remarkable for local legislation on procedure probably because of the efforts by diocesan tribunals to digest and assimilate the vast material of the universal law. Of late however individual courts have exhibited evidence of fairly complete assimilation and supplementary law is appearing on every side. In America for example the synodal laws of recent years have been devoting considerable space to such procedural legislation.[21]

Similarly mandates of appointment of officers, especially of *officiales*, are presenting more or less complete instructions from local ordinaries to their representatives in judicial fields.

5. While not a part of this history but nevertheless a parallel development and a source of material for future diocesan constitutions, there are the modern constitutions for the tribunals of the Holy See.[22] The reform of these great courts was accomplished

21. Thus the Diocese of Fargo, *Liber Synodalis Fargensis* (1941), Statutes 372, 374, 376, pp. 72-73 and also ¶¶ 792-801 of Article 49 of the second part, pp. 162-166; the Diocese of Spokane, *Synodus Dioecesana Spokanensis Prima* (1939), Statutes 104-105, p. 40 and appendix XII, pp. 83-85; the Diocese of Harrisburg, *Synodus Diocesana Harrisburgensis Octava* (1928), Statutes 389-391, p. 133 and appendix XI, pp. 149-152; the Diocese of Richmond, *Synodus Dioecesana Richmondiensis Tertia* (1932),Statutes 35-43, pp. 14-15; the Province of Portland in Oregon, *Acta et Decreta Concilii Provincialis Portlandensis in Oregon Quarti* (1932), Decrees 112, 152, 153, 311 and 312.
22. It is the mind of the universal legislator that these *Normae* be considered models for local customs and laws — cf. c. 20; Pius X, const., 29 iun., 1908- —, *AAS,* XLI, (1908), 425-426; cf. also the commentary on the *Normae a.* 1934 in the Jus Pontificium, (Romae, 1921- —), XIV (1934), 305.

by means of the magnificent constitutions of 1908, 1910 and 1912.[23] That these had great influence on the legislation of the Code affecting diocesan courts is evident from the footnotes of the Gasparri edition of the Code. But since the Code one document in particular has been prepared that may even more specifically serve as a prototype of the future constitutions for diocesan courts, the *Normae* of the Sacred Roman Rota of 1934.[24] Stripped of much universal legislation, which is preserved for all courts in the Code, the *Normae,* with its supplement on fees and taxes of May 26, 1939,[25] are today a strictly "local" constitution for one individual court, the Sacred Roman Rota, and in this sense are the model in form and material for future constitutions for diocesan courts.

23. *Lex propria S.R. Rotae et Signaturae Ap.,* 29 iun. 1908 — *Fontes,* n. 6459; *Regulae servandae in iudiciis apud S.R. Rotae Tribunal,* 4 aug. 1910 — *Fontes,* n. 6461; *Regulae servandae in iudiciis apud Suprem. Signaturae Ap. Tribunal,* 6 mart. 1912 — *Fontes,* n. 6462; *Ad regulas servandas in iudiciis apud Supremum Signaturae Apostolicae Tribunal,* 28 iun. 1915 — *Fontes,* appendix of Tome VIII (after n. 6462).
24. *Normae S. Romanae Rotae Tribunalis,* 22 iun. 1934 — *AAS,* XXVI (1934), 449-492 (henceforth referred to as *Normae a.* 1934).
25. *Tariff of Fees of the Tribunal of the Sacred Roman Rota* of May 26, 1939 — *AAS,* XXXI (1929), 622.

CHAPTER II

THE NATURE, VALUE AND SOURCES OF A CONSTITUTION FOR DIOCESAN COURTS

6. A constitution for the diocesan court is a set of rules drawn up and promulgated by the legislative power within the diocese regulating the functions and practises (the *modus operandi*) of the court in greater detail than the universal law.

7. A constitution is a natural consequence postulated by the existence and the nature of a diocesan court and may be found operating, at least in equivalent form, in practically every other similar organization throughout the world. The Supreme Apostolic Signatura and the Sacred Roman Rota, tribunals of the Holy See, have their own constitutions by which they govern themselves within the scope allowed by the universal law.[1]

Each federal court of the United States (i.e. each type of federal court) has its rules of court which are the equivalent of the statutes of a constitution.[2] Finally the courts of the individual

1. Cf. ¶ 5 of this dissertation. In the introduction to the *Normae a.* 1934, Cardinal Massimi, then dean of the Sacred Roman Rota, emphasized the need and purpose of the constitution for the S. R. Rota in these words: "Codice promulgato et observato rerum usu, visum est Auditoribus novas conscribere normas, quibus plura definirentur spectantia ad constitutionem Tribunalis et ad officium Auditorum aliorumque Tribunali addictorum, de iudiciis vero generales Codicis leges indoli atque stylo Rotae aptarentur" — *Apollinaris,* (Romae, 1928-—), VII (1934), 429.
2. These are all published in one volume (Vol. XI), entitled *"Court Rules,"* of the *"Digest of the United States Supreme Court Reports,"* (11 Vols. with four supplements to bring these rules down to February 15, 1943), Rochester, N.Y.: The Lawyers Co-operative Publishing Co., 1939). They include: 1. Revised Rules of the Supreme Court of the United States, pp. 5-58; 2. Rules of Practice in Admiralty for the Courts of the United States, pp. 59-84; 3. Rules of the Court of Claims of the United States, pp. 185-203; 4. Rules of the United States Courts of Appeal, pp. 205-358 (this includes rules for the ten circuit courts of appeal and of the District of Columbia Court of Appeal); 5. Rules of Civil Procedure for the District Courts of the United

state, governed though they are by universal procedural practice, by state constitutions and by state laws, nevertheless have their individual rules of court to regulate activities within the scopes of the jurisdiction given to them.

Furthermore the administrative departments of the dioceses are encouraged to have and some actually do have regulations governing their activities.[3] Also each religious order, congregation and society is governed and directed by its constitution.

8. So necessary and natural is a constitution to regulate in any agency the innumerable details of active existence, sometimes untouched by universal law and sometimes presented in general terms, that possibly every diocesan court in America has the beginnings of a constitution in scattered regulations found in varied places from synodal laws to loose leaf notes deposited in various files about the office. Few, if any, courts have drawn these rules into formal constitutions as yet because of the need of time and experience since the publication of the Code of 1918 to assimilate universal law and to recognize the manner in which it may be supplemented.

9. The scope of the constitution is set by the place of the diocesan court in the organization of the Church. In the first place it acts as a supplement only to the universal law. Its field is that vast realm of possible laws and regulations on judicial activities left to the local lawmaker. The diocese is an integral unit of the universal Church and therefore its departments are governed primarily by the common law. For the diocesan court, this common or universal law is the Code of Canon Law of 1918.[4] The constitution

States, pp. 363-505. As a background to these and a most interesting example of constitutional rules of various kinds are the regulations affecting all federal governmental agencies as they appear in *"The United States Code"* (Fifty Titles, St. Paul, Minn.: West Publishing Co.). In this vast compilation, Title 28, in nine volumes, sets forth the *"Judicial Code and Judiciary."*

3. C. 356. For example, synodal laws for sick priest funds, for cemetery organizations, etc.
4. Cf. Schmidt, John, *The Principles of Authentic Interpretation in Canon 17 of the Code of Canon Law,* (The Catholic University of America

may not disregard or change any regulation of universal law. Its rules will always presuppose a thorough knowledge and a careful application not only of the Code but also of the authentic interpretations of it and of the Instruction of 1936.

10. Within the diocese, the field of the court, and therefore of its constitution, is limited. This occurs first in relation to the bishop. The court is, after a manner, his *alter ego* in judicial matters. Being in this sense the same person with him, there is no strict appeal from the court to the bishop. The constitution might record that the judicial power rests in the bishop and that he is exercising it *per alios*. The bishop may make whatever provisions he wishes for supervision, for example a semi-annual or annual report, and these can be incorporated in the constitution. Furthermore the bishop has full power to dispense from, change or abrogate the laws of the constitution.

11. The court is limited by and has its relationship to the other curial departments and to the diocese as a whole. There may be at times an overlapping with the administrative departments of the curia, for example both may employ the same canon law library or the same archive room or the same stenographical staff, but the constitution should be careful not to confuse the functions of the one with the others.

12. The constitution when it is made law by the bishop

Canon Law Studies, n. 141; Washington, D.C.: The Catholic University of America Press, 1941), p. 62. To the Code will be added the authentic interpretations of the Code Commission. In the classification of doctrinal interpretation, and therefore not new law, may be placed the Instruction of 1936. This can be considered only doctrinal interpretation because the Sacred Congregation of the Sacraments does not have either legislative power or the power of authentic interpretation — Schmidt, *op. cit.*, p. 61. It can be noted also that the diocesan court as such is not directly regulated by the Instructions of 1923 and of 1931. In the causes and petitions which form the precise subject matter of these Instructions, the Congregations alone are competent and the diocesan judicial personnel, instructing them, act only as delegates of the Holy See and not as a court exercising ordinary power.

primarily affects the officers of the tribunal. But because of the court's relationship to the entire diocese some at least of the laws may have their effect on the clergy and laity in general. For example, the constitutions will probably present some regulations on the preliminary handling of causes. A practical regulation forbidding priests to give any assurance to the interested parties of a favorable decision in a possible cause would be a law affecting all priests of the diocese. Such a rule could be incorporated in both the constitution and the synodal statutes.

13. Many reasons might be given for the development of constitutions for diocesan courts. Such a constitution, as supplementary law, is presupposed by the universal law of the Church. The latter is necessarily made for the whole Church, for European, Asiatic, American, African mentalities, for the world wide scope of the Roman courts, the seldom functioning courts of religious communities, the diocesan courts, for the tribunals of large and small dioceses, etc. Under the circumstances it cannot enter into as much detail as desirable. The result and the cause of consequent complaint has been a certain state of confusion as to policy and detailed procedure existing among the diocesan courts of the world. Thus officers of courts hesitate on courses of action on disputed points or grow weary of constantly consulting the ordinary because they have not certain powers they feel should belong to their offices. This confusion is in no way the fault of the universal legislator who no doubt foresaw many at least of the difficulties but was constrained by his obligation to the universal Church to keep his rules general and who left it to the local lawmaker to prepare and promulgate more specific laws according to the conditions and circumstances of his territory. It may be said that the confusion is the result of the hesitancy of local lawmakers to exercise their divinely given power to make the detailed laws necessary for their dioceses.

14. The Code in unmistakable terms refers to local laws that are peculiar to tribunals. For example, C. 1625, in regard to punishments for neglect of duty and violation of secrecy on the part of judicial personnel, uses the expression: "*salvis peculiaribus statutis.*"

C. 1864, referring to the length of written defenses, says: *"nisi de hoc peculiari tribunalis lege sit cautum."* C. 1865 also mentions the observance of the rules of local courts. C. 1591 and C. 1805 both have references to local judicial customs while C. 1638 § 1 and C. 1909 command public decrees for the judicial department, one for a schedule of set times when the court may be approached and the other for a schedule of taxes and fees.

15. Furthermore in the universal law there is given much freedom to use or not to use certain institutes, to make definite many indefinite terms and even to compose entirely new legislation according to circumstances. Thus a court *may* use auditors;[5] a court makes definite regulations on indefinite terms like *"congruis poenis"* and *"per turnum"* appointments;[6] the proper authorities draw up schedules of fees;[7] the court makes regulations on preliminary reception of causes, etc. The constitution is the specific embodiment of the exercise of this freedom, and, according to local circumstances and conditions, makes laws to supplement the universal law.

16. Much inconvenience has been experienced by the necessity imposed by the universal law of petitioning the bishop of the diocese in various situations for permission to exercise a power or for delegation of such power. The universal law chose to leave certain powers entirely in the office of the bishop rather than to grant them also to the officers of the court. For example the *officialis* has no authority in universal law to make substitutions for judges withdrawing from a *"turnus"* because of suspicion.[8] This reservation of power to the bishop was no doubt carefully made. It leaves to the individual bishop, motivated by circumstances and local conditions, of which he is the best judge, to determine to what extent he personally will enter into the work of the court. Thus he may choose to keep a very close supervision of the work as it proceeds by continuing to reserve these powers to himself or by granting delegation for individual cases only. Or he may choose to keep a

5. C. 1580.
6. C. 1625 § 1 and c. 1576 § 3.
7. C. 1909 § 1.
8. C. 1615 § 2; *Instructio a.* 1936, Art. 19 ¶ 1.

less close supervision by granting general delegations of these powers. In large dioceses especially the innumerable calls upon the time and energy of the ordinaries impel some of them to grant many general delegations. The constitutions is the natural instrument for the granting, the uniform applying and the preserving of the record of such grants of power.

Authors have long felt that it would be practical for the *officialis* in many cases to have at least some of the powers which the Code reserves to the ordinary. Some of them, instead of advocating the granting of these powers to the *officialis* for example in a diocesan constitution, have at times "extended" the term "ordinary" to include, in practise if not in theory, the *officialis* — possibly forgetting that the terms of the Code were carefully chosen. As was said above, the universal law reserves certain activities to the ordinary so that he, who is most familiar with the circumstances and needs of the diocese, may determine whether to keep them to himself or to grant them to the *officialis* by delegation.

17. In any healthy institute, there is a natural growth of law. The Church not only expects this but encourages it. Thus she commands that councils and synods be held frequently to meet the needs of the locality through legislation.[9] Experience often teaches new and better ways of accomplishing ends and purposes. Many tribunals have learned by experience the value of a solemn opening of the court season each year. Others have seen the value of recording the impression the court receives of a particular witness (*animadveriones judicis, delegati,* etc.) Also peculiar circumstances and national mentalities often demand local legislation. Thus in some places civil laws may forbid technical citations; the presence of a predominately non-Catholic population may demand a greater lenience in hearing witnesses outside the hall of sessions; American minds, responding differently to questions in court because of civil law training and practises, may call for more detailed questionnaires. Such national mentalities are sometimes well reflected in civil law rules and procedure. Moreover new regulations coming into being in one department of Catholic life naturally affect other departments.

9. C. 281; c. 283; c. 356 § 1.

Thus the comparatively recent laws on pre-nuptial investigations and on pre-ordination oaths naturally demand legislation on the presentation of these when the marriage or the ordination in question is being attacked. The many contacts today of one court with another bring about mutual influences on rules of court. Thus the example of the Rota and of other well organized courts in compiling a court library is influencing many courts to gather and preserve source books and commentaries. National and regional meetings of canon law societies serve as mediums of exchange for progressive ideas and central schools become powerful factors in directing and in unifying progress as it is achieved. At times this natural development among diocesan courts has a marked influence on universal law.[10]

18. In every constitution there are matters inherently proper to such a document and valuable to the body for which the constitution was made as guides for the orderly conducting of business. In the constitution for the individual diocesan court there should be mention of the place of the hall of sessions; rules on material equipment such as archives, seals, record books; regulations on times as to sessions, as to consultations, as to seasons of the year, as to holidays; detailed specification of duties of officers over and above those imposed in the universal law; an exposition of the jurisdiction of the court and finally a mention of the court to which appeal is to be made. These regulations are found in great detail in rules of court of higher ecclesiastical tribunals and of civil tribunals. An added advantage of the constitution is that it safeguards, preserves and stabilizes the smallest details of this "*modus operandi.*"

19. Sometimes there develop practises in dioceses that are contrary to universal law, that show neglect of universal mandates or that are at least useless. Thus the practice of appointing purely honorary judges who never function on succeeding "*turni*"; the failure to reappoint judges after ten years in office with consequent invalid trials and sentences; the repetition of unnecessary oaths each year; the inclusion in the acts of much useless material. These

10. Cf. ¶¶ 2 and 3 of this dissertation.

and many other neglectful and embarrassing practices can be done away with by the constitution even at times by the repetition of universal legislation.

Finally a not undesirable effect of constitutions throughout the country would be a development of uniformity among the dioceses, especially in procedure intimately affecting all. Thus in America today there is noticeable lack of uniformity in methods of fulfilling rogatory commissions. One tribunal will send a single individual for testimony and another will send a full court; one will fulfill the bare letter of the law by asking only the questions of the interrogatories and another will zealously develop pertinent points by *ex officio* questions. A court sending a rogatory request would like the assurance of full cooperation from its sister court. The adoption and the observance of constitutions would assist in developing this cooperation.

20. Other reasons might be given for the adoption in America of constitutions for diocesan courts. For most trained specialists in the field of law affecting tribunals it is sufficient to note that the drafting of constitutions is according to the mind of the Church. Reasons might be presented against them. Some practitioners desire the greatest possible flexibility in court practice. Any law naturally restricts freedom of action to a certain extent and in an individual instance may even work a slight hardship. In answer to this, it may be said that the good accruing to the many from a reasonable and opportune law far outweighs the inconvenience consequent in the case of the occasional individual. Furthermore the tribunal authorities in drawing up a set of rules will naturally use ingenuity in their composition and foresee possible points of friction. Finally it is not unexpected that the first attempt at legislating on local rules of court would in individual laws be somewhat stringent. These minor mistakes can be remedied by the legislator in time and his own and subsequent generations will have profited by the development through legislation of practices in conformity with both the universal law and local circumstances and mentalities.

21. Besides the commands of the universal law, which obviously must always be at least an implicit element, the sources of

the material for the constitution (i.e. of suggestions only since the bishop as sole legislator is the only source of diocesan law itself) will include the recommendations of the universal law, the practices of other courts, especially the Roman courts, the suggestions of recognized authors and the customs of the court for which the constitution is made.[11]

22. The universal law as a source of suggestions commands certain things that should be explicitly incorporated into the constitution. Thus Canon 1909 orders the provincial council or the meeting of the bishops of the province to draw up a program of judicial fees and taxes. Again Canon 1638 declares that in each diocese the ordinary by public decree sets the days and hours when the tribunal can be regularly approached in quest of justice. The results of these commands would well be included in the constitution. The universal legislator at times merely recommends certain procedures. Thus Canon 1576 § 2 suggests the submission of certain difficult causes, other than those commanded in § 1 of that Canon, to courts of three or five judges. The constitution may make more definite regulations on recommended points. The universal law at times gives a choice of action and the diocesan law may decide on the course to be pursued in that particular diocese, for example, the use of auditors and their permanent or temporary appointments.

Sometimes officers of the court and even the authors dispute as to powers granted by law to particular offices. Thus the question is raised as to the right of the individual judge (not the presiding judge) of a collegiate tribunal to hear witnesses, without a mandate as auditor, in individual cases when the other judges are prevented from being present. Such disputed powers may be given to these officers by the constitution, at least "*ad cautelam*" or to remove doubt from individual minds. Finally the local legislator would do well to check the practices of his own court for neglected points and *contra legem* customs and repeat an occasional precept of the

11. C. 20; cf. also the commentary on the *Normae a.* 1934 — *Jus. Pontificium* XIV (1934) 303.

universal law. Too much repetition would possibly defeat the purpose. The constitution ordinarily presupposes a full knowledge of and compliance with universal law.

23. The practices of Roman courts especially are sources of material for the constitution. Canon 20 recommends the style and practice of the Roman Curia as a manner of acting when no law exists on a point and *a fortiori* this style and practice should be a source of suggestions for permanent modes of action through law.[12] It will be noted that this dissertation quotes frequently from the practices of the Sacred Roman Rota. Some practices of the Rota must by their very nature remain distinctive to that body but many of them can be and are guides to inferior courts.[13]

The Instructions drawn up by the Sacred Congregation of the Sacraments for causes affecting Holy Orders and for petitions for dispensations from ratified non-consummated marriages, while given

12. In a doubtful situation over which he has legislative power or the ability to delegate, the ideal is not that the bishop use parallel law or the practice of the Roman Curia alone to solve a difficulty but that he also use his legislative or delegating powers and make the situation definite for his diocese through a law or through a delegation. The rules of C. 20 are guiding norms in situations that continue in doubt. The bishop can remove the doubt in many cases by an exercise of his powers. If he is desirous, for example, that the *officialis* exercise a power apparently reserved to the bishop in the Code, it is hardly the mind of the lawgiver that the bishop quote the practice of the Sacred Roman Rota or even parallel law as a basis for action by the *officialis* and then do nothing more. Rather he should give a definite delegation of power to the *officialis*. This can be accomplished in a stable manner through a constitution.

13. There is a difference in the organization of the Sacred Roman Rota and the diocesan court. The S. R. Rota is a College having existence and functions apart from the individual "*turni*." Not so the diocesan court. Also the Dean of the S. R. Rota is president of the College and as such has many functions in relation to it that the *officialis* does not have in relation to the diocesan court. The *officialis* is primarily a presiding judge and as such is to be compared to the *ponens* on a rota "*turnus*" rather than to the Dean. The bishop may give the *officialis* some of the powers of the Dean by delegating these to him as a delegated moderator of his court. Cf. ¶¶ 28 and 33 of this dissertation.

to delegated courts, may offer alternatives for the tribunal functioning by ordinary power.[14]

Moreover, as similar sources of alternative suggestions, this dissertation quotes frequently from the practices of some of the well organized courts of the country. To avoid embarrassment the actual source is seldom mentioned and the quotations are given in general terms. Regional conferences of canon law societies can be practical media for interchanging comments on helpful practices of court procedure and thus be depositories of points available for incorporation in court constitutions.

24. Recognized authors, men of wide experience, can make many practical suggestions. Thus Muniz urges that fixed norms for drawing up original written documents and instruments in a diocese be established.[15] Little can be said here of the practices of the court for which the constitution is being composed. Officers drawing up the individual constitution will be aware of their presence and of their great value. Custom "*juxta legem*" is the best interpreter of the law.[16] Synodal laws have recorded some customs that are most practical.[17]

25. Concerning the material of this dissertation as a possible source of suggestions for regulations in the constitutions, it can be stated as a matter of course that it naturally has no greater force than its original sources. For example, when a synodal law is quoted, that law is noted merely as having force only in the diocese for which it was made. Thus much of the material is couched in such words as "the constitution may" or "the constitution would do well to" or occasionally "the constitution should." The dissertation endeavors to present alternatives but definitely makes no claim to exhaust the possible options. Many extremely detailed suggestions are made but this detailed method need not be adopted by the legislator in making an actual constitution. These minute

14. *Instructio a.* 1923; *Instructio a.* 1931.

15. *Procedimientos Eclesiasticos,* III, n. 364; cf. ¶ 239, footnote 149, of this dissertation.

16. Canon 29.

17. Cf. ¶ 4 (footnote) of this dissertation for quotations.

recordings may however serve as a valuable background for the constitution. It might be added that many of the points themselves, as well as the details within the points, may be ignored lest the constitution become too cumbersome. Finally experience in court practice may suggest many other points not even mentioned in this work as possible laws of a constitution. The local legislator will be governed by the conditions and circumstances of his diocese in adopting or rejecting any suggestions offered. Needless to say, considerable study will be required to complete a satisfactory constitution. A completed constitution becomes law for the diocese by the mere signature of the bishop.[18] It may or may not be adopted at a synod and probably needs no vacation between its adoption and the date it becomes effective (to be determined by the bishop). Promulgation will be determined by the material of the constitution. If some of the prescriptions (and these will be as a rule few) affect all priests of the diocese, these portions can be included in the synodal laws or in some other way be made known to all concerned. The portions affecting only the court can be promulgated by presentation to its officers. The entire work may of course be presented to the diocese by inclusion, for example, in publications containing the acts and the statutes of synods.

18. He is the sole legislator in his diocese — C. 329; c. 335; c. 362.

CHAPTER III

THE ORGANIZATION OF THE COURT

ARTICLE 1. THE INTRODUCTORY RULES

26. Like the regulations governing the Sacred Roman Rota, the rules for the individual diocesan court may well begin with a definition of the court and its territorial limits.[1] The specific constitution can mention for which diocese it is drawn up, and the nature of the court it is to govern, i.e., whether it acts as a court of first instance only or as a court of first and second instances (with mention of the dioceses whence appeals may come). The diocesan court as such is an ecclesiastical tribunal of one or more judges and of other lawfully appointed officers, endowed with ordinary jurisdiction[2] to adjudicate in formal trial contentions and criminal causes[3] within its competence under the supervision of the ordinary.

27. Mention should be made of the manner of official promulgation of the constitution, of the persons upon whom and the manner in which it is binding, of the authorities who can interpret its laws and of whatever provision is desired on individual dispensations from its rules.

28. Mention might be made of the power of the court in the

1. *Normae a.* 1934, Art. 1.
2. C. 1578; Roberti, Franciscus, *De Processibus,* (2 vols. in 1, Romae: apud Aedes Facultatis Iuridicae ad S. Apollinaris, 1926), I, n. 103. The same officers may at times be employed on ordinary and delegated tribunals, but there is a definite distinction. The delegated court is not diocesan as such but (as a rule) a representative of the Holy See.
3. The term "cause," following the terminology of the Code, will be employed throughout the dissertation to designate the object of formal procedure (judicial and otherwise) to the exclusion of the term "case" which designates the object of the summary procedure of C. 1990, of lack of form cases, of Pauline Privilege cases, etc. Cf. the index of the Gasparri edition of the Code under *"causae"* and under *"casus."*

diocese, that in judicial matters it represents the bishop[4] and that commands and requests from it are to be considered as commands and requests from him. Hence it could provide that any command to a pastor to undertake a commission for the court or any request to him for information must be fulfilled with the care and promptness accorded communications from the ordinary. The constitution might include in this summary of judicial authority in the diocese a command from the ordinary that priests honor with dispatch any request from another diocesan court for certificates, copies of pre-nuptial investigations, etc.[5]

29. The moderator of the entire court is the bishop.[6] As moderator, he has the right to advise and instruct officers, to examine the records at all times, with the exception of the opinions and *vota* of the judges in the session of the sentence, and to see that all rules of procedure are observed.[7] Some authors speak of the *officialis* as moderator of the court in this sense.[8] Possibly he has some few powers over and above those of presiding judge but in calling him a full moderator they are giving him an office he does not have by universal law. The recent *Normae* for the tribunals of the Philippine Islands, issued by the Sacred Congregation of the Sacraments, is most definite in speaking of the archbishops as moderators of the provincial tribunals permitted in the Islands.[9] It is true the

4. C. 1572 § 1; c. 1573 § 2.
5. An example of such a command may be found in the synodal statutes of the Archdiocese of San Francisco: "Quandocumque ad parochum vel sacerdotem pervenerit mandatum aut petitio a Cancellaria Nostra vel a dioecesi aliena, ut reddat vel procuret testimonium in aliqua causa matrimoniali, jubemus ut munus tanti momenti fideliter et quam celerime praestet" — *Statuta Archidioecesis Sancti Francisci in Synodo Secunda,* (San Francisco, 1936).
6. C. 363; c. 1572 § 1; *Instructio a.* 1936, Art. 21.
7. *Instructio a.* 1923, Reg. 100; *Instructio a.* 1931, Art. 71.
8. Roberti, *De Processibus,* I, p. 166; Tobin, *De Officiali Curiae Dioecesanae,* (Romae: apud Aedes Pontificiae Universitatis Gregorianae, 1936), n. 395 (henceforth referred to as *De Officiali*); Doheny, *Canonical Procedure,* p. 41.
9. The title of Chapter I of the *Normae* is: De tribunalis provincialis moderatore, iudicibus et ministris. Article I reads: Tribunal pro-

provincial court as such is an unusual concession. Nevertheless this court employs an *officialis* and Article 4 of the *Normae* speaks of his appointment apparently with no restrictions of his rights and duties. In speaking of the archbishop as moderator, the document simply says he has "all the rights and duties which belong to the local ordinaries as regards their own tribunals. . ."[10] It is possible that the universal law deliberately refrains from speaking of the *officialis* as moderator in order to leave full freedom to the bishop to follow a course in this regard best suited to the conditions of his diocese. The bishop himself may wish to exercise the functions of moderator. Again, the *officialis* may not be in a position to do so because, for example, he is a pastor who is not too frequently at court and therefore the bishop may wish to give some duties of a moderator to another.

30. Among the introductory rules for the diocesan court, mention should be made of the relationship of the vicar general to the judicial department. By universal law, the vicar general has no part in strictly judicial functions as such and it would seem to be contrary to the spirit of the law to associate him with these.[11] However appointments of permanent officers, to the permanent lists as opposed to appointments to *"turni,"* is an administrative act and not judicial. Therefore he could, and possibly should, have a

vinciale subest auctoritati archiepiscopi loci in quo ipsum sedem habet, qui, proinde, idem regit et moderatur nomine omnium Provinciae Episcoporum, eidemque omnia iura et officia attribuuntur quae Ordinariis locorum, ad normam sacrorum canonum et *Instructionis* Sacrae huius Congregationis de disciplina Sacramentorum diei 15 augusti 1936, circa proprium tribunal competunt, nisi aliter infra cautum sit vel subiecta materia exigat — *AAS*, XXXIII, (1941), 364-365.

10. Translation of the phrase is by Bouscaren, *The Canon Law Digest*, II, 536.

11. C. 1573 § 1; *Instructio a.* 1936, Art. 3 ¶ 2. Coronata says that the vicar general has both administrative and judicial ordinary power but that he may not lawfully exercise his judicial power if there is an *officialis* in the diocese — *Institutiones Iuris Canonici,* (5 vols., Taurini [Italia]: Marietti, vol. III, 1933; vol. IV, 1935; vol. V, 1936; vols. I, II, 1939), III, n. 1116 (hereafter cited Coronata, *Institutiones,* III). Tobin, quoting many authors, denies that the vicar general has latent judicial power — *De Officiali,* n. 278.

function here. Emergencies can always arise when there may be urgent need to appoint an *officialis,* or at least a *vice-officialis,* when the bishop is not available. Thus someone, preferably the vicar general, should be able to name a *vice-officialis* when the *officialis* has to withdraw because of suspicion, illness, etc., and neither a *vice-officialis* nor the bishop is available, especially since some dioceses do not have *vice-officiales.*[12] Canon 152 declares that the vicar general cannot appoint to an ecclesiastical office without a special mandate. The constitution may be the instrument used to confer this special mandate granting the vicar general the authority to appoint an *officialis,* or a *vice-officialis,* in case of necessity.[13] This grant of authority may be extended to include, possibly for an emergency only, the naming of other officers. The bishop may prefer to give this latter power only in a restricted form and possibly to the *officialis* rather than to the vicar general.

Ordinarily the vicar general would have nothing to do with naming the "*turnus*" of a cause. His power to do so is disputed and therefore the constitution may grant him this authority in the absence of the bishop for causes the naming of whose "*turni*" is reserved to the bishop. Briefly the vicar general could be empowered in emergencies to represent the bishop in every way in those causes and cases reserved to the bishop.

Article 2. The Officers of the Court Roster

31. For the sake of cataloguing concepts, the title of this article suggests the term "roster" for the lists of permanent court officers in the diocese. It is used somewhat as the "*Normae*" of the Sacred Roman Rota employs the term "college" for the list of

12. C. 1613; c. 1614; c. 1615.
13. C. 1573 § 3; the *officialis* by common law most probably cannot delegate his power either permanently or in individual cases. "...putamus potestatem officialis delegandi suam potestatem ordinariam, etiam in singulis casibus, esse valde dubiam, ne dicamus vanam — 'in dubiis abstine'" — Tobin, *De Officiali,* n. 263. Doheny says that by universal law the *officialis* cannot delegate his power as *officialis* because it is granted to him *industria personae* — *Canonical Procedure,* pp. 38-39.

permanent auditors of the Rota[14] in contrast to the term *"turnus"* for an active court hearing a cause. The roster includes permanently appointed judges, notaries, auditors, promoters, defenders and minor officers, excluding procurators and advocates who are one with the parties rather than with the court.

32. As a safeguard, the constitution may command that officers acting on a *"turnus"* must observe the solemnities and formalities of formal trials as well as prescriptions of the constitution most exactly. If for any reason they depart from them, the constitution may demand that an account of the matter with the reasons prompting the departure be put in the records.[15] This may prevent unnecessary delay on appeals. The Sacred Roman Rota, for example, may return a cause for explanation of irregular procedure or with instructions to follow the law on the point whereas it would have accepted the departure if reasons for it had been given. C. 209 does not supply for the omission of *solemnities.*

33. The synodal laws of the diocese of Richmond contain a provision which some dioceses may wish to include in their constiutions for courts. It reads: "Officialis gaudebit praecedentia supra omnem clerum diocesanum excepto vicario generali."[16]

14. *Normae a.* 1934, Articles 4 ¶ 3; 7 ¶ 2; 10 ¶ 1; 13 ¶ 1. The term "roster" naturally has a broader connotation and is used with no intention of giving to the roster an entity such as the Sacred Roman Rota enjoys as a college. The Rota definitely has existence as a college (Articles 10 ¶ 1; 11 ¶ 2; 13 ¶ 1 of the *"Normae"*). This is not true of the diocesan court. The law never speaks of the complete group of judges and other officers having either existence or functions as a board or college. The diocesan court exists and functions only as a *"turnus"* actively judging a particular cause.

15. *Instructio a.* 1931, Art. 71. Mention of the fact and reasons for it can be made as a rule orally during the session and can thus be recorded in the minutes of the session.

16. *Synodus Dioecesana Richmondiensis Tertia* (1932), Stat. 36. Cf. also the commentary on the *Normae a.* 1934 — *Jus. Pontificum,* XIV (1934), 307. The bishop can give the *officialis* a precedence — Tobin, *De Officiali,* n. 198. The Code (C. 363 § 2) names him in the list of curial officials after the vicar general.

34. The constitution is the logical instrument for granting special powers and faculties to the *officialis*.[17] In the following list of possible powers which may be given to the *officialis* there may be some repetition of the universal law, especially if there is the slightest dispute on a point, but it may be of value to include these in the constitution.[18] The bishop may desire that there never be even the slightest question as to the *officialis'* power to care for all ordinary judicial affairs in their entirety without necessity of recourse to him, even at the cost of an occasional repetition of universal law. One

17. The *officialis* once appointed possesses vicarious ordinary power, — c. 1573 § 1; Tobin, *op. cit.*, n. 208; the bishop has a strict obligation to appoint an *officialis* — Tobin, *op. cit.*, n. 139; it is at least preferable that he be not a religious, unless the diocese has been given over to the religious — Tobin, *op. cit.*, n. 173; a secularized religious may not be appointed *officialis* without a special indult of the Holy See — Tobin, *op. cit.*, n. 174; cf. also c. 642 § 1 n. 3; it is preferable at least that he be not related to the bishop — Tobin, *op. cit.*, n. 181; and the *officialis* may be either a priest of the diocese or an *"extraneus"* — Tobin, *op. cit.*, n. 182. The *officialis'* power is not suspended if the bishop happens to incur such a penalty — Coronata, *Institutiones*, III, n. 1116. A dispute exists on the power of the *officialis* when the new bishop arrives. Some (Coronata, *Institutiones*, III, n. 1116; T. Muniz, *Procedimientos Eclesiasticos*, [2. ed., 3 vols., Sevilla: Lib. de Sobrino de Izquierdo, 1926], I, 126) say his power ceases *ipso facto;* others (Roberti, *De Processibus*, I, 98; Dugan, Henry, *The Judiciary Department of the Diocesan Curia*, [The Catholic University of America Canon Law Studies, n. 26; Washington, D.C.: The Catholic University of America, 1925], p. 40 [hereafter cited as Dugan, *The Judiciary Department*]) say that he may validly act until removed. Tobin, (*op. cit.*, n. 142) is of this latter opinion.

18. A grant of power or authority (i.e. a faculty) may be (1) jurisdictional, upon the use of which the validity of certain acts depend; (2) *"gratiae"* or *"licentiae"* which is a permission *"ad licite agendum;"* and (3) *"ad cautelam,"* which is an assurance to the doubting agent that his act receives the approval of authority. The last of the three is not a faculty in the full meaning of the term, although *de facto* it may become a real faculty when "objectively the conditions for validity are wanting and the faculty supplies" — Motry, Hubert L., *Diocesan Faculties according to the Code of Canon Law*, (The Catholic University of America Canon Law Studies, n. 16; Washington, D.C.: The Catholic University of America, 1922), p. 20.

of the purposes of the constitution is to so arrange the "*modus operandi*" of the judicial department that it will function smoothly and efficiently even on occasions of prolonged absences of the bishop, as for example, on his visitation to Rome.

35. The *officialis* may be given at least some rights of a delegated moderator over the court roster.

A) The power to appoint (not just name from the roster to a "*turnus*") a *vice-officialis* in an emergency should probably be given to the vicar general and left in his hands.[19]

36. B) He could be given the power to supervise the work of all officers of the court even those serving on "*turni*" under *vice-officiales*.[20]

37. C) The concession to the *officialis* of the right of supervision of all work may necessitate extending his coactive powers. As presiding judge, he possesses certain powers to punish.[21] The bishop may wish to extend some of these powers to him as delegated moderator so that he may employ them even when he is not the presiding judge. Included in the delegation might be a power similar to that of c. 2222 § 1 and c. 2222 § 2, enabling him to punish with an appropriate punishment the transgression of any law even though no sanction is attached to the law.[22] This could include the power

19. Cf. ¶ 29 of this dissertation. In his formularies for bishops, Joseph Mothon mentions the naming and the substituting of a *vice-officialis* for an individual cause as a power that may be given to the *officialis* — *Institutions Canoniques,* (3 vols., Paris: Desclee de Brouwer, 1924); vol. III, *Formulaire et Table Analytique,* pp. 22-23.

20. This is a duty inherent in the office of the Dean of the Rota as president of the college of the Rota — *Normae a.* 1934, Art. 13 ¶ 1. It is at least appropriate that the bishop grant it to the *officialis*. Cf. Tobin, *De Officiali,* n. 398.

21 C. 1640 § 2, to keep order in the court; c. 1916, to force an advocate to assist a poor person; c. 1743 § 3 and c. 1755 § 3, to punish perjurers and those inducing to perjury; c. 1766 § 2, to punish contumacious and disobedient witnesses; c. 1845 §§ 1-2, to punish disobedient parties; c. 1625 § 3, to punish officers violating the rules of secrecy. Cf. Tobin, *De Officiali,* nn. 266-272.

22 Cf. Tobin, *De Officiali,* n. 273.

to apply pecuniary fines (c. 2291, 12°), penal remedies (c. 2306) and penances (cc. 2312-2313).

38. D) Sometimes the bishop has occasion to name delegated judges (*iudices delegati*) to a "*turnus*."[23] There would seem to be no occasion for delegating this power to anyone. However the *officialis* probably should be delegated to appoint all other officers in emergencies for single causes at least. (Appointment is used in the sense of an original designation of one not already holding office in contradistinction to the mere nomination[24] of permanent officers of the roster to individual "*turni*.") This could include the authority to appoint any qualified person as defender of the bond, promoter of justice, auditor, judicial adviser, notary, messenger or bailiff (*apparitor*).[25]

39. E) The *officialis* has the power from universal law to name judges, and *a fortiori* other officers, to his own "*turnus*" from the roster.[26] Whether this includes the authority to name judges to the "*turnus*" of the *vice-officialis* could be disputed. To remove any possible doubt, the *officialis* could be given the power to name

23 Cc. 1606-1607.

24 E.g. § 39 of this dissertation.

25. Cf. ¶¶ 46; 50; 66; 67; 171 of this dissertation.

26 C. 1576 § 3; Pontificia Commissio Interpretationis, 28 iul. 1932 — *AAS*, XXIV, (1932), 314; *Instructio a.* 1936, Art. 14 ¶ 4; Tobin, *De Officiali*, n. 396. C. 1576 § 3 says the ordinary chooses the judges "*per turnum.*" The *officialis* is not included in the term "ordinary" (c. 198) and therefore he could not by the Code lawfully appoint the "*turnus.*" To say that such an appointment would have been invalid might be too extensive because the judges chosen were already judges of the roster. But the appointment was not of the realm of the *officialis*. The Code Commission on July 28, 1932, declared the *officialis* could appoint the "*turnus.*" This declaration could mean (1) that the *officialis* could validly appoint to the "*turnus*" in the sense mentioned above, or (2) that the *officialis* could both lawfully and validly appoint the judges to the "*turnus*" and that henceforth this was to be the ordinary procedure (an extensive interpretation and therefore new law). The 1936 Instruction speaks of the *officialis* appointing to the "*turnus*" as a normal thing and not as an extraordinary measure. The Instruction is not new law. Therefore it would seem to affirm that the 1932 declaration was new law.

judges of the "*turnus*" of the *vice-officialis* and for the sake of order could be asked to name officers of all "*turni.*"

40. F) The *officialis* has not the authority by the universal law to make a substitution for a judge of the "*turnus*" who withdraws from an established "*turnus*" because of suspicion and possibly also because of other reasons, for example for sickness.[27] The authority to substitute judges, even the presiding judge, i.e. for himself or for the *vice-officialis,* as well as notaries, defenders of the bond and promoters of justice could be given to him in the constitution. Substitution in this paragraph means to name another officer from the roster to the "*turnus*" only.

41. G) He should be empowered to change, for a good cause, the "*per turnum*" appointment of judges, and of other officers if their appointments are regulated by the constitution, to the "*turnus.*"[28]

42. H) Advocates and procurators for marriage causes and advocates for all causes need both the approval of the ordinary and mandates of the parties to act.[29] The *officialis* should be given the authority to grant this approval for individual causes especially for procurators. The ordinary not only approves but names the procurators for moral persons if there is a conflict between the rights of the moral persons and their rectors or administrators.[30] The ordinary may desire to reserve this power to himself although he may delegate it.

43. I) The *officialis* may be empowered to change the chronological order of the calendar in an individual instance and for a

27. C. 1615 § 2; *Instructio a.* 1936, Art. 19 ¶ 1 and Art. 32 ¶ 2. Article 19 ¶ 1 of the 1936 Instruction seems to confirm the viewpoint that the *officialis* may not make substitutions. It speaks of the bishop substituting. Article 32 ¶ 2 uses the term "*ordinarii*" in referring to this power as does c. 1615 § 2.
28. C. 1576 § 3; Tobin, *De Officiali,* n. 396, is of the opinion that he has this power by universal law but it is difficult to see this without extending the term "ordinary" — C. 1576 § 3.
29. C. 1658 § 2; c. 1659; c. 1661; *Instructio a.* 1936, Art. 48 ¶ 4.
30. C. 1649.

good cause.[31] The constitution may demand an explanation in the protocol book as to why this was done.

44. J) He could be authorized to choose, constitute and substitute guardians (*tutores vel curatores*) for minors and those lacking use of reason and to either approve or substitute for guardians named by civil authorities.[32]

45. K) The *officialis* can be authorized to receive requests for rogatory commissions from other dioceses, to constitute and to delegate, in accordance with the instruction from the other diocese, the desired commissions and to return them with the so-called *votum episcopi.*[33]

46. L) The *officialis* should be certain of his power to name, even for the "*turnus*" of the *vice-officialis,* auditors, including priests not permanently designated as such on the roster, and judicial advisers.[34]

47. As presiding judge, the *officialis* may receive further delegations.

A) The constitution may well be used to define the extent of the *officialis'* authority. For example, a regulation may read that he has the right to preside at all causes, contentious or criminal, whether of clerics or of laymen, coming to the diocesan court under any title whatsoever.[35] This would be a grant of universal jurisdiction but even this includes the implicit understanding that the bishop may in individual causes assume the responsibility of presiding himself.[36] The grant of universal jurisdiction implies that when the bishop reserves an individual cause he will do so specifically and expressly. On the other hand the bishop may choose to reserve

31. C. 1627; Tobin considers the *officialis* has this authority by universal law — *De Officiali,* n. 400. He quotes the precedent of the Sacred Roman Rota — *Normae a.* 1934, Art. 13.
32. C. 1648 §§ 2-3; c. 1651 §§ 1-2.
33. C. 1570 § 2; c. 1770 § 1 n. 3.
34. C. 1580; c. 1575.
35. C. 1573 § 1; Mothon, *Institutions Canoniques,* III, 22-23.
36. C. 1573 § 2. The bishop may of course appoint a "*judex delegatus*" to represent him as presiding judge of a "*turnus*" — c. 199 § 1.

to himself certain types of causes and these might be mentioned in the constitution.[37] Some dioceses prefer to add further restrictions for all causes in which the plaintiff is a non-Catholic, or an apostate, renegade or unworthy Catholic. Permission must be obtained in these dioceses from the bishop before the petition can be sent to Rome or the cause can be accepted. This is a protection against scandal in the cases of unworthy Catholics and against insincerity in the cases of non-Catholics.

48. B) The *officialis* may be given the authority to receive the oaths and professions of faith of individuals named to the roster or to a "*turnus*" directly but not from the roster by the bishop himself.[38]

49. C) Mention can be made of his right to choose and to delegate commissions to fulfill judicial acts within the diocese for causes being heard in the diocese.[39]

50. D) The *officialis*, as presiding judge, could be given the

37. C. 1573 § 2; a dispute exists as to the interpretation of the phrase of this canon "sed nequit iudicare causas quas episcopus sibi reservat." Augustine says "the power of the *officialis* is entirely subject to the will of the bishop" — (Bachofen), Charles Augustine, *A Commentary on the New Code of Canon Law,* (8 vols.), Vol. VII, *Ecclesiastical Trials,* (3. ed., 1930, St. Louis: Herder), p. 31 (henceforth cited as Augstine, Commentary, VII). Most authors affirm that the bishop cannot reserve to himself so many causes that the power of the *officialis* becomes practically less than ordinary power. Thus he can reserve a certain type of cause, for example, civil and criminal causes against the vicar general, but he cannot reserve to himself a whole category of causes, for example, all matrimonial causes. Cf. Tobin, *De Officiali,* n. 255; Doheny, *Canonical Procedure,* p. 38; Joseph Noval, *Commentarium Codicis Iuris Canonici,* Liber IV, *De Processibus,* Pars. I, *De Iudiciis,* (Augustae Taurinorum — Romae, 1920), n. 114 (henceforth cited Noval, *De Processibus,* I); Coronata, Institutiones, III, n. 1116; D'Angelo, S., *La Curia Diocesana a Norma del Codice di Diritto Canonico,* (Giarre, Sicilia: Casa Editrice D. Pietro Lisi, 1922), I, p. 61; Dugan, *The Judiciary Department,* p. 38.
38. C. 1621 §§ 1-2; c. 1623 § 1; *Instructio a.* 1936, Art. 20.
39. C. 1770 § 2 n. 4; cf. ¶¶ 217-226 of this dissertation.

authority to appoint as notaries[40] messengers[41] and procurators, individuals not of the roster thereby facilitating the delivery of citations and the collection of evidence in unusual situations. Sometimes the court is called upon to employ individuals in these capacities who are not permanently associated with the tribunal and therefore the *officialis* should have the authority to designate them as officers for individual causes.[42]

51. The constitution would do well to make some regulation concerning the proper person to hear causes requiring only one judge. For example, it could mention that the *officialis* hears them all; or that the *officialis* determines who is to hear them; or that the *officialis* and the *vice-officiales* hear them in turn.

52. A consideration of possible delegations to the *officialis* in criminal causes, Roman causes and cases, exceptional cases of C. 1990, lack of form cases, Pauline Privilege cases and proof of death cases will be found in Chapter VIII of this dissertation under these various titles.

53. The constitution may desire to impose further duties on the *officialis* especially as presiding judge and even at times to reiterate some of the prescriptions of universal law. Thus the *officialis* may be asked:

A) To make himself available at definite times to give to the priests and laymen who wish to consult him concerning possible causes the benefit of his specialized knowledge of canon law.[43]

B) To shorten trials as much as justice and charity will allow by refusing useless and delaying petitions, by keeping time limits as short as possible, by urging immediate cooperation from the officers, etc.[44]

C) To personally check all mandates required in a trial.[45]

40. C. 373.
41. C. 1591; c. 1592.
42. Cf. ¶ 171 of this work.
43. *Normae a.* 1934, Art. 19 ¶ 3.
44. *Normae a.* 1934, Art. 19 ¶ 2.
45. *Normae a.* 1934, Art. 19 ¶ 2.

D) To supervise the attempts at reconciliation and to approve the conditions if the attempts are successful.[46]

E) To supervise the recording of facts, calling attention to unusual but pertinent things to be recorded and even at times to dictate what is to be written.[47]

F) To edit the remarks of parties and witnesses when these are confused, especially verbose or irrelevant parts, taking care however to preserve the full essence of each statement.

G) Before closing a cause, to go over the acts carefully to see if any matter is missing, incomplete, contradictory or ambiguous.[48]

H) To prepare a short animadversion of his impression of any party, witness or expert heard during the trial thereby facilitating the work of the court of appeal.

I) To care for all rogatory and other requests coming to the diocese from outside.

54. The Code allows freedom in the use or non-use of *vice-officiales*.[49] The constitution, considering the size of the diocese and the number of causes handled, may specify that *vice-officiales* will be appointed only for individual causes or that one or two or more *vice-officiales* will be appointed permanently to the roster.[50]

55. The constitution should make definite the powers and

46. *Normae a.* 1934, Art. 19 ¶ 2.
47. *Instructio a.* 1923, Reg. 44 ¶ 2.
48. *Instructio a.* 1923, Reg. 96 ¶ 2.
49. C. 1573 § 3.
50. If no *vice-officialis* is used, the *officialis* in person must preside at every trial — cc. 1573, 1577, 1578; *Instructio a.* 1936, Art. 14; Roberti, *De Processibus,* I, n. 103; Tobin, *De Officiali,* n. 315; Doheny, *Canonical Procedure,* pp. 37 and 46. This presupposes that the *"turni"* are not special collegiate courts such as those mentioned in ¶¶ 60, 86 and 87 of this dissertation. For such unusual *"turni"* the bishop can appoint delegated judges as *"praeses."* It also presupposes he has not named a personal representative as delegated *"praeses"* of an ordinary *"turnus"* (mentioned in the second footnote of ¶ 47 A of this dissertation).

jurisdiction of the *vice-officialis* or *vice-officiales*.[51] The extent of the jurisdiction may be determined once and for all by the bishop in the constitution and henceforth an appointed *vice-officialis* would know the limitations of his faculties as dependent on diocesan law.

56. Along with the powers the *vice-officialis* receives from the universal law, he may also receive as many of the delegated powers of the *officialis* as the bishop deems necessary or useful for an efficient court.[52] The bishop may be especially inclined to give the *vice-officialis* all powers delegated to the *officialis* as presiding judge.[53]

57. If permanent *vice-officiales* are employed by the diocesan court, a regulation should be made in the constitution determining their relation to the *officialis* and to the *"turni."*[54] They may be called upon, for example, by the *officialis* only when needed; or they may be given causes in rotation with the *officialis;* or they may be asked to handle certain types of causes. A priest familiar with a foreign language prevalent in the diocese may be assigned as *vice-officialis* for all causes involving those speaking this language. The advantages of a presiding judge questioning in the language of the party or witness are self evident. The individual questioned is

51. Augustine and Coronata say that the *vice-officiales* do not have ordinary power and may not be looked upon as quasi-judges *in solidum,* but only as assistants to the *officialis* in case of need — *Commentary,* VII, p. 31; *Institutiones,* III, n. 1116. Tobin holds the far more common view that the *vice-officiales* have ordinary power — *De Officiali,* n. 433. Agreeing with this opinion are Muniz, *Procedimientos Eclesiasticos,* I, n. 126; Roberti, *De Processibus,* I, n. 97. Doheny says: "The common opinion is that they enjoy ordinary jurisdiction in a manner similar to the *officialis.* Therefore, it is our opinion that wherever the Instruction authorizes the *Officialis* to perform some judicial act, a *Vice-Officialis* acting in the capacity of a *Vice-Officialis,* is empowered to perform similar functions, *congrua congruis referendo" — Canonical Procedure,* p. 38.
52. ¶¶ 34-52 of this dissertation.
53. ¶¶ 47-50 of this dissertation.
54. The diocese of Richmond has the following law: "Vice-officialis, ex commissione Officialis, fungetur eius munere, quo tamen sessiones ordinarias Tribunalis in civitate Episcopali convocabit" — *Synodus Diocesana Richmondiensis Tertia,* Stat. 39.

naturally more capable of expressing himself and is more at ease while, on the other hand, the judge grasps shades of meaning lost in translations. Again a *vice-officialis* may be asked to care for causes in a particular section of the diocese. Some dioceses have large cities and vast territory far from the episcopal city. It does not seem contrary to universal law to have in such distant places a second hall of sessions and court officers presided over by a *vice-officialis*. This would not be a separate court[55] but a portion of the one diocesan court that is the judicial department of the diocese, a "*turnus*" that, because of unusual circumstances, is not chosen "*per turnum*" for the causes it hears.

58. The constitution may wish to say something of the precedence of the *vice-officiales* in regard, for example, to the synodal judges of the diocese.

A regulation may determine that the *officialis* appoint members of all "*turni*" or that each *vice-officialis* appoints his own "*turnus*," following the rules of the constitution on rotation.[56]

59. The Code gives many specific regulations on the synodal and pro-synodal judges, from the permanent lists of whom the associate judges of the "*turni*" are drawn.[57] As a rule, the associate judges of the "*turni*, two or four, depending on the cause, must be chosen "in turn" from the lists.[58] Therefore the practice in some dioceses of having honorary, non-functioning judges would seem to be "*contra legem*." The constitution may be more specific in defining the method of the choice of judges "*per turnum*." The Sacred Roman Rota, for example, varies the membership of successive "*turni*" by choosing the first three members for the first cause, i.e. Numbers 1, 2 and 3; the second cause does not call for Numbers 4, 5 and 6

55. Tobin says that all authors agree there can be but one *officialis* under pain of nullity — *De Officiali*, n. 197.

56. From the discussion mentioned in ¶ 55 above, it would seem that most probably at least the *vice-officialis* has the right by universal law to do this. The constitution can of course make this definite. Also it may regulate that he not use this power by assigning to the *officialis* the duty of arranging the "*turni*."

57. C. 1574; c. 1576; c. 385; c. 386; c. 387; c. 388.

58. C. 1576 § 3.

but for Numbers 2, 3 and 4; and the third for Numbers 3, 4 and 5, etc.[59] The diocesan court may determine on a "1-2; 2-3; 3-4" choice, the presiding judge always being the *officialis* or the *vice-officialis*, or on a "1-2; 3-4; 5-6" choice or on any other method providing the judges are chosen in turn.[60] The choice by turn may be determined according to seniority, or by combining one senior judge with one junior judge or in any other way decided upon by the bishop.[61] On occasions the *"per turnum"* appointment may be varied. The constitution may require that reasons for this be entered for example, in the book of appointments. Knowledge of languages may be one of many factors dictating a departure from the regular order.

60. There are times, especially for criminal causes, when the bishop may wish to use priests not of the roster and even priests not of the diocese as judges on special *"turni."* These priests are appointed by him as delegated judges and named then to the *"turni."*[62] From the nature of these situations the bishop will probably reserve all appointments and designations of delegated judges to himself.

61. Some confusion exists in places concerning the possibility of the associate judge of a *"turnus"* acting as auditor without a mandate to receive testimony in an emergency. The constitution, to remove any doubt, might grant all judges this power. All recognize that the ideal is to have all three or all five judges present at the hearing of any party, witness or expert. However circumstances may at times militate against this. For example, all judges may have planned to be present for a hearing in preference to employing an

59. *Normae a.* 1934, Art. 15; the Dean of the S. R. Rota does not always preside since he is not present on every *"turnus."* Therefore three auditors or judges of the Rota are chosen in turn, one of whom is made the presiding judge.

60. C. 1576 § 3.

61. Augustine, *Commentary,* VII, 35; the use of juniors and seniors on the same *"turnus"* might be arranged by a "1-7; 2-8; 3-9" method or by a "1-12; 2-11; 3-10" method. The important thing seems to be that it follow a predetermined order thereby distributing the work and excluding merely honorary judges.

62. Cc. 1606-1607.

auditor but one or more may have been prevented at the last minute from attending. Could the remaining judge or judges continue with the instruction of the cause, no auditor having been appointed? Some places, to care for such situations, constitute all judges as permanent auditors. Others require the presiding judge to appoint the *ponens*, for example, as auditor of the cause or even both associate judges as auditors or one as *ponens* and the other as auditor. The constitution should at least make mention of this situation to remove any doubt from the minds of the judges.

62. The constitution may make a further regulation safeguarding the necessary reappointment of judges at the end of a ten year period.[63] C. 356 § 1, which demands that a diocesan synod be held every tenth year, is a safeguard required by universal law. The appointments and reappointments must be cared for at each synod. Another safeguard may be in the annual report to the bishop. The constitution may require special care in compiling this report in noting the date of appointment and the number of years of service of each judge with special mention to the ordinary of the fact when reappointments are in order. A third method might be a rule requiring the recording in the acts of each cause of the date of appointment of all judges of the "*turnus.*"

63. Many courts in the United States are availing themselves of auditors to collect evidence and otherwise to instruct causes.[64] The constitution by statute may set the number of permanent appointments of auditors to the roster and may determine more specifically when they may or may not be used. Permanent appointments of auditors to the roster must be made by the bishop unless he delegates this power[65] but instructions might be given to the *officialis* regarding occasions when he may name for individual

63. C. 387 § 1 says that the office ceases at the end of ten years unless the appointment is renewed. Judges serving beyond this ten year limit without reappointment are holding office invalidly — Doheny, Canonical Procedure, p. 44. C. 209 would probably supply jurisdiction in most cases because of common error.

64. C. 1580-c. 1583; *Instructio a.* 1936, Art. 23-25; Roberti, *De Processibus,* I, 179-180.

65. C. 1580; *Instructio a.* 1936, Art. 23.

causes auditors who are not on the roster.[66] The constitution will determine whether auditors are to be named to "*turni*" from the roster by rotation, at the discretion of the *officialis*, according to the nature of the cause, etc. The bishop might appoint all the judges of the roster as permanent auditors thus giving the *officialis* a wide choice and thus facilitating the naming of a judge of the "*turnus*" as auditor. The constitution may withhold the power of permanent auditors to act on certain causes, for example, criminal causes, without special mandates. The tenure of office may be limited, for example, from synod to synod, and reiteration of the universal law rule that oaths must be taken by auditors on assuming office even though these oaths were taken by them previously on entering their office of judge would not be out of place.[67]

To facilitate their work, all auditors might be given a general permission in the constitution to proceed as the head of a commission to collect testimony on occasions outside the hall of sessions. The constitution may require of course that before he do this he obtain permission of the *officialis*. Likewise rules may be given regulating the power of the auditor to name and delegate commissions of which he is not a member to collect testimony for him at distant points.

64. Further duties may be specified for auditors. For example, they may be required to prepare statements of their impression of all parties and witnesses heard (*animadversiones auditoris*). Included in these statements should be the impressions made as to the sincerity, and other attitudes of those being heard such as flippancy, hesitance, noticeable instability of mood. These are to be preserved in the acts of the cause and may be placed at the end of each deposition.

65. Judicial advisers (*assessores*) are recommended by the Code for causes being heard by a single judge.[68] The constitution may suggest that they be used on occasions by judges of the collegiate courts. Regulations may be made determining their appointment or non-appointment as permanent members of the

66. C. 1580 § 3; *Instructio a.* 1936, Art. 23 ¶ 1.
67. C. 364 § 2 n. 1; cf. ¶ 83 of this dissertation.
68. C. 1575.

roster or advisers appointed for individual causes or as both. The judges of the roster are *ex officio* permanent advisers.

66. The judicial advisers (*secreti*) of the Sacred Roman Rota have, among other duties, the following obligations which may be of assistance in setting forth a rule for local judicial advisers. (A) They must study the judicial acts, both of the cause and of the process, and report on these either orally or in writing. At least five days before the definition of the cause they must bring to their judges opinions with reasons in law and in fact.[69] (B) They must come to the judges whom they are assisting on the day and at the hour prescribed by them either for a discussion of the cause or for any other study required by him.[70] (C) They must, after the definition of the cause, restore all writings and summations to the judge.[71]

67. Many dioceses have felt the need of more than one defender of the bond.[72] There are evident advantages in the appointment of more than one defender of the bond. The constitution, mindful of the needs of the diocese, could determine not only the number of defenders of the bond to be permanently appointed but also the relationship of the defenders to each other and the method of their appointment, viz., from the roster to the "*turni,*" i.e. according to types of causes, by rotation or at the discretion of the *officialis*. Some diocesan regulations attribute equality to all the defenders of the bond but the Sacred Roman Rota uses only a substitute defender to supply when necessary.[73] The regulations may determine that the defender of the bond take all causes and instruct him to ask the *officialis* to call in the second defender of the bond when the number of causes becomes too great. The constitution may determine, in smaller dioceses especially, that only one

69. *Normae a.* 1934, Art. 50 a and d.
70. *Normae a.* 1934, Art. 50 b.
71. *Normae a.* 1934, Art. 53.
72. In 1943 Philadelphia had six; Brooklyn, three; St. Louis, seven; Chicago, two; Detroit, four; Los Angeles, three; Boston, two; Cleveland, one; San Francisco, one — *The Official Catholic Directory,* (New York: P. J. Kennedy, 1822-1943), 1943.
73. *Normae a.* 1934, Art. 5.

defender of the bond be designated permanently and mention that the bishop will appoint temporary defenders of the bond for individual causes if the need arise, with delegation to the vicar general or to the *officialis,* for example, to make this appointment in case of necessity. Some dioceses have a defender of the bond who is a specialist in Roman causes for example, and he confines his work to these. Some have the defender attached to the presiding judge, i.e., one defender cares for all causes presided over by the *officialis,* and another for all causes of the *vice-officialis.* This is naturally appropriate if the *vice-officialis* hears causes in another part of the diocese. Language also may influence the appointment of defenders of the bond to causes. Nothing prevents the designation of the promoter of justice as a permanent, but preferably subordinate, defender of the bond and vice versa.[74]

68. The universal law is both definite and detailed in presenting the duties of the defender of the bond. The local lawmaker however may wish to clarify or add to these universal prescriptions and the following suggestions may be helpful.

(A) When the Code says the defender of the bond is to be heard on a point, he must present, if possible, arguments and reasons in opposition.[75]

(B) If the basis of the competence of the court is quasi-domicile, he must check carefully the reasons why the cause was not introduced in the court of domicile and in other ways assist in the fulfillment of the Instruction of 1929 on this point.[76]

(C) He must obtain, if possible, copies of pre-nuptial investigations and pre-ordination oaths.[77]

(D) He must suggest to the judge new questions in the course of the examinations especially if he discovers contradictions.[78]

74. *Normae a.* 1934, Art. 5 ¶ 2; C. 1588.
75. *Normae a.* 1934, Art. 30 and 37.
76. S.C. Sacr., instr., 23 dec. 1929, Title II — *AAS,* XXII, (1930), 168.
77. *The Jurist,* (Washington, D.C., 1941-—) in reply to a question, declares that the pre-nuptial investigation record is to be preserved in both the parish and the diocesan archives — II (1942), 161-162.
78. *Instructio a.* 1923, Reg. 28; *Instructio a.* 1931, Art. 22.

(E) Throughout the trial, he must watch the form of the process and the merits of the cause and make his objections soon enough that defects may be corrected. He is not a prosecutor who has interest in his side of the question only.

(F) Before he declares that there is no more to be offered in defense of the bond, he must carefully go over the acts and determine whether they are complete.[79]

(G) In drawing up his animadversions, he represents the Church with the greatest diligence. Therefore he limits himself to arguments in favor of the bond only and at no time expresses himself in favor of dissolution of the bond even if he is convinced of the need of this. However he must not at any time resort to sophistry, misrepresentations or sharp practices in his work.[80]

69. The promoter of justice is in a position similar to that of the defender of the bond. However the ordinary diocese seldom needs more than one promoter of justice. The constitution could include occasions when the promoter of justice must appear by diocesan law in causes other than those mentioned in the Code. The *Normae* of the Sacred Roman Rota has many regulations for the promoter of justice and among these the following especially may be of help to the diocesan promoter. (A) When the Code speaks of hearing the promoter of justice, he is bound to adduce motives, actions and arguments in defense of the public good.[81] (B) The promoter of justice is to be heard on occasions involving the question of granting or denying gratuitous patronage.[82]

70. In several dioceses of America there has gradually come into being a new office, a notary whose responsibility continues apart from causes and who is known as the secretary of the court.[83] This distinction between the secretary of the court and the *actuarius*

79. *Instructio a.* 1923, Reg. 96 ¶ 3.
80. S.C. Sacr., litt. priv., 5 ian. 1937 — Bouscaren, *Canon Law Digest,* (2 vols., 1934 and 1943, Milwaukee: Bruce Publishing Co.,) II 541-542.
81. *Normae a.* 1934, Art. 30.
82. *Normae a.* 1934, Art. 31.
83. The S.R. Rota has a similar officer entitled the notary attached to the protocol — *Normae a.* 1934, Art. 6 ¶ 2; Art. 39; Art. 62.

of a cause is not found in the Code but it is in no way contrary to it. The office answers a specific need in some dioceses and bishops are free to institute such an office by diocesan law if they desire to do so. In smaller dioceses especially the chancellor or the secretary of the bishop could well be designated to take over the duties of this office.[84] In larger dioceses the secretary of the court could be made a vice chancellor, for example, to facilitate his work as archivist. He should of course be made at least a notary.

71. Among the duties to be assigned to the secretary of the court might be the following:

(A) To assist the *officialis* in all his judicial and administrative activities.

(B) To care for all correspondence of the court.

(C) To care for records of appointments by entering these in the register of the roster.[85]

(D) To note in the protocol book the day and hour of the reception of causes, commissions and documents as well as the date of fulfillment of causes and commissions.[86]

(E) To be present at and record in the register of the roster the oaths of all permanent officers.

(F) To care for the seal and to check the presence of the seal and signatures on all documents.[87]

(G) To prepare the annual reports for the Holy See and for the bishop.

84. Prince includes among the duties of the chancellor many of those that might be assigned to the secretary of the court. Thus he says the chancellor should countersign the appointments of judges; the rejection or admission of the *libellus;* and the nomination of delegated judges. "... in fact," he says, "any decree that issues from the bishop and not from the *officialis* should bear the counter signature of the diocesan chancellor" — *The Diocesan Chancellor,* (The Catholic University of America Canon Law Studies, n. 167, Washington, D.C.: The Catholic University of America Press, 1942), p. 84.

85. *Normae a.* 1934, Art. 39 a.

86. *Normae a.* 1934, Art. 39 b and c, Art. 40 a.

87. *Normae a.* 1934, Art. 39 d.

(H) To fulfill other duties given him by the bishop or the *officialis,* such as notifying officers of their appointments to "*turni.*"

72. C. 373 § 1 implies that the bishop should appoint a number of notaries, as it were a diocesan list. The constitution can designate this list, along with the chancellor, the vice chancellors, the assistant chancellors and the secretary of the court as the list of notaries who may be called upon as *actuarii* of trials. The bishop makes the appointments to this list although he may desire to delegate the power to name notaries at least for individual causes.

The office of notary in itself does not entitle a priest to act as *actuarius* of a cause. This requires a further designation for the specific cause by the ordinary, the *officialis* or the presiding judge.[88]

The constitution may determine the method of this designation as *actuarii.* Most probably the designation of the chancellor and possibly of the vice chancellors will be only for more serious causes and especially for more secret causes. The others may be chosen after any manner set forth in the constitution, for example, in turn, according to the discretion of the *officialis* or according to language.[89]

73. Lest there be any confusion between the office of *actuarius* and that of the secretary of the court, the constitution might mention that the former performs everything demanded by the Code during the actual trial itself. He cares for the portfolio of the cause and keeps all records and documents therein. Likewise he notifies all officers of the time and place of sessions, if necessary, and carefully keeps the minutes of the sessions even though a stenographer is employed to record the testimony being heard.

74. Every court should have an archivist (*scrinarius*) although this office may be combined by the constitution with another. Some would say that the chancellor should be the archivist[90] and he is naturally the logical choice because of his access to the diocesan

88. Bouix, D., *Tractatus de Iudiciis Ecclesiasticis,* (2 vols. Parisiis, 1855), I, 480; Prince, *The Diocesan Chancellor,* p. 84; Augustine, *Commentary,* VII, p. 40.

89. The notary for judicial acts is called the *actuarius;* for non-judicial acts simply the notary — Coronata, *Institutiones,* III, n. 1123.

90. C. 372 § 1; Prince, *The Diocesan Chancellor,* p. 68.

archives. Most chancellors in America however are concerned with more important things. The officer chosen as archivist, for example, the secretary, can however be designated a vice chancellor.[91]

It is the duty of the archivist to see to the protection of the archives, to put completed and suspended causes in them at the order of the presiding judge and to make indices of all archive material in accordance with the system employed by the court.[92]

75. The Sacred Roman Rota employs a librarian[93] and it is most natural that the diocesan court have one also to care for its library. Again this office might well be combined with another, for example, with that of the secretary.

The constitution may wish to specify the duties of the librarian. For example, it may declare that it is his duty to care for the law books of the court, to preserve and ultimately to have bound all official magazines subscribed for by the court, to purchase new books under the direction of the *officialis,* to keep an index of all books and magazines and to hand out books and magazines to those who wish to consult them, recording the names and dates.[94]

76. The constitution can determine who is to perform the duties of treasurer. Among these duties will be the recording of moneys due, the reception of fees and taxes, the care of the ledger book and the distribution of the moneys under the direction of and according to the instructions of the bishop or of the *officialis.*[95]

77. The Code recommends the appointment of an "*apparitor*" or bailiff.[96] The principle duty of the bailiff would be to escort desired parties, witnesses or experts into the courtroom from the waiting room and to usher them out when hearings have been completed. This office could be given by the constitution to the *actuarius* of the cause. He should take particular care lest those already heard have communication with those about to be heard.

91. C. 372 § 2.
92. *Normae a.* 1934, Art. 46.
93. *Normae a.* 1934, Art. 6 ¶ 2.
94. *Normae a.* 1934, Art. 43.
95. *Normae a.* 1934, Art. 45 and 46.
96. C. 1591.

78. The messenger in many dioceses is a priest. The purpose of this is to encourage cooperation from witnesses and especially from respondents in trials.[97] The priest-messenger in these dioceses not only delivers documents to persons and places according to directions and records the fact, time and place of the delivery, but also gives assurance that no great inconvenience will be encountered by the parties cited by appearance in court and even at times gathers information invaluable in clarifying the joinder of issue.

79. Regulations should be made by the constitution concerning stenographers to be employed by the court. Persons of practical experience are agreed, for example, that it is most undesirable to have female stenographers for actual court sessions themselves. Special attention should be paid in the choice of stenographers to the obligation of secrecy. Among the duties of the stenographers might be mentioned the obligations to make copies of documents and transcriptions of causes and cases according to directions received, to take care that all writings and transcriptions are executed without defects and without mistakes and to examine thoroughly all papers for such defects and mistakes prior to returning them to the *actuarius*.[98]

Article 3. Rules for the Roster

80. The constitution may specify that all permanent appointments to the roster be made by the local ordinary of the place. The universal law requires this for the *officialis*, the *vice-officialis*, the judges, the defender of the bond, the promoter of justice and the notaries, but the constitution, to insure greater stability, may require it for the other officers also such as the librarian and the secretary of the court.[99]

81. Permanent appointments to the roster should always be in writing.[100] This is necessarily so for the offices that are such

97. C. 1591; cf. especially ¶¶ 168-172 of this dissertation.
98. *Normae a.* 1934, Art. 41.
99. C. 1573 § 1 and § 3; c. 385 § 1; c. 373 § 1; c. 1589.
100. C. 364 § 1; c. 159; "Non est ad validitatem" — Tobin, *De Officiali*, n. 141.

in the strict sense but may be made to include offices in a broad sense and even for the very minor offices like that of the librarian established by diocesan law. Rules should be made concerning the recording of appointments and the preservation of this recording. In ¶ 105, reference is made herein to a record book of permanent appointments, i.e., the register of the roster, which each court may and should have. The fact of appointment and the date may be placed in this book whence information is easily obtainable for the records of the individual causes.

82. Diocesan law may determine that all permanent officers except judges and possibly the *officialis* and *vice-officialis* be re-appointed, for example, every three years.[101] Appointment of judges must be for a term extending from synod to synod or, if no synod is held, for a ten year period.[102] Some have suggested the renewing of the appointment of all officers, even the judges, every year at the solemn opening of court. This could be done for other officers but would seem to be out of accord with the universal law for judges. The term of their appointment is set by universal law and hence the particular law cannot restrict it to one year.

83. On being appointed to office, each officer must take the required oaths. This is demanded of most officers by universal law and the constitution may require it of appointees to lesser offices created by itself. Included among the oaths required by universal law are the oaths of office, of secrecy in some causes and against modernism.[103] The constitution may mention the anti-modernist oath. The Code does not because of its temporary character but this oath and the profession of faith accompanying it are still of universal obligation.[104] The officers of the tribunals to take the

101. This period is suggested for the Philippine Islands — *Normae* for Tribunals of the Philippine Islands, Art. 5 — *AAS,* XXXIII (1941), 365; Bouscaren, The Canon Law Digest, II, 537.

102. C. 1574 § 2; cc. 385-388.

103. C. 1621; c. 1623; S.C.S. Off., 22 mart. 1918 — *AAS,* X (1918), 136; S.C.S. Off., const., *"Pascendi.,"* 8 sept. 1907 — *Fontes,* n. 680; S.C.S. Off., motu proprio., *"Sacrorum Antistitum,"* 1 sept. 1910 — *Fontes,* n. 689; Tobin, *De Officiali,* n. 200.

104. S.C.S. Off., 22 mart. 1918 — *AAS,* X (1918), 136; the officers of the

anti-modernist oath and the profession by universal law include the *officialis*, the *vice-officialis*, the chancellor, the vice chancellors, the promoters, the defenders, the judges, the auditors, the notaries, the messengers and the bailiffs (*apparitores*).[105] This oath is required for reappointments and for appointments to each distinct office even though taken previously upon the assuming of another office.[106] The fact that the oaths and professions of faith were taken must be preserved. This is done in some places by having the officers sign printed copies of the oaths and professions and these are preserved in the archives. Mention of the fact in the register of the roster would be sufficient.

The constitution may make its own regulations concerning oaths of appointees to offices of its own making.

84. Precedence among court officers is determined by the office held. Within the same office, precedence is determined by prior appointment and, this being equal, by prior ordination to the priesthood and finally by greater age.[107]

85. Officers of the roster may resign for a just cause.[108] A resignation must be made either in writing or orally before two witnesses,[109] the record of which should be preserved in the record book of permanent appointments. For validity the resignation must be accepted by the appointer, his successor or his superior, who

diocesan court are not mentioned among those required to make the profession of faith in C. 1406 § 1. However the motu proprio, "*Sacrorum Antistitum*" of Pope Pius X says: "Officiales in curiis episcopalibus et ecclesiasticis tribunalibus, haud exceptis ... iudicibus" — *AAS*, II (1910), 668-669. Tobin, *op. cit.*, n. 201.

105. Canavan, Walter, *The Profession of Faith*, (The Catholic University of America Canon Law Studies, n. 151, Washington, D.C.: The Catholic University of America Press, 1942), p. 114.

106. C. 1406; Canavan, *The Profession of Faith*, p. 114. Oaths and professions need not be read completely by each one of a group taking them but may be read by one and the others need repeat only the last line.

107. *Normae a.* 1934, Art. 3 ¶ 1; Commentary on the *Normae a.* 1934, — *Jus Pontificium* XIV (1934), 307.

108. C. 184.

109. C. 186.

should not accept the resignation except for a just and proportionate cause.[110] The office does not become vacant until notice has been received of the approval of the resignation.[111]

Article 4. Rules of the *Turnus*

86. The bishop of the diocese possess the right to judge or to assist in judging any cause coming to his court.[112] The dignity of office will suggest otherwise in nearly all cases. He may feel constrained to reserve certain causes however to his own judgment and the diocesan constitution could list the causes thus reserved. On such occasions, if a collegiate court is required, he presides in place of the *officialis*.

87. The diocesan constitution may determine both who chooses the officers of the "*turnus*" and how they are chosen. The bishop has every right to reserve the designation of officers of the "*turnus*" to himself for every cause but it seems more in keeping with the dignity of his position to allow subordinates to handle routine details such as this. However he may well reserve to himself the appointment of the officers of the "*turni*" in criminal causes and in certain more serious contentious causes. The constitution could list the causes in the case of which "*turni*" appointments are reserved to the bishop. Mention might be made of the authority of the vicar general or of the *officialis* to appoint for these in cases of necessity.

When the bishop does not exercise his right of appointing, the *officialis* appoints the officers of the "*turni*" over which he presides.[113] The diocesan constitution may determine to what extent the *vice-officiales* appoint their own officers. The constitution can determine in what order officers are to be chosen from the roster.[114]

88. The synodal laws of Richmond include a regulation which the constitution may desire to adopt: "Ad tribunalis sessiones conveniant omnes judices et administri qui ab officiali vocantur."[115]

110. C. 187; c. 189.
111. C. 190.
112. C. 1572 § 1.
113. P. C. I., 28 iulii 1932 — *AAS*, XXIV (1932), 314.
114. Cf. ¶¶ 59-60; 63; 65; 67; 69; 72 of this dissertation.
115. *Synodus Dioecesana Richmondiensis Tertia*, Stat. 37.

89. Once the *"turnus"* is set up, it is stable. So much so that, even though the *officialis* chose the original members of the *"turnus,"* if one of the major officers, for example, a judge, becomes sick, withdraws because of suspicion, or for any other reason cannot act after the trial has started, the *officialis* may not under the restrictions of universal law make the substitution required.[116] Possibly the lawmaker by this rule is expressing his desire for definite stability in each established *"turnus."* The constitution may delegate the *officialis* to make these substitutions and naturally will require that the reasons for them be made in the acts of the causes.

Substitute officers should sign all papers as substitutes and all references to them in the acts should mention the substitution by designating them as, for example, substitute judge, substitute defender of the bond.[117]

90. Record of all appointments and substitutions to the *"turni"* must appear in the acts of the causes. The constitution may adopt any method desired for accomplishing this. For example, some courts insist that the original decree of appointment, as a rule a separate paper, be placed among the acts. Others have the decree read at the first session of the trial and thereby it is incorporated directly into the minutes of the session. The latter method makes for greater compactness in the acts, for more completeness of detail and for simplicity in making copies of the acts.

91. Oaths of officers of a *"turnus"* should not be renewed if they were taken on the assumption of office. The constitution may mention that the oaths of officers appointed for individual causes only be taken at the first session of the trial immediately after the reading of the decree setting up court. The advantage of a set time mentioned in the constitution is to prevent neglect of oaths through inadvertence. Delegation might be given in the constitution to the presiding judge to receive the oaths of officers named to the *"turnus"* by the bishop himself.[118]

116. C. 1615 § 2; *Instructio a.* 1936, Art. 19 ¶ 1 and Art. 32 ¶ 2; cf. ¶ 40 of this dissertation.

117. *Instructio a.* 1923, Reg. 18; *Instructio a.* 1931, Art. 10.

118. C. 1621 § 1.

CHAPTER IV

REGULATIONS ON EQUIPMENT, TIME, PLACE, CONDUCT AND REPORTS

ARTICLE 1. EQUIPMENT OF THE DIOCESAN COURT

92. The constitution may specify that the court have a library with at least a minimum number of essential books for consultation.[1] It can designate the location, preferably in or near the hall of sessions for convenience in consulting it, and make rules concerning the index of the library, the borrowing of books, expenses of books, the purchase of new books and the binding of magazines.[2]

93. Each court must have at least two archives and regulations should be made in the constitution concerning these. Both the general archive and the secret archive would seem to be portions of the regular diocesan general and secret archives.[3]

94. When secret causes are complete, the constitution may require that they be sealed in an envelope and filed in the diocesan secret archives. The filing must be done by the bishop and the

1. This is a practice of the S.R. Rota — *Normae a.* 1934, Art. 6, ¶ 2 and Art. 43. The Fourth Provincial Council of Portland prescribes a library for each diocesan curia — *Acta et Decreta Concilii Procialis Portlandensis in Oregon Quarti,* Stat. 112.
2. The tribunal library should contain at least the Code, the *Acta Apostolicae Sedis,* some good commentaries, and some general and particular civil law books. Highly recommended, among many works that could be mentioned, are the decisions of the S.R. Rota, the *Fontes,* a good canon law magazine, dissertations, for example, of The Catholic University of America, and Bouscaren's *The Canon Law Digest.* It would be most difficult to interpret the present law without some good commentaries on the law prior to 1918.
3. C. 375 and c. 379, for example, speak of the documents of criminal causes as being retained in the diocesan secret archive. Cf. Louis, W.F., *Diocesan Archives,* (The Catholic University of America Canon Law Studies, n. 137, Washington, D.C.: The Catholic University of America Press, 1941) p. 49 and p. 71.

vicar general.[4] This archive should have an inventory containing a brief summary of documents contained therein.[5] To protect the secrecy of criminal trials especially the contents of the archives should be surveyed each year and the documents of the processes destroyed by burning after the deaths of the principals or after the lapse of ten years.[6]

95. It would be inconvenient to place documents of pending secret causes in the diocesan secret archives and therefore the constitution may suggest a special secret archive for such causes under the care of the *officialis* for example.[7]

96. C. 1871 § 2 would seem to indicate that the conclusions of individual judges in solemn trials are to be placed with the original documents of the acts and yet kept secret. This might be accomplished by placing them in a sealed envelope. Probably they could be placed, sealed and in proper order, in the special secret archive mentioned in ¶ 95 of this dissertation.

97. General archives of completed causes (stationary archives) are treated as part of the diocesan general archives by authors.[8] The chancellor has charge of these archives and hence the desirability of making him or a vice chancellor archivist for the diocesan court.[9] Separate general archives for the court, in charge of the tribunal archivist, probably would not be contrary to the law providing precautions against fire, intruders, dampness, etc., are taken.[10] Any method may be employed for the filing of causes within the archives but a natural division according to protocol number suggests itself.[11] Larger dioceses may find need of a more extensive division into various types of causes. This filing may be correlated

4. C. 379 § 3.
5. C. 379 § 2.
6. C. 379 § 1; *Normae a.* 1934, Art. 143; Louis, *op. cit.*, p. 72.
7. The S.R. Rota has its own secret archive — *Normae a.* 1934, Art. 143.
8. C. 1645 § 2; Louis, *Diocesan Archives*, p. 48.
9. Prince, *The Diocesan Chancellor*, pp. 64-65, p. 68; cf. ¶ 70 of this dissertation.
10. Louis, *Diocesan Archives*, p. 44-47.
11. Louis, *op. cit.*, p. 54.

with the card indices mention in ¶ 100. All of which can be regulated in the diocesan constitution.

98. To avoid inconveniences, some tribunals have temporary (current) archives for pending causes.[12] The many developments of the present day, for example, in steel filing cabinets, make this a simple expedient and the diocesan constitution may make regulations concerning it. Causes would be transferred from the current to the stationary archive only at the command of the presiding judge.

99. A most convenient archive for any tribunal is one that has been termed the "*instruenda*" file. In it, with cross references to all parties involved, are records of all interviews on prospective causes and cases. The purpose of this file is not only the preservation of information but also a protection against duplication and fraud. It has been known for example that persons, meeting with discouragement at the hands of one consulting officer, have returned to another with a different story. Prevention against this fraud is but one of many reasons for this file which is referred to by each consulting officer prior to the presentation of a cause or a case. When a possible cause or case meets a favorable reception and proceeds to the introduction of the *libellus* or the petition,[13] the information and material of the *instruenda* file can be removed, given a protocol number and filed in the current archive.

100. Canon 375 § 2 requires an inventory or catalogue of documents contained in the archive. No particular form is suggested. It may be in a bound book; on sheets of loose paper placed in a portfolio; on index cards, etc.[14] The index cards have a marked advantage because of modern scientific methods of making and of preserving these. Some dioceses have excellent systems of cross references in their files with separate cards and sometimes even distinct colors to record causes and cases by number, type, and names of both parties. The inventory and cross filing can begin, for example, with the transfer of documents from the *instruenda* file to

12. Louis, *op. cit.*, p. 47.
13. Cf. ¶ 140 of this dissertation.
14. Louis, *Diocesan Archives*, p. 57.

the current archive but must be made not later than the transfer to the stationary archive.

101. The diocesan constitution can make specific regulations on how the injunction of C. 376 § 1 is to be carried out. This canon insists that inventories be kept up to date. The local statute may require, for example, a compiling of causes as they are added to one or the other archive, a general compiling at the beginning or end of each month or again a general compiling at the beginning or end of each year.[15]

102. The constitution may desire to specify details about the portfolio (*fasciculum*, format) of the individual cause,[16] the placing of documents therein, the recording therein of writings going out of the office and the identification of the specific portfolio by designation on the outside with the protocol number and the names of the parties especially. The index of this portfolio will be dealt with in ¶ 256.

103. Regulations should be made concerning access to both the current and the stationary archives and to the removal of documents therefrom. C. 377 forbids ingress to the diocesan general archives without permission of the bishop or of the vicar general and of the chancellor. Possibly the constitution could grant a general delegation to the *officialis* and to the secretary of the court (not needed if he is vice chancellor). Removal of documents by others requires permission of the bishop or of the vicar general and the signing of a receipt.[17] Access to the current archives might be reserved to the *officialis* and the secretary of the court.

104. Each court should have its own seal.[18] Some authors declare that the tribunal seal ought to be distinct from that of the *curia* mentioned in C. 381 § 2.[19] Some courts of second instance

15. Louis, *Diocesan Archives,* p. 58.
16. C. 1644 § 1; cf. also ¶ 152 of this dissertation.
17. C. 378 § 2.
18. C. 1643 § 1; c. 1715 § 2; *Normae a.* 1934, Art. 39 d.
19. Tobin, *De Officiali,* n. 199; Connolly, Thomas, *Appeals,* (The Catholic University of America Canon Law Studies, n. 79, Washington, D.C.: The Catholic University of America, 1932), p. 101.

have a second seal for use on appeal causes only.[20] Many courts expedite the transcription of documents by use of a special rubber stamp which prints "*concordat cum originali*" with a line for the signature of the notary. This might be called the "*attestatur*" stamp.[21]

105. The record books of the diocesan court are most essential. Among these might be (A) a register of the roster for the recording of permanent appointments of officers and the dates of their assumption of office through the taking of oaths;[22] (B) the protocol (docket, journal) book in which are kept records of causes, including the dates of their receptions, the dispatching of citations, officers of the "*turni*," commissions sent out and returned, the dates of decisions, rogatory requests received and fulfilled and in a word all information on causes, cases and commissions necessary for the annual report;[23] (C) a date book in which the day and hour of each future session or appointment are recorded; (D) a minute book, although most courts prefer to keep minutes of sessions on loose leaf paper thus making easier the combination of the minutes with the rest of the acts of a cause; (E) a ledger for finances in which money received, money due, money paid out, library expenses, rogatory expenses, and gratuitous patronage are recorded;[24] (F) a source book of private replies from the Holy See;[25] (G) a loose-leaf book for communications from the ordinary; (H) a court

20. Tobin says that the court of appeal ought to have a second seal for its appeal work — *De Officiali*, n. 199.
21. Cf. ¶ 155 of this dissertation.
22. The register of the roster should be mindful of the information desired in Form III of the annual report to the Holy See — cf. Doheny, *Practical Manual*, p. 236.
23. A printed protocol book based on Form I and mindful also of the information desired in Form II of the annual report to the Holy See would be most convenient. Cf. Doheny, *Practical Manual*, p. 228.
24. *Normae a.* 1934, Art. 46 ¶¶ a nn. 1-7; a finance ledger should be mindful of the information desired in Form I of the annual report to the Holy See.
25. Some dioceses have a system whereby they exchange private replies received from the Holy See and these are preserved for directions to themselves in difficult situations.

ritual possibly in loose leaf form containing typewritten copies of oaths of office, the oath against modernism, the profession of faith, the oath of parties, witnesses and experts gathered from various sources and placed herein for convenience; (I) the book of Gospels which custom in the United States has long interpreted as the Bible.

106. Finally among their equipment, some courts include various forms and blanks.

Article 2. Regulations on Time

107. Some courts follow the custom of the Sacred Roman Rota in setting aside a vacation period every year.[26] Appropriately associated with this could be a solemn opening of the court season each year at the close of this vacation period. If the constitution chooses to adopt this practice, it could specify the date and the ceremonies of the opening. This would also be an excellent opportunity to check the dates of appointments, especially of judges, and to receive the oaths of newly appointed permanent officers.[27] Also related to the vacation period could be an official closing of the tribunal year. The constitution could make this an occasion for completing indices and inventories and for reports to the ordinary. The summer holiday closing should not be so absolute as to prevent all access to court officers. Arrangements can be made by the constitution whereby at least one consulting officer would always be on hand and whereby correspondence could be continued.[28]

108. Canon 1639 states that days of precept and the last three days of Holy Week are holydays on which court activities are forbidden.[29] Under the old law formal judicial activities were

26. A decree of July 3, 1913, set the S.R. Rota *"Feriae Autumnales"* from August 21 to October 14 — *AAS,* V (1913), 378. Roberti recommends a vacation and says the bishop determines the time by decree — *De Processibus,* I, n. 185.
27. The practice of having all officers renew oaths each year at this time seems to be contrary to the principle of avoiding unnecessary and useless oaths.
28. Roberti, *De Processibus,* n. 185.
29. Coronata, *Institutiones,* III, n. 1160; Roberti, *De Processibus,* I, n. 185.

invalid on these days but the Code has lifted this invalidating clause. It might be mentioned that Canon 1248 includes court activities along with manual labor as forbidden on days of precept.[30] The constitution could require an explanation in the acts if necessity or charity required judicial activities on these days. For the sake of uniformity through the years, further regulations might be made concerning court work during the unusually busy early days of Holy Week and during the Christmas season.[31] Local conditions will naturally determine whether such regulations are needed or desirable.

109. Canon 1638 § 1 demands a set time, determined by public decree, when the court may be approached and the regulations on this point might well be incorporated in the constitution.[32] Included here will be not only the hours when consulting officers may be approached but also the times when the *officialis* is available.[33] In larger dioceses the court may wish to have set times for sessions, for example, once or twice a week, thus giving officers of the court the opportunity to plan on such hours and to regulate their court work and other work accordingly.[34] Difficulties will be encountered if several "*turni*" are at work at the same time. Therefore the constitution may desire to leave the schedule to the judgment of the *officialis* with instructions that dates be set regularly if possible and sufficiently in advance to enable the officers to plan for the occasions. It might be observed that at any given hour, sessions of several causes could be held depending on the work to be accomplished and upon which witnesses, parties and experts could be on hand at that hour. Care should be taken to keep sessions of different causes technically distinct.

30. Ayrinhac, H. A., *Administrative Legislation in the New Code of Canon Law,* (New Lork: Longsmans, Green, 1930), p. 106.
31. Coronata, *Institutiones* III, n. 1160.
32. Roberti, *De Processibus,* I, n. 186; Coronata says the ordinary issuing this decree may be the vicar general — *Institutiones,* III, n. 1160, Footnote 2. This duty could be delegated to the *officialis.*
33. Cf. ¶ 125 and ¶ 53 A of this dissertation.
34. The Diocese of Richmond decreed that its court meet twice a month — *Synodus Dioecesana Richmondiensis Tertia,* Stat. 38.

Article 3. Regulations on Place

110. The constitution may determine upon the location of the tribunal's hall of sessions or at least give the address of this hall. C. 1636 gives a latitude in choosing this place[35] and excludes only places under the jurisdiction of exempt religious. The Code prescribes only two things for the hall of sessions, a crucifix and a book of gospels, but needless to say the more fitting a hall of sessions the greater dignity can be given judicial work and the greater respect can be demanded for the tribunal.[36] Tables for the judges, the *actuarius* and the defender of the bond and a witness stand can be determined by local conditions.

Article 4. Regulations on Conduct in Court

111. The constitution may make a further provision on who may be present during a court session. It would be bad taste, for example, to have female stenographers present at some sessions at least. C. 1640 § 1 says "*extranei*" are to be excluded. Article 128 of the 1936 Instruction affirms that ordinarily neither the parties nor their procurators or advocates may assist at the examination of witnesses.[37] Because of the practice in the United States of employing only priests as advocates, whose primary interest is simple justice as opposed to any interest in fees, it would not seem contrary to the spirit of the 1936 Instruction, which allows their presence in individual cases, if the constitution would urge these advocates to request permission to be present at all sessions hearing

35. Coronata, *Institutiones,* III, n. 1159; Roberti, *De Processibus,* I, n. 184.
36. Roberti, *De Processibus,* I, n. 184; Coronata mentions the Code as necessary and also includes in this category "*aulae distinctae pro expectatione et pro notariis.*" The waiting rooms for witnesses should be so arranged that those examined may not speak to those yet to be examined. He recommends also separate halls for contentious causes and criminal causes, or at least that there be separate archives for these — *Institutiones,* III, n. 1158 ¶ 3.
37. Coronata declares the session is public in the sense that all the activities are preserved in writing but not in the admission of persons who have no relation to the cause. He gives many reasons for excluding the public — *Institutiones,* III, n. 1161; cf. also Roberti, *De Processibus,* I, nn. 165-166.

witnesses and urge judges to grant this request whenever possible. This would greatly facilitate the work of the advocates.

112. The constitution may choose to make regulations about court etiquette, for example, about proper clerical dress in the court room, smoking during sessions and about silence. Or it may impose on the presiding judge a watchfulness about these things. It may demand that the judge open and close each session with a prayer, which, aside from its value as a petition for enlightenment, serves to call the session to order in place of the civil court use of the gavel and impresses all present with the seriousness of the work that is about to begin. In addressing the court, some officers employ the civil law term "honorable court" and others the appropriate term "reverend court."

Article 5. Annual Reports

113. Each year the diocesan court must submit a report on its activities in matrimonial causes and cases to the Sacred Congregation of the Sacraments through the Apostolic Delegation.[38] The constitution may designate the secretary of the court as the officer bound to make out this report with instructions that it be submitted upon completion to the bishop. Properly arranged books and registers of the tribunal would be of great assistance in compiling such a report.[39]

114. The constitution may demand that for example an annual or a semi-annual report covering all causes and all cases be made to the bishop.[40] The secretary could be appointed to make out this report also and in it emphasis could be placed, among other things, upon the completion of causes within the required two years, upon court finances, upon the recording of results of all matrimonial procedures in marriage and baptismal records, upon such needs as reappointments, new officers and new equipment.[41]

38. S.C. Sacr., litt., 1 iul. 1932, *AAS,* XXIV (1932), 272.

39. Cf. ¶ 105 of this dissertation.

40. The Diocese of Richmond demands a semi-annual report, in January and July — *Synodus Dioecesana Richmondiensis Tertia,* Stat. 42.

41. Marx, Adolph, *The Declaration of Nullity of Marriages Contracted Outside the Church,* (The Catholic University Canon Law Studies, n. 182, Washington, D.C.: The Catholic University of America Press, 1943), p. 110 (henceforth cited as *The Declaration of Nullity*).

CHAPTER V

THE PARTIES, THEIR PROCURATORS AND THEIR ADVOCATES

115. In determining the right of a person to stand in court, the laws of the Code and, for matrimonial causes, their interpretation in the Instruction of 1936 are to be carefully observed.[1] Court officers may be advised to give these laws as broad an interpretation as the law and well recognized authors permit lest they interfere with a strict right of individuals to seek justice through the diocesan court.

116. The universal law makes some reservations of rights of certain persons to act in court.[2] Some dioceses prefer to extend this restriction in order to further protect the sacredness of the sacraments and of the court by requiring permission of the ordinary before certain petitions may be entertained. Thus the *officialis* in these dioceses is not permitted, on his own authority, to forward applications of non-Catholics to Rome, to receive the applications of non-Catholics in lack of form or in the summary cases of C. 1990. Permission in each case must be obtained from the bishop. Court officials in places have requested such a restriction to protect themselves from those who might be designated as "bargaining" non-Catholics, who would become Catholics if they are permitted to marry certain Catholics.

Again, to assure himself that the faith of individuals is protected and that scandal is avoided, the bishop may demand that the court obtain permission from him before considering any action by an apostate Catholic,[3] a Catholic adhering to a non-Catholic sect or to a forbidden society, a formally excommunicated person and a public sinner.

1. Cc. 1646-1654; cc. 1970-1972; *Instructio a.* 1936, Articles 34-42; S.C.S. Off., 27 ian. 1928 — *AAS,* XX (1928), 75; S.C.S. Off., 22 mart. 1939 — *AAS,* XXXI (1939), 131; private letter of the Apostolic Delegate of Sept. 23, 1938 — Bouscaren, *The Canon Law Digest,* II, 531.
2. For example, non-Catholics may not act as plaintiffs in matrimonial *causes* without permission of the Holy Office — *Instructio a.* 1936, Art. 35 ¶ 3.
3. A decision of the Holy Office of Jan. 15, 1940, places apostate Catholics in the category of non-Catholics — *AAS,* XXXII (1940), 52.

The bishop may choose also to reserve to himself an approval of causes requiring special procurators by ruling that he himself is to appoint these procurators.[4] These include the causes of minors and moral persons in case of conflict between the rights of their administrators and their own rights.[5] He may require that permission be obtained before any priest or religious be admitted to institute an action in his court. Finally, in certain dioceses especially, he may choose to make some regulation concerning application of Orientals for consideration of their causes by the Sacred Congregation for the Oriental Church.

117. Advocates and procurators are employed in diocesan courts and a double authorization is needed for them in most cases. Advocates in all causes and procurators in marriage causes must be appointed to these offices by the proper authorities[6] while authorization by the parties must be given through mandates for every individual cause.[7] The first appointment is generally made by the bishop and the names of those appointed are published in a list (*album*).[8] The Sacred Roman Rota publishes such a list each year.[9] The constitution may choose to adopt this or any regulation concerning the list that is better suited to local conditions.[10] It may rule on the place where this list is to be preserved, for example in the register of permanent appointments, and on the manner in which it will be made available to those requiring it. The bishop may of course delegate this power of original authorization of advocates and procurators. Again he may prefer to reserve to himself all appointments for causes in general and delegate to the *officialis*, for example, the power to authorize them for individual causes. It can be noted

4. This power to appoint these procurators may of course be delegated to the *officialis* as was suggested in ¶ 44 of this work.
5. C. 1648 § 3; c. 1649; Hogan, James, *Judicial Advocates and Procurators,* (The Catholic University of America Canon Law Studies, n. 133, Washington, D.C.: The Catholic University of America Press, 1941), p. 75.
6. C. 1658; *Instructio a.* 1936, Art. 48 ¶ 4; Hogan, *op. cit.,* 94-95.
7. C. 1659; c. 1661.
8. *Instructio a.* 1936, Art. 53.
9. Hogan, *op. cit.,* p. 96; Doheny, *Canonical Procedure,* p. 119.

that this delegation refers only to the approval and not to the mandate to act. It might be useful also to grant to the *officialis* the right to subdelegate the power to appoint procurators in individual causes in order more easily to obtain at least a minimum cooperation from obstinate respondents especially.[11] Regulations should be made concerning the recording of recognition of such appointments for individual causes either in the acts of the cause or in the register of appointments or in both.

118. In some dioceses it is not always possible to have all advocates and all procurators as fully equipped with degrees and other legal qualifications demanded by the Code and by the 1936 Instruction.[12] The law provides for relaxation in exceptional cases and in these necessity is the determining factor. "In the case of the advocate it is the ordinary who will judge whether or not such necessity really exists, while in the case of the procurator, except for matrimonial trials, the decision will be referred to the judge."[13] The bishop may wish to authorize the *officialis* to make this judgment, for advocates in all causes and for procurators in matrimonial causes, in individual cases at least.

119. The mandates authorizing action in an individual cause come as a rule from the parties in the cause.[14] The constitution may demand that some officer, the secretary of the court for example, shall check these mandates in every cause and, if this has not been done by the pastor, witness the designation by his signature[15] as well as properly preserve these mandates for the acts. Care should be taken lest possible witnesses be chosen for either of these offices.

120. The constitution could rule that procurators and advocates whose names are listed in the register are bound to accept appointments given to them or approved for them by the *officialis;*

10. Hogan, *op. cit.,* p. 96.
11. Cf. ¶ 171 of this dissertation.
12. C. 1657; *Instructio a.* 1936, Art. 48.
13. Hogan, *Judicial Advocates and Procurators,* p. 84; Noval, *De Judiciis,* p. 178.
14. C. 1659; c. 1661; *Instructio a.* 1936, Art. 49.

that all who serve in either capacity in the court for which the constitution is operative are bound to follow not only the regulations of the universal law but also those of the diocesan constitution;[16] that their work is subject to the supervision of the *officialis* and that the *officialis* is authorized to punish them for negligence or disrespect. In order to give force to the latter point, the constitution may extend any power of coaction given by the Code to the *officialis* and may specify the type of punishment, for example pecuniary fines, for individual occasions.

121. The advocates and even the procurators may be encouraged to request permission to be present at the hearing of parties, witnesses and experts, as was seen in ¶ 111. If necessary the court can always bind the advocates and procurators with oaths of special secrecy.[17]

122. The Rota demands an oath of office for procurators and advocates.[18] The constitution also may ask a formal oath of secrecy and of office of all advocates and procurators if it deems this necessary as an added safeguard of the natural law secrecy of office in C. 1755 § 2 n. 1.[19]

123. Fees for procurators and advocates are to be established in a schedule by the bishops of the province.[20] If this has not been done, they are to be determined by the judge or by the ordinary.[21] The constitution may make it definite by delegating this entirely to the *officialis* until such time as the provincial schedule is drawn up.

15. C. 1659 § 1; *Instructio a.* 1936, Art. 49 ¶ 1; Hogan, *op. cit.*, 105.
16. The S. R. Rota has a law like this — *Normae a.* 1934, Art. 56 ¶ 1.
17. *Instructio a.* 1936, Art. 130.
18. *Normae a.* 1934, Art. 54; Hogan, *op. cit.*, p. 62.
19. Hogan says that they are bound by the universal law to take an oath and gives c. 1621 § 1 as a reference (p. 132). It is possible that this is an extensive interpretation of C. 1621 § 1 since advocates and procurators are one with the parties rather than with the tribunal. Art. 130 ¶ 1 of the 1936 Instruction seems to imply that no previous oath was taken.
20. Hogan, *Judicial Advocates and Procurators*, p. 171; cf. also ¶ 339 C of this dissertation.
21. Coronata, *Institutiones*, III, n. 351; Roberti, *De Processibus*, II, n. 538; Hogan, *op. cit.*, p. 172.

CHAPTER VI

JUDICIAL PROCEDURE

ARTICLE 1. THE PRELIMINARY RECEPTION OF CAUSES

124. The universal law of the Church is as a rule silent on potential causes prior to their formal introduction through the *libellus.* Individual dioceses have included rulings on this point in their synodal laws and the diocesan constitutions should set forth some guiding norms for pastors and laymen, as well as for officers of the court, in regard to preliminary preparations.

A. The Pre-Libellus Consultation

125. For example, the constitution may suggest or even require that the plaintiff and possibly his adviser, who would most often be the pastor or any priest whom he has consulted, meet with a consulting officer or group of officers in an informal non-judicial conference for a discussion of the possible cause and for instructions on how to proceed.[1] For this purpose the constitution could determine certain set hours when the designated officers could be approached, for example during the morning hours of each week day.

126. The constitution would do well to give in this place a few practical rules for priests of the diocese who will naturally be called upon to advise their people concerning legal actions. In most cases parishioners approach their pastors first and the constitution could suggest this possibly without making it obligatory. The adviser is not a judicial personality as such.

127. The first practical rule to be remembered by these priest-advisers is that it is "unwise to present cases without first

1. The term "consulting officer" is arbitrary. Some may prefer, for example, "special advocates," *"advocati pauperum"* or just "notaries." Their identity would vary with the various dioceses; in some places they would be possibly four of the notaries; in others possibly four of the advocates; and in smaller dioceses the secretary and possibly the *officialis* might be the consulting officers.

studying the matter thoroughly."[2] This presupposes a certain preliminary inquiry. This inquiry is non-judicial in every way; oaths may not be given and testimony received can be introduced later only if original judicial testimony cannot be had and then only as enjoying the authority of a private document or of hearsay testimony. This inquiry must necessarily be very limited because of the danger of prejudicing individuals as to the testimony they will give later. The Fargo Statutes rightly declare that witnesses are not to be interrogated "lest the case be thereby prejudiced."[3] The constitution for the court may include instructions similar to those of the Fargo Synodal Laws: "The evidence of witnesses is not to be taken until it is requested by the... court, except in cases of contumacy, or unless, because of the probable death or departure of a witness, such testimony cannot safely be deferred to a proper time and place."[4] Testimony taken in an emergency without delegation from the court may be submitted later but only as enjoying the authority of a private document and its value will be judged by the precautions taken to insure the complete truth.

128. A second practical rule for priest-advisers can also be taken from the Fargo Statutes: "It is imprudent and strictly forbidden to promise or give any assurance to the interested parties of a favorable decision at any time previous to the final curial decision."[5] The reason for this in matrimonial causes is given. Making promises or expressing opinions "causes irreparable harm; for, experience shows that the least word indicating the likelihood of a favorable decision is frequently magnified by the interested parties and interpreted by them as a practical assurance of a forthcoming decree of nullity. In keeping with the mind of the Church an attitude tending to uphold marriage, and not to destroy it, should be maintained by all priests in connection with matrimonial cases.

2. *Liber Synodalis Fargensis*, n. 792, p. 162; Donovan, James, *The Pastor's Obligation in Pre-Nuptial Investigation*, (The Catholic University of America Canon Law Studies, n. 115, Washington, D.C.: The Catholic University of America Press, 1938), p. 132.
3. *Liber Synodalis Fargensis*, n. 793, p. 164.
4. *Liber Synodalis Fargensis*, n. 793, p. 164.

Nevertheless, great care should be taken lest one's right to seek redress before the ecclesiastical tribunal be denied him."[6]

129. The Constitution may empower the consulting officer to make inquiries at the preliminary conference concerning possible reconciliation of the parties and to institute action to bring about this reconciliation if it is possible.[7] The constitution may mention when this is to be omitted, for example when a civil divorce and a subsequent civil marriage have intervened in marriage causes. It may indicate that if he deems reconciliation and elimination of court action possible, he shall proceed with prudent and pastoral charity in tactfully offering advice and exhortation.[8] He may be empowered to commission a pastor or another priest or even a layman to attempt the reconciliation. The constitution may ask that these attempts at reconciliation be made prior to the submission of the *libellus*, if possible, and that a record be kept of the attempts. This record, either of the attempts or of the reason for their omission, should be presented at the first session of the court in order that the acts of the cause may be complete.

130. The consulting officer cannot be empowered to reject presented causes at this discussion or conference but naturally he can inform the petitioner when the request is evidently useless and even sometimes ridiculous.[9] Under these circumstances he can use his powers of persuasion to influence the individual to pursue the action no farther. But if the party insists on a formal presentation through a *libellus* to the court this request must be granted because only the court in its official capacity can reject a request for justice.[10] In matrimonial causes this means a collegiate court of three judges.[11]

131. The constitution may ask the consulting officer to give instructions on the choice of a procurator and of an advocate and on

5. *Liber Synodalis Fargensis*, n. 792, p. 163.
6. *Liber Synodalis Fargensis*, n. 792, p. 163.
7. *Instructio a.* 1923, Reg. 10.
8. *Instructio a.* 1923, Reg. 10.
9. Roberti says that even the *officialis* cannot admit or reject judicial petitions — *De Processibus*, I, n. 97.
10. C. 1709; Doheny, *Canonical Procedure*, p. 134.
11. *Instructio a.* 1936, Art. 61-67.

the drawing up of the mandates. The diocese has its list (*album*) of procurators and a choice may be made at this time from this list by the plaintiff. If the latter desires that his adviser act as procurator in the cause, as is often the case, the *officialis* could be empowered by the constitution to give him official approval as procurator for the cause if he is not listed in the diocesan "*album*" and if he deems it prudent.[12] The date of this appointment, or of the permanent appointment recorded as a rule in the register of the roster, could be mentioned in the mandate. The diocesan list of advocates may be presented on this occasion to the party and a choice of advocate made. In the instruction on the mandates of the procurator and of the advocate by the consulting officer, the rules laid down in the Code and in the Instruction of 1936 are to be minutely observed and mention may be made that the mandates should be very brief and may be placed at the end of the *libellus*, properly signed and notarized.

132. The consulting officer may then give instructions on the *libellus*.[13] The advocate may be employed to assist in its composition but he does not sign the completed document.[14] The constitution determines how it is addressed to the court and to what address it is to be forwarded on completion. Concerning the contents, the object, the grounds, the formal request, the reason for the request, etc., the rules of the Code and of the Instruction of 1936 are to be carefully followed. A limit may be set by the constitution for the length of the ordinary *libellus*. While the *libellus* should contain a full and accurate account of essentials of the cause,[15] nevertheless the *libellus* is not the place for the presentation of proofs. Since there may be several occasions when the *libellus* is to be read at court sessions, it should not be, exclusive of lists of witnesses, more than a page or two in length.

133. The party can be told to send the list of witnesses with

12. ¶ 42 of this dissertation.
13. Cc. 1706-1710; *Instructio a.* 1936, Art. 55-57.
14. Hogan, *Judicial Advocates and Procurators*, p. 138.
15. *Instructio a.* 1923, Reg. 6 ¶ 1.

their addresses with the *libellus.*[16] The libellus should also be accompanied by a petition that these witnesses be called to give testimony, by *"articuli"* or points of information known to the party upon which the witnesses may be questioned and upon which the defender of the bond may base at least some of his questions in his questionnaires,[17] by letters of introduction to witnesses if these will be helpful and by releases from professional secrecy if these are necessary. Naturally the constitution will leave a certain freedom in supplementing this list at later dates. This early presentation of a completed list of witnesses will allow the court to arrange its plans accordingly and hasten the completion of the cause.

134. The constitution may insist that ordinarily a letter or document of information from the pastor be presented to the court with the *libellus.*[18] Instructions on this may be given by the consulting officer at the preliminary conference especially if the pastor is the plaintiff's adviser and is present. If the pastor is not at this conference, the constitution may direct that the petition for these *"informationes"* be sent to the pastor directly rather than through the party.[19]

The letter should contain the pastor's statements of his knowledge of the parties, especially as to their character, the reasons for their present action in coming to court, the presence of scandal, the future danger of scandal if the cause is pursued, the possibilities of reconciliation, any pertinent circumstances and something of the financial status of the parties if they are requesting gratuitous patronage. This letter is not a judicial document and may or may not be included as a private document in the trial itself. Assurances should be given the pastor if necessary that the information con-

16. *Instructio a.* 1936, Art. 59; *Synodus Dioecesana Spokanensis Prima,* n. 145 a.
17. Cf. ¶ 183 of this dissertation.
18. This letter might be compared to the *"informationes"* of the bishop in the petition for dissolution of a ratified non-consummated marriage — *Instructio a.* 1923, Reg. 9.
19. Tobin, *De Officiali,* n. 304, nota 163; Doheny, *Practical Manual for Marriage Cases,* (Milwaukee: Bruce Publishing Co., 1938) p. 137 (hereafter cited *Practical Manual*).

tained therein will be kept secret. If the letter contains pertinent information, it is preferable that the pastor be called as a witness during the trial rather than that his letter be entered as a private document. The purpose of the *"informationes"* is to aid the court in its decision to accept or reject the *libellus*, to guide it in directing the attempts at reconciliation, to determine the presence of scandal and to decide on any petition for gratuitous patronage.

135. The consulting officer could be asked to give the plaintiff information on documents that should be submitted with the *libellus*, even though, if necessary, they may be admitted at a later date. Information should be given on needed certificates, contracts, private letters and documents, etc. Also the party can be informed of the need of identification during the trial and of the fees and expenses of judicial procedure. Many dioceses insist that down payments and guarantees be submitted with the *libellus*.[20]

136. If the plaintiff is desirous of gratuitous patronage or a reduction of fees, the consulting officer may direct him to present his petition, with the reasons, with his *libellus*.[21] This will enable the court to consider his request at either the first or the second session. The consulting officer may be authorized and even commanded to make whatever investigation is necessary.[22]

137. The consulting officer may be delegated by the constitution to gather the data at the preliminary conference on which the decision as to the competence of the court will be based and on which the determination of the right of the parties to act in court will depend. Special care should be taken to secure full information on the domiciles of both parties and on the place of contract. The consulting officer should make a record of all information gathered, to be presented to the court at the first session. He may be asked to give his own conclusions with the data if the situation presents difficulties. If the information is evidently unfavorable, i. e. showing either that the court has no competence or that the party has no

20. For example, *Liber Synodalis Fargensis*, n. 795, p. 164.
21. C. 1915 § 1.
22. C. 1915 § 2; *Instructio a.* 1936, Art. 238 ¶ 2.

right to plead, he cannot be empowered to make a definite decision on these points but he may be delegated to inform the plaintiff of the situation before the latter presents his *libellus* and to use persuasion with him to direct his petition to a competent court for example or to abandon his desire to sue.

138. Naturally all causes will not fit into the above suggested pattern of procedure. For such causes additional arrangements and instructions can be given by the constitution on the procedure as for example when the promoter of justice is compelled to plead in place of the party or when a preliminary conference cannot be held. In the latter case, for those living too far away for a personal interview, the constitution may well ask that a petitioning letter be sent by mail. All or much of the above suggested information could be sent to the party or to his adviser in the place where he is. Local circumstances will naturally determine the appointments of procurators and advocates in these cases. Care should be taken lest the pastor of the party, for example, be asked to serve as procurator and at the same time as a member of the commission delegated to hear the testimonies or that he be asked to assume an office connected with the cause if he is to be a witness in the trial.

139. The consulting officer may be requested to place his information, with cross reference cards, in the *instruenda* file, regardless of the possibilities of continuing the cause or the case.[23] This will be a protection against duplication and possible fraud.

B. From the Reception of the Libellus to the First Session

140. The constitution can proceed with directions on the activities of officers when the *libellus* and its accompanying documents come to the tribunal office. The cause is then removed from the *instruenda* file, officially docketed by entrance in the protocol book and placed in the current file. The constitution may designate the manner of docketing, indicating for example that the secretary shall enter the information in the protocol book according to the

23. Cf. ¶ 99 of this dissertation.

proper form,[24] give the cause a protocol number and note the time of reception. The order of handling causes is to be determined by the date of this act of docketing and therefore special care may be prescribed on entering the day and even the hour.[25]

141. Each court may adopt its own method of numbering its causes. Thus some courts, in smaller dioceses especially, number causes successively over long periods of time. Others choose to number them by the year and thus the protocol number reads, for example, 5|44 or 44|5. Still others number in succession within types of causes. The constitution may determine that *cases* handled, for example those of C. 1990 and lack of form cases, be given a different numbering than the causes, although many courts do not discriminate thus.

142. The *libellus* with its accompanying documents is to be placed in its folder or portfolio, on the outside of which may be placed identifying marks such as the protocol number, the names of the parties and the type of the cause.[26] The Sacred Roman Rota, in its rules, sees fit to mention that when documents are placed in its protocol, they are considered as belonging to the tribunal for the duration of the trial and that they may not be taken away while the cause endures. Temporary removal requires the consent of the other party and a decree of the court.[27] The documents to be placed in the portfolio depend on the nature of the cause but care should be taken that the mandates of the procurator and advocate be present and properly drawn up.[28]

143. The cause being docketed, the bishop, the *officialis* or the *vice-officialis* according to the requirements of the constitution, establishes the "*turnus*" for the cause observing the rules of the universal and local laws.[29] The constitution may specify that the

24. Cf. ¶ 105 of this dissertation.
25. C. 1627.
26. Cf. ¶ 102 of this dissertation.
27. *Normae a.* 1934, Art. 61.
28. *Normae a.* 1934, Art. 62 ¶ 1.
29. The Dean of the S.R. Rota issues the decree drawing up the individual "*turnus*" of that tribunal — *Normae a.* 1934, Art. 63.

presiding judge shall appoint the *ponens* and name the auditor at the time at which the "*turnus*" is constituted. If it is foreseen that special mandates may be needed by officers of the court, these could be drawn up at this time also.[30]

144. All officers of the "*turnus*" should then be notified of their appointments and of the time, and place if need be, of the first session of the court. A regulation may be given on the manner of notifying the personnel. The constitution may demand, for example, that the secretary of the court forward with the notification a copy of the *libellus* in order that the judge or judges may study it and make a review if necessary of the legal background involved in the cause before coming to the session for accepting or rejecting the *libellus*.

145. It may be arranged that the presiding judge, assisted by the secretary or the *actuarius*, cite at this time the defender of the bond and the promoter of justice, if these enter into the trial. This will serve as a general citation for the whole trial. For individual sessions these officers can be notified, as are the other officers, of the time and place of the sessions. If sessions are held regularly, once or twice a week, for example, it can be presumed they know of these and no notification need be given except for extraordinary sessions. Moreover, if the presiding judge gives the time and place of the next session in his decree closing the previous session, this notification suffices.[31]

146. The plaintiff will be notified as a rule at this time of the names of the officers of the court and will be given instructions on his right to raise exceptions against them. The respondent will naturally be notified at the time of his citation for the session of the joinder of issue.[32] The constitution may determine that the information concerning the right of exception against the personnel be given to the parties by their advocates.

30. Cf. ¶ 63 of this dissertation.
31. *Instructio a.* 1923, Reg. 35.
32. The Code asks that exceptions respecting the personnel be proposed and settled before the joinder of issue — C. 1628 § 1.

147. Finally, when setting up the *"turnus,"* the presiding judge may issue his decree calling the first session. It may be ruled that this be in writing to be read at the first session and thereby recorded in the acts.

Article 2. The Acts

148. By judicial ecclesiastical acts are understood the records drawn up during the process of an ecclesiastical trial. While the cause endures, the judicial acts or any part thereof "cannot be taken away except it be a document useless to the cause or unless it can be restored very soon and then only with the consent of the other party and with a decree" of the presiding judge.[33]

The cause being finished, the documents ought to be restored to the parties with the consent of the presiding judge, unless the public good demand their retention. The Code does not specify which documents are to be returned to the parties; but it obviously refers to documents given to the court by the parties themselves. The judge can retain such documents only in criminal causes.[34]

149. Because of the sad experiences of some courts in the past, the constitution would do well to emphasize that court records be kept so exactly and in such detail that the meaning of every item and of every step be clear, not just to those present who have seen the cause unfold, but especially to the judges of the courts of appeal and to judges having occasion to review the cause at a distantly future time.[35] The constitution may indicate that this is a special charge of the presiding judge who should at times even stop the proceedings if necessary to dictate an important item for the minutes.

33. The above quotation is from the *Normae a.* 1934, Art. 61 (translation by the writer).

34. Coronata, *Institutiones,* III, n. 1166, footnote 1.

35. Coronata says the main reason for minute care in keeping acts is that the cause must be "juridically established," i.e., in the acts. "Quod non est in actis, non est in mundo." — *Institutiones,* III, n. 1163; Roberti, *De Processibus,* I, nn. 163-164.

150. Minutes of individual sessions, the *acta sessionis,* are the guides to the whole judicial process. They not only answer the questions of "where," "when" and "who," but give explanations and preserve essential information like dates for *fatalia*, interruptions, oral notices of appeal, explanations of presumptions, etc. If there is an interruption, if a rule of court cannot be followed, if exceptions are instituted, these are explained in the minutes. They record the progress of the cause by *mentioning* decrees of the process, for example, for the joinder of issues, for the publication of the process, for the conclusion. The dispatching of rogatory requests can be therein recorded as well as the return of the completed commission and its inclusion in the cause. Important words of the presiding judge are preserved in them, as well as special oaths, refusals to testify, oral discussions, etc. Considering the neglect of this important procedure in some courts, the constitution would do well to legislate on the keeping of minutes and could rule that this is the joint responsibility, for example, of the notary of the cause and of the presiding judge, who naturally recognizes the more essential points and can direct the notary to record these. In the completed acts, the minutes introduce the material of each session and explain the position in the trial of each document. Since nothing comes into a trial except through actual mention in a session, the minutes become a perfect guide to the process. The more perfect the minutes, the better understood will be the cause in the court of appeals. Whenever this dissertation uses the term "minutes" it is referring to these *"acta sessionis."*

151. Considering the importance attached to the distinction by the Code, the constitution might direct the *actuarius* to distinguish in a chosen way between the *"acta causae"* and the *"acta processus."*[36] C. 1738, for example, declares that only the *acta pro-*

36. C. 1642 § 1. The *"acta causae"* are those concerned with the cause as such. The *"acta processus"* are those concerned with the process. The writer, conscious that his inclusion of some acts in one group as opposed to the other may be disputed, that the value of some acts is not the same in every cause and that his list does not include all possible acts, suggests the following division. The *"acta causae"* may include the *libellus;* the minutes of the sessions; documents pertinent to proofs; testimonies of parties, witnesses and experts; character

cessus are extinguished by abatement.[37] C. 1890 speaks of the *acta causae* being forwarded to the court of appeal and the Sacred Roman Rota rules mention receiving the *acta causae.*[38] The decision of the Code Commission of January 31, 1942 declared that all judicial acts, not just the *acta causae*, are to be forwarded to the court of appeal.[39] Nevertheless the specific mention of the *acta causae* in C. 1890 indicates the far greater importance of these over the *acta processus*. The improper inclusion of the non-essentials of the *acta processus* makes the acts cumbersome and hinders the work of the judges. The general attitude of higher officials has been to exclude unnecessary material.[40] The constitution might rule, for

testimonials and affidavits; completed commissions; procedural acts on exceptions pertinent to the cause and on incidental questions; decrees pertinent to the cause such as on the joinder of issue; briefs, animadversions and rebuttals of advocates and defenders; summations by the *ponens;* the sentence. The *"acta processus"* may include memoranda of the non-judicial consulting officer; decrees appointing and changing *"turnus"* members; mandates of procurators, advocates, auditors, guardians and *"tutores;"* proofs of the dates of the process such as return receipts of registered citations, envelopes of refused or undelivered citations; citations; notifications; signed oaths; *"articuli"* or *"positiones"* of parties; letters not pertinent to the cause such as those introducing individuals, informing parties of court personnel, releasing from professional secrecy, expressing appreciation, etc.; decrees not pertinent to the decision on the cause, for example, for the *conclusio in causa* and the publication of the acts; all decrees and records on finances, etc. This division presupposes very complete minutes for each session. Cf. ¶ 150 of this dissertation.

37. Coronata, *Institutiones,* III, n. 1163.
38. *Normae a.* 1934, Art. 61.
39. "An sub verbis *acta causae,* de quibus in Canone 1890, veniant omnia acta iudicialia?" R. "Affirmative." — *AAS,* XXXIV (1932), 50.
40. At the end of the appendix of formulas to the Instruction of 1931, the Sacred Congregation of the Sacraments includes the following: "In transcribing the record to be sent to Rome according to c. 1644, it is not necessary to include every detail of the original record. It is enough that the ordinary in his written report can certify that the court was duly organized in accordance with these rules, that the summonses were duly made, that the oath was taken by those making up the court, by the party and the witnesses, and that he report on their credibility" — *AAS,* XXIII (1931), 457; Bouscaren, I, 832-833. This applies to causes involving Holy Orders but the principle could

example, that (1) the minutes of the sessions, which are part of the *acta causae*, be carefully kept so that they will be a guide to the trial; (2) that the *acta processus* in turn be divided into essential and non-essential papers and that only the former be copied into the transcriptions of the cause, although both may be preserved in the portfolio of the original documents; (3) that the essential papers of the *acta processus* be not scattered through the *acta causae* but placed together at the end of the *acta causae*. In this way judges are delivered from much useless thumbing of non-essential pages and the parties are saved the expense of copying many unnecessary papers.[41]

152. An excellent method of caring for the acts, employed by an eastern court, preserves the originals of all acts in a folder or portfolio. As the cause proceeds copies are immediately made of the *acta causae* and of the essential papers of the *acta processus* and these are properly arranged and numbered with a single successive pagination. Three transcriptions (copies, retypes) are made, each neatly bound in a format, which are then used by the judges and, when the cause is complete in the court of first instance, are almost immediately ready for the court of appeal. In this system the originals of documents are seldom handled and need rarely, if ever, be removed from the hall of sessions. Some courts make as many as five transcriptions on thin onion paper which preserves even lengthy causes from too great bulkiness.

153. Some courts employ memoranda to introduce information gathered in some non-judicial, or at least non-ecclesiastical, procedure. These are introduced as private documents when original testimony cannot be had. Thus the consulting officer makes a memorandum of the information he collects and of such activities as the attempts at reconciliation. At times a canon law expert reviews the testimony preserved in the records of civil trials and makes a memorandum of pertinent facts. Again a memorandum

be applied to all causes with the exception that the minutes of the sessions and not the ordinary testify to the fulfillment of these things.

41. *Instructio a.* 1936, Art. 234 ¶ 1 warns against unnecessary and useless acts.

may be made of the facts of a former ecclesiastical process, other than those derived from direct evidence, which may be of use to the present court.

154. The constitution may specify that it is the duty of the *actuarius* to stamp each page of original writings and documents with the court seal.[42] The notary, actually present when the minutes, testimonies, etc. were taken[43] signs each page first.[44] A rubber stamp does not seem to be admissable for the signature.[45]

155. The constitution may designate, if it desires to descend to such detail, the number of copies or transcriptions to be made. Carbon copies may be used.[46] The law requires that there be an attestation by a notary that the copy is a faithful transcription of the original.[47] Some courts stamp each page with a rubber stamp "*concordat cum originali*" and the notary signs each page. This involves much labor especially if a cause is long and three or four transcriptions are made.[48] The writer ventures an opinion that an

42. C. 1643 § 1; Coronata, *Institutiones,* III, n. 1164.

43. Although the law permits two witnesses to supply the presence of a notary in the writing of certain acts (c. 1017 § 1; c. 1659 § 2; c. 2143 § 1; c. 2225; c. 2309 § 3), it is the opinion of Coronata that two witnesses cannot fulfill the office of the notary in the process of a trial — *Institutiones,* III, n. 1123. He especially maintains that the decretal law permitting this was abrogated by c. 1585 § 2. Roberti is of the same opinion — *De Processibus,* I, n. 115. Wernz-Vidal, however, seems to admit the contrary opinion — *Ius Canonicum,* (8 vols., Romae: apud Aedes Universitatis Gregorianae), Vol. VI, *De Processibus,* (1927), n. 103, note 49.

44. The judge does not sign each page as the notary does, but only the completed acts — Coronata, *Institutiones,* III, n. 1164, footnote 8; the "*datatio,*" i.e., the day, month, year and place, must be attached to each individual act, i.e., to each testimony, each *acta sessionis,* not to each page — Coronata, *Institutiones,* III, n. 1164, note 8; the signature should be followed by the office of the one signing, at least the first signature — Coronata, *Institutiones,* III, n. 1164.

45. Augustine, *Commentary,* VII, p. 40 and p. 92.

46. Coronata, *Institutiones,* III, n. 1165; Augustine, *op. cit.,* VII, 92.

47. C. 374 § 1 n. 3.

48. Coronata seems to require this — *Institutiones,* III, n. 1165. He also speaks of putting the seal on copies, which would seem to be super-

affidavit at the beginning or at the end of each transcription attesting the faithfulness of the entire work and signed by the notary would be sufficient, especially if the transcriptions are sent directly to the court of appeals and never are in the hands of the parties.[49] At least since the second and third copies are duplicates of the first, the stamp and signature, if placed on each page, need be on only the first copy.

156. The cause should have an index and the constitution may designate the officer to make this index.[50]

157. Each court decides on its own system of pagination. Some places use a double pagination, one for the entire cause and one for individual documents, e.g., testimonies, within the cause. Others in making copies, find little use for a second pagination, employing a straight numbering from beginning to end. In this system occasionally a document, for example, a rogatory commission, may happen to arrive after the compilation. These may then be inserted with the occasional double pagination, for example, 22a, 22b, 22c.

ARTICLE 3. SESSIONS AND DECREES

158. The constitution may choose to give some general rules on sessions. A session of court is any legitimately convened assembly of the court personnel for successive steps of the cause.[51] The complete trial is naturally divided into sessions although sessions may be combined even to the extent of having the entire trial in one session.[52]

159. As a precaution the constitution could insist that every possible portion of the trial come into the acts through a session.

fluous especially if the *"concordat cum originali"* is used. Some courts however place both the *"concordat"* stamp and the seal on each page of each copy.

49. Augustine speaks of the "attestation" in the singular accompanying each bound copy of the acta — *Commentary,* VII, p. 92.

50. C. 1644 § 1; most courts introduce each transcription with an index, which is naturally most convenient.

51. *Instruction a.* 1923, Reg. 33 ¶ 1.

52. *Instructio a.* 1923, Reg. 34 ¶ 2; *Instructio a.* 1931, Art. 25 ¶ 2.

Thus things accomplished before the first session could be introduced at the first session; thus also fulfilled commissions could be specifically mentioned at a session on their return.

160. Because of the danger involved, the constitution may demand an explanation in the minutes of why the business begun in one session, for example, the hearing of a party, a witness or an expert, was not completed in that session and may ask for a presentation of the precautions taken against collusion.[53]

161. The constitution may ask that the acts of each session (minutes) precede the material of the session in the completed acts as an explanation of it. Some places have printed formularies for sessions. These are beneficial as introductions but the body of the minutes will naturally vary according to the activities.[54] C. 1642 § 2 asks that Latin be used, but also mentions that a just cause will excuse from this. A just cause could be the desire to keep very complete minutes with detailed explanations that would require for some much time and effort to render properly in Latin.

162. The constitution may ask the presiding judge to exercise special care in issuing decrees and commands. The course of the trial is directed by these pronouncements of the judge.[55] Most decrees within a session can be and should be given orally and recorded thus in the minutes. This does away with many useless pages in the completed acts and hence with much work in copying these pages. The bishop may of course command that decrees be in writing and on separate pages, and it would be well that this be done in the case of all decrees issued outside a session as such, but the obligation of so completing them would arise from diocesan and not from universal law. Decisory decrees should propose reasons in law and in fact with the decision.[56]

53. C. 1781; *Instructio a.* 1936, Art. 107.

54. "The notary shall accurately record... everything worthy of note which may occur..." — *Instructio a.* 1923, Reg. 45; c. 1779.

55. C. 1868 § 2; c. 1840 § 3; *Instructio a.* 1936, Art. 196 ¶ 2.

56. Lemieux, Delisle, *The Sentence in Ecclesiastical Procedure,* (The Catholic University of America Canon Law Studies, n. 87, Washington, D.C.: The Catholic University of America, 1934) p. 38 (hereafter cited *The Sentence*).

Article 4. The Session for Considering the Libellus

163. To avoid misunderstanding on the point, the constitution may reiterate the universal law's command that all judges of the cause participate in the decision on the *libellus*. This cannot be delegated to the auditor.[57] The constitution may require the presence of the defender of the bond at this session in matrimonial causes although this is not a requirement of the universal law.[58]

164. The constitution, in harmony with the Instruction of the Sacred Congregation of Sacraments of March 27, 1929, may require mention in the minutes of the process employed in identifying the plaintiff.[59]

57. C. 1709 § 1; *Instructio a.* 1936, Art. 61; Doheny, *Canonical Procedure,* p. 134; Kealy, John, *The Introductory Libellus in Church Court Procedure,* (The Catholic University of America Canon Law Studies, n. 108, Washington, D.C.: The Catholic University of America, 1937), pp. 51-52.
58. A possible procedure for this session, neither necessarily complete nor logical in sequence, would be: a) prayer; b) reading of the *libellus,* for example, by the presiding judge — *Instructio a.* 1923, Reg. 34 ¶ 1; c) reading of the decree setting up the *"turnus"* — *Instructio a.* 1923, Reg. 34 ¶ 1; d) reading of the decree citing the court; e) recording in the minutes of the dates of the permanent appointments and the permanent oaths of the officers, if this is desired; f) oaths of officers if not already taken; g) report of the investigations of the consulting officer; h) reading of the *"informationes pastoris;"* i) report on the motives of the plaintiff in seeking court action; j) report on the attempted reconciliation; k) proofs of the identity of the plaintiff; l) consideration of the right of the party to plead; m) consideration of scandal as involved in the particular cause; n) consideration of the right of the court to hear the cause; o) objections of officers against their own appearance because of suspicion; p) decree of acceptance or rejection of the *libellus* with mention of the rights of the plaintiff to plead and the court to judge; q) reading of petition of plaintiff for particular witness if the *libellus* is accepted; r) acceptance of documents given with *libellus;* s) if necessary, order compelling separation — *Instructio a.* 1936, Art. 63; or of sequestration or injunction — cc. 1672-1678; t) appointment of guardian for respondent, if necessary; u) decree ordering next session; v) decree citing parties for next session; w) decree closing session; x) signing of the minutes; y) prayer.

165. A complete report in fulfillment of the Instruction of the same Congregation of December 23, 1929 may be required if the competence is based on quasi-domicile.[60] The constitution could determine that the consulting officer report such a cause immediately to the *officialis* when it first comes to his office; that the *officialis* determine who is to make the investigation and the report; that the report be completed before the session for considering the *libellus*.

166. If the cause is matrimonial, the constitution might reiterate that special notice be taken in the preliminary investigation of the culpability of the plaintiff and that if any suspicion of culpability is present the promoter of justice be informed of the situation immediately and that he be ordered to make his investigation and present his report at the session for considering the *libellus*.[61]

167. The constitution will determine how the party is to be informed of the decision of the court in regard to the *libellus*. It may ask that, if the decision is unfavorable to him, the court inform the party of his right to appeal within ten days. If the decision is favorable, the notification may well be accompanied by the citation of the plaintiff to the session for the joinder of issue.

168. The constitution would do well to make some regulations on the citation of the respondent and on receiving his objections to officers, his list of witnesses and his "*articuli*" for questioning the plaintiff and the witnesses. Since this citation is so very important, some courts, unless they are certain of cooperation, rely entirely on priest-messengers to deliver it. This gives the priest an opportunity to explain the situation and most often cooperation is obtained in this way when it probably would have been refused if the citation, even with an explanation, were sent through the mails. That the reports drawn up by the messenger may be public documents, he should be legally appointed to this position.[62]

59. *AAS*, XXI (1929), 490.
60. *AAS*, XXII (1930), 168.
61. C. 1971 § 2; *Instructio a.* 1936, Art. 37 ¶ 4; P.C.I., *Responsa*, 17 febr. 1930 — *AAS*, XXII (1930), 196, et 17 iul. 1933 — *AAS*, XXV (1933), 345.
62. C. 1593; *Instructio a.* 1936, Art. 18.

169. The diocesan tribunal of Cleveland, for example, presents this instruction to its designated priest-messenger: "Kindly explain that there are no legal entanglements, no publicity, no obligations, no unpleasant embarrassments; there is merely an obligation to answer truthfully a few questions in the interest of justice and religion in a matter affecting the consciences of a number of people." It adds these prescriptions for the benefit of the messenger: "The following instructions are to be literally observed since this is a formal trial: (1) deliver citation enclosed; (2) fill out report completely and return to the diocesan tribunal within five days of the receipt of this appointment; (3) return copy of citation with your report."[63] The messenger is instructed to return a report on the day and the hour, to whom and where the citation was delivered and to state whether the cited person will appear and when. If there is a refusal, the messenger presents the reason for this.[64]

The citation to be delivered by the messenger could have a place reserved for the signature of the one receiving it.[65]

170. The constitution may designate registered mail, for example, as the preferred method of delivering citations when messengers are not used and may give instructions on the care of the return receipt, which, in most places, is stapled to the preserved copy of the citation.[66] Finally it could designate the diocesan paper, for example, as the medium for citation by edict.[67] If this method is used, the press advertisement is to be preserved in the acts.[68]

171. Many diocesan courts have met with difficulties in ob-

63. These quotations are taken from prepared forms of the Cleveland tribunal received by the writer through the kindness of the Right Reverend Monsignor F. L. Begin, *officialis;* cf. also cc. 1721-1722.

64. C. 1718.

65. C. 1721 § 2; *Instructio a.* 1936, Art. 81.

66. C. 1719.

67. C. 1720 § 1.

68. Article 68 of the *Normae a.* 1934 reads: Quoties locus esse debet citatione per edictum, decretum citationis inseri potest in commentario officiali *"Acta Apostolicae Sedis,"* non exclusis aliis modis qui ad finem tutius et efficacius obtinendum inserviunt, tempore congruo assignato, ut ad notitiam rei conventi pervenire possit.

taining cooperation from respondents. Too often the latter have refused to appear for the joinder of issue and have been therefore declared contumacious. At a later date however the courts have sent auditors to them and found them willing to testify providing they were not inconvenienced thereby. This testimony could not then be received however without purifying them of their contumacy.[69] This can be done of course although it seems to reflect carelessness and furthermore the declaration of contumacy may further antagonize the party. The tribunal of one mid-western diocese, to offset this, has arranged the following ingenious method. The priest-messenger bears the citation to the respondent and, after a diplomatic explanation of the situation, delivers the citation. He then fills out his report as *cursor*. If the party shows signs of refusing to cooperate however he, according to the terms of his appointment, ceases to be *cursor* and becomes a notary. As notary he is authorized to ask the party sufficient questions to establish the joinder of issue.[70] These questions being recorded, he, according to the terms of his appointment, ceases to be notary. He then asks the objecting party if he, the priest, may represent him, the respondent, as procurator for the trial. If the answer is in the affirmative, the former cursor-notary obtains if possible the signature of the respondent on the mandate of procuratorship. As procurator he returns to court prepared to represent the respondent and the joinder of issue is held without the inconvenience of a declaration of contumacy.[71] The testimony of the respondent may then be obtained by a commission at a later date and legally presented in court.

The procedure is unusual and would be used only when ordinary methods have failed but the court mentioned above, because

69. *Instructio a.* 1936, Art. 90; Doheny, *Canonical Procedure,* pp. 173-176.
70. Without necessarily showing the *libellus,* he asks the respondent's position on reaction to the allegations of the plaintiff, as a rule in question and answer form.
71. The information gathered by the priest as notary, plus the authorization to act as procurator, is sufficient to carry on the joinder of issue because a mere statement, signed but not necessarily witnessed, sent by the respondent is sufficient, according to many authors, to join the issues — Doheny, *Canonical Procedure,* p. 172.

of it, has seldom had to declare a respondent contumacious. Furthermore its unusualness is justified by the difficulties confronting American courts working among a predominantly non-Catholic population. One of the reasons for diocesan constitutions is the development of legal procedures to care for unique conditions of a particular territory. The above procedure is legal throughout because the priest is not a court officer and a representative of one party *at the same time.*[72] These offices may be held successively.

The framers of diocesan constitutions will naturally consider circumstances of their own dioceses before adopting these suggestions on citations. According to circumstances, they may wish to incorporate them in whole or in part, they may wish to vary the procedure, for example, to send two priests on this mission to the respondent, one as cursor-notary-procurator and the other as auditor with permission to take a complete deposition, or they may wish to adopt an entirely different procedure. The predominance of non-Catholics in America seems to make it imperative that the diocesan constitutions employ further means than those of the universal law to elicit cooperation in procedural work.

172. The constitution may wish to give some definite regulation on procedure when contumacy has evidently been shown. Thus the Sacred Roman Rota gives the following regulation to its presiding judge: "If notice comes to the tribunal concerning the correct delivery of the citation to the respondent, and if perchance he has refused to accept it or he refuses to appear before the tribunal or does not give any or an insufficient excuse for not appearing, it will be the duty of the *ponens* [who is the presiding judge on a Rota "*Turnus*"] to decide whether (a) the joinder of issue should be delayed and a new citation sent to the respondent; or (b) there ought to be a proceeding toward stating the formula of doubt, with or without a declaration of contumacy."[73] The constitution may ask that the presiding judge, ordinarily at least, make

72. The office of notary is incompatible with that of procurator — Roberti, *De Processibus,* I, n. 115. This is evident if both are held at the same time.

73. *Normae a.* 1934, Art. 70 ¶ 1 (translation by the writer).

further efforts to elicit cooperation, for example, by sending the citation again through a close friend of the respondent or through a person of dignity.[74]

173. The Sacred Congregation of the Sacraments, in its instructions for delegated officers, includes this statement, which may be of use to the diocesan courts: "It will usually be prudent to abstain from coercive measures to overcome contumacy."[75]

Article 5. The Session for the Joinder of Issue

174. The constitution may propose that all officers of the "*turnus*" be present for the joinder of issue. This seems to be the safest practice because of the need of a full court if a discussion arises.[76] The third session, for hearing the parties, is often joined to this second session and the presence of the full "*turnus*" at this session is highly recommended.[77]

74. *Instructio a.* 1923, Reg. 38 ¶ 2; *Instructio a.* 1931, Art. 29 ¶ 2.
75. *Instructio a.* 1931, Art. 29 ¶ 2; *Instructio a.* 1923, Reg. 38 ¶ 2.
76. *Instructio a.* 1936, Art. 92 ¶ 2.
77. A routine may be proposed lest some important item be omitted: a) prayer opening session; b) reading of decree calling session; c) substitution of officers and oaths of new officers, if necessary; d) reading of decree citing parties; e) consideration of mandates of advocates and procurators — *Normae a.* 1934, Art. 62; f) taking of oaths by advocates and procurators, if this is to be done; g) proof of identity of respondent; h) consideration of exceptions of parties to each other and to officers of the court; i) consideration of the joinder of issue; j) decree on the joinder of issue; k) consideration of expenses; l) reading of petition for gratuitous patronage or for a reduction of fees if this was presented and also reading of the letter of pastor or report of consulting officer on the worthiness of the petitioner for this reduction; m) decree on expenses; n) depositing of required sum; o) appointment of auditor if used and if not already appointed; p) presentation of list of *ex officio* witnesses and witnesses of respondent; q) decree ordering presentation of names of respondent's witnesses and of *ex officio* witnesses, if this is desired, to the party or parties for objections; r) setting time limits for objections and proofs of objections to witnesses; s) decree ordering next session; t) decree citing parties to this session; u) decree closing second session; v) signing of minutes; w) prayer.

175. No special formalities are required for the actual joinder of issue.[78] The constitution may propose or suggest a mode of procedure. For example, it may require that in the presence of at least the presiding judge or the auditor, the notary, the defender of the bond and both parties or their procurators, the *libellus* be read in its entirety; that the plaintiff or his procurator then make further proposals if he wishes; that the respondent or his procurator make his denials and counter proposals; that the discussion and the conclusion then follow with the judge giving his approval to the proposed agreement and issuing a decree containing the formula.[79] If no agreement can be reached by the parties, the full "*turnus*" must *ex officio* settle on the formula of doubt.[80]

176. The formula of doubt ought to cover the merits of the case in its entirety[81] and cannot be changed except by a new decree of the judge or of the "*turnus*," according to which of the two approved it, for a grave cause, at the instance of a party or of the defender of the bond or the promoter of justice, after a hearing given the other party or the parties and after the reasons have been given.[82]

177. The decree of the joinder of issue may be given orally and recorded in the minutes.[83]

178. The Sacred Roman Rota wisely requires a consideration of expenses at this stage of the trial.[84] The constitution may require a definite listing of ordinary fees involved in the cause in the decree on expenses.[85] Mention may be made in the constitution that provisions for extraordinary expenses which may be incurred will be cared for in the decree on the sentence.[86] If the party has

78. C. 1727.
79. C. 1727; *Instructio a.* 1936, Art. 88.
80. *Instructio a.* 1936, Art. 92 ¶ 2.
81. *Normae a.* 1934, Art. 77 ¶ 1.
82. C. 1729 § 4; *Normae a.* 1934, Art. 77 ¶ 1.
83. Roberti, *De Processibus,* I, n. 302 ¶ 4.
84. *Normae a.* 1934, Art. 78.
85. C. 1909 § 1; *Instructio a.* 1936, Art. 233 ¶ 1; Art. 235 ¶ 1.
86. *Instructio a.* 1936, Art. 236 ¶ 1.

made a petition for gratuitous patronage or for a reduction of fees[87] the promoter of justice and the defender of the bond should be present for the discussion of expenses unless their opinion has been secured beforehand by the judge.[88] The constitution may require a letter from the pastor of the party attesting the party's inability to bear the expenses and affirming his worthiness to receive gratuitous patronage.

179. The constitution may well suggest the joining of this session with that for examining the parties if this is possible in a particular cause. This would both shorten the trial and reduce the expenses and the inconveniences of the parties. Under these circumstances no second summons of the parties is needed.

Article 6. Judicial Examinations in General

180. Many rules have been given for the examination of persons in court, especially since the practical and masterful Instruction of the Sacred Congregation of the Council of August 22, 1840.[89] Nevertheless even today "a great deal is left to the customs and regulations of tribunals as well as to the good judgment of judges and auditors."[90] Some at least of these "customs and regulations" may be incorporated into the constitution.

181. Ordinarily the questioning in court is done by the judge or auditor alone.[91] The constitution may wish to emphasize the questioner's obligation to develop by *ex officio* questions points not clearly brought out by the questionnaire or points that develop during questioning; that he must break up difficult and complex questions; that he see that every point is answered in full;[92] and that he may omit repetitious questions if prudence suggests this.

87. ¶ 136 of this work; *Normae a.* 1934, Art. 177 ¶ 1.
88. C. 1915 § 2; *Instructio a.* 1936, Art. 238 ¶ 2; *Normae a.* 1934, Art. 178 ¶ 2.
89. *Fontes,* n. 4069.
90. Doheny, *Canonical Procedure,* p. 204.
91. C. 1773 ¶ 2.
92. *Instructio a.* 1931, Art. 33.

182. The constitution may rule on the method of presenting questions by others in court, for example, that they hand them in writing to the judge,[93] that they then be asked by him, according to his (the judge's) judgment and prudence, after the completion of his own questioning from the questionnaire. It may recommend that the judge allow the persons to develop points in their own words rather than answer with single words or single sentences. If necessary it may permit him to edit the answer for the records, omitting non-essential material but submitting the results to the individual questioned for approval.[94]

183. Very few rules are given in universal law on the "*articuli*" or "*positiones*" of parties and diocesan law would do well to develop this point according to local conditions.[95] These *articuli* are necessary for probing the knowledge of opposing parties and of witnesses. They are the basis of the questions of the defender of the bond and the judge. The Rules of the Sacred Roman Rota call these "*interrogatoria*" (questionnaires) and give this rule: The parties can propose questionnaires for each other for the purpose of eliciting a confession of fact. These can be proposed not only by the litigating party himself, but also by his procurator, in the manner permitted him in his special mandate.[96]

The constitution may demand that these *articuli* be handed in with the list of witnesses,[97] that they be immediately forwarded by the secretary to the defender of the bond, that the latter in turn forward them to the judge or auditor some time before the session

93. This is for dignity only — Wanenmacher, F., *Canonical Evidence in Marriage Cases,* (Philadelphia: Dolphin Press, 1935), n. 233, (hereafter cited *Canonical Evidence*), n. 233; cf. c. 1773 § 2.

94. C. 1778; c. 1780 § 1.

95. C. 1745 ¶ 1; *Instructio a.* 1936, Art. 70; 101; 125 ¶ 2; Doheny, *Practical Manual,* p. 168; Wanenmacher, *Canonical Evidence,* n. 227; Krol, John, *The Defendant in Contentious Trials,* (The Catholic University of America Canon Law Studies, n. 146, Washington, D.C.: The Catholic University of America Press, 1942) pp. 127-129 (hereafter cited *The Defendant*).

96. *Normae a.* 1934, Art. 99 ¶ 1.

97. Cf. ¶ 133 of this dissertation; *Synodus Dioecesana Spokanensis Prima,* Stat. 145 a; Wanenmacher, *Canonical Evidence,* n. 227.

for the examination. This latter practice enables the judge or auditor to develop his own thoughts on the issues involved and therefore to ask more useful *ex officio* questions.[98] Likewise it serves as a check on the defender of the bond, forcing a full development of both sides of the issue. Parties have a right to have their questions asked directly and not as changed about by the defender of the bond if the judge so rules and the possession of these *"articuli"* of the parties by the judge or auditor may assist in fulfilling justice in this regard.[99] Experience may teach individual courts more practical methods of obtaining the *"articuli."* Thus some may prefer that the views of the party concerning the opposition and particular witnesses be obtained through an interview with the consulting officer or with the defender of the bond. The constitution may then rule, for example, that notes be kept on these interviews and that a report be made on them. Also the rules may ask that these *"articuli"* or reports be placed, after their use, in the files, for example, among the non-essential documents of the *acta processus,* until the end of the trial.[100]

184. The constitution may give some suggestions and directions to the defenders of the bond and promoters of justice for their questionnaires.[101] For example, that they should remember the American mentality of those who will be answering questions in court, that civil law practice has trained them to brief answers, that a certain rigorous examination is expected and therefore that greater detail in questionnaires is sometimes needed. It may remind them that not only should the questions probe for the direct knowledge of the person but also its source (whence, how, when) and that questions should probe for reasons behind activities, especially for reasons for entrance into court, as well as for relationship of the witness to parties, for his opinions on the character of the

98. Wanenmacher, *Canonical Evidence,* n. 227.

99. C. 1773 § 2; *Instructio a.* 1936, Art. 101; Art. 114.

100. Wanenmacher says: "the judge may communicate to the adversary the various questions and points on which either one proposes that the witnesses be examined" — *Canonical Evidence,* n. 227.

101. C. 1968 § 1; c. 1981; *Instructio a.* 1936, Art. 71 ¶ 2.

parties or, in the case of a party to the action, of the other party.[102] The *"specialia"* or questions other than those identifying the person should be given to the judge in a sealed envelope after the session opens.[103]

185. The notary might be required to record not only when a question is asked *ex officio* but also by which officer it was proposed. In recording answers, the exact words should be given and in the first person rather than in the third, even when the judge has edited the answer to eliminate superfluous material.[104]

186. The constitution may require that at the end of each testimony, the judge or auditor give his impression of the person testifying especially as to sincerity and that he record any unusual features occurring during the examination such as hesitancy and change of attitude.

187. The oath used in court for persons testifying can be approved once and for all in the constitution.[105] A form other than that of the American civil court should be suggested because of the shameless abuse of this oath in American courts. A change of form may render the oath more impressive.

The second oath of truthfulness may be omitted at the discretion of the judge.[106] An explanation of the secrecy in the second oath, especially as to how long it endures, would not be out of place both to avoid scrupulosity in some and carelessness in others and could be given prior to the second oath. It might be mentioned also that "the publication of the sentence does not release them from the bond of secrecy relative to the information that would be of a prejudicial or deleterious character if it were published."[107]

188. The constitution may demand the signature of the one testifying on each page of the testimony and not merely at the end.

102. *Instructio a.* 1936, Art. 100; *Instructio a.* 1923, Reg. 56; Wanenmacher, *Canonical Evidence,* n. 237.
103. *Instructio a.* 1923, Reg. 28 b; *Instructio a.* 1931, Art. 19 and 50.
104. *Instructio a.* 1923, Reg. 44, ¶ 1; c. 1778.
105. C. 1622 § 3; Wanenmacher, *Canonical Evidence,* n. 223.
106. C. 1768; Wanenmacher, *Canonical Evidence,* n. 225.
107. Quotation from Krol, *The Defendant,* p. 118, note 140; cf. also Coronata, *Institutiones,* III, n. 1150.

Article 7.

The Session for the Judicial Examination of the Parties

189. Some time may have to elapse between the hearing of the plaintiff and the hearing of the respondent to give the defender and possibly the judge an opportunity to formulate further questions for the respondent based on the testimony of the plaintiff.[108]

108. A tentative program for the session at which the parties are examined may be suggested: a) prayer; b) reading of decrees ordering session and citing parties; c) giving of report, if necessary, on refusal of respondent, with consequent activities of the officers of the court; d) introduction of plaintiff; e) delivery of questionnaire by defender of the bond; f) asking of general questions and proof of identity (not needed if established at prior session); g) sermon on oath and taking of oath by plaintiff; h) asking of special questions; i) asking of *ex officio* questions, for example, of defender of the bond and questions of parties if these were not included in questionnaire; j) reading testimony back to plaintiff, corrections of testimony, etc.; k) instructions on secrecy and oath of truth and and secrecy; l) signing of testimony by plaintiff and his departure; m) introduction of respondent; n) delivery of questionnaire to which are added questions suggested by testimony of plaintiff; p) asking of general questions and proof of identity; q) taking of oath; asking of special questions; r) asking of *ex officio* questions; s) reading testimony back, corrections of testimony, etc.; t) reading of *libellus* and all or parts of testimony of plaintiff if this is desired; u) explanation of secrecy, taking of oath, signature and departure; v) the court may choose at this point to give its impression of parties when testifying; w) decree recalling plaintiff, with order on time and place, if this is deemed necessary; x) consideration of objections to witnesses; decree settling objections one way or the other; decree calling witnesses (although the time set for each will probably be different) and decree ordering session for hearing witnesses; y) it might be well at an early stage to issue decree ordering experts, matrons, etc., if these are needed; decree communicating names of experts to parties and defender, with a time limit for presentation of objections — *Instructio a.* 1936, Art. 145; and finally decree on instruction of experts, on time for inspection and on time limit for returning written report; z) decree ordering commissions for gathering evidence, if needed; decree closing session; the signing of minutes and of testimonies; prayer.

190. The ordinary procedure is that the plaintiff be heard first. If husband and wife are both plaintiffs, the court may follow the rule given for non-consummation causes and hear the wife first.[109]

ARTICLE 8.

THE SESSION FOR THE JUDICIAL EXAMINATION OF WITNESSES

191. The diocese of Spokane has the following practical rule which may be of use in the constitution: "The actor and the procurator, and all unauthorized persons, should beware of interrogating or tampering with witnesses beforehand, lest they prejudice the case."[110]

109. *Instructio a.* 1936, Art. 110; Art. 113 ¶ 1; *Instructio a.* 1923, Reg. 50 ¶ 2.

110. *Synodus Dioecesana Spokanensis Prima,* ¶ 147 a. Any tentative program for sessions at which witnesses will testify will be mindful of the possible many sessions necessary for hearing witnesses. The following will be varied accordingly: a) prayer; b) reading of decree ordering session and decree citing witnesses; c) explanation of refusal of any witness to appear; d) introduction of first witness by Bailiff; e) delivery of questionaire; f) asking of general questions and proof of identity; g) sermon on oath and taking of oath; h) asking of special questions; i) asking of *ex officio* questions and questions of parties, if not already asked; j) reading back of testimony, corrections, etc.; k) reading of parts of testimony of parties, if desired, and request for opinion on these and possibly on character of parties; l) instruction on secrecy and taking of second oath; m) signing of testimony and departure of first witness; n) consideration of proofs of credibility and court opinion of witness; o) decree on financial reimbursement of witness; p) introduction of second witness, etc., etc.; q) decree on rehearing of any witness, if necessary; r) introduction of returned commissions, of non-judicial testimony, of character testimonials; s) decree communicating testimony to parties (at this time or later); t) consideration of objections to experts if any and decree rejecting either experts or objections; u) introduction of written reports of experts; v) decree on session for judicial examination of experts; w) decree citing experts to appear at the session; x) decree closing session for witnesses; y) signing of minutes and testimonies; z) prayer.

192. The constitution may demand that the party asking for a witness secure the consent of that witness to appear or at least give the court a letter of introduction to him and guarantee a cordial reception of requests for cooperation. Finally a written, signed and notorized release from professional secrecy will be necessary in some cases, for example, for doctors, lawyers, etc.

193. The Instruction on ordination causes gives a rule on the order for the examination of witnesses that may be of assistance to the diocesan constitution: "The examination of witnesses begins with those called by the petitioner, and first with those closely related to him who are presumed to be the best informed; next, those not related to him are examined if there be such. This order however in the hearing of witnesses is not essential; the judge may change it."[111]

194. The constitution may demand an explanation of the non-appearance of requested witnesses, of the exemption of witnesses and of the exclusion of witnesses.[112]

195. The constitution, as a precaution, may ask that the record clearly state for whom each witness is testifying, if he is a character witness or a *"de scientia"* witness; that it should also set forth any unusual dignity in a witness, for example, that he is a priest, a pastor, a professional man, or, on the contrary, any feature that would detract from the value of his testimony. Care should be taken to note carefully if a debarred, unfit, suspected witness has been admitted, why this was done and what precautions were taken to obtain the truth in the case.[113]

196. Court rules should make some regulation on the proper sequestration of witnesses. Special care should be taken that those already examined be not returned to the same room with those to be examined.

111. *Instructio a.* 1931, Art. 49 (translation by Bouscaren, *The Canon Law Digest*, I, 825-826); Wanenmacher, *Canonical Evidence*, n. 130.
112. *Instructio a.* 1923, Reg. 26.
113. Wanenmacher, *Canonical Evidence*, p. 120.

197. All objections to witnesses and the disposal of them should be recorded for the benefit of the court of appeal. The decrees disposing of most of them at least, with the reasons for the decision, can be given orally with the activities of an individual session.

198. Some courts send letters of appreciation to witnesses. The practice is commendable but copies of these letters should not encumber the acts.

199. Reimbursement of witnesses may be made for expenses only and never for the act of testifying as such.[114] The constitution may regulate the procedure for the awarding of expense payments. Thus, for example, the consulting officer may be called upon to inform the parties of their duty in this regard, a deposit may be required to cover the costs and a discussion of expenses with the witness prior to appearance may be suggested.

200. Commissions, containing depositions of witnesses, should be formally introduced to the trial by presentation at a session when they are returned. Mention of this should appear in the minutes. Introduction of evidence by witnesses that is not strictly judicial, for example, letters, extra-judicial confessions, testimony given in civil court, testimony taken prior to the joinder of issue, should also take place at a formal session.

201. The communication of testimony of witnesses to the parties is accomplished by most courts by a letter to the parties informing them that the testimony is at the hall of sessions and that it may be read if desired.[115]

Article 9.

The Session for the Judicial Examination of Experts

202. The naming of experts, their instruction and the presentation of their names to the parties are mentioned in the footnote to ¶ 189 (under subdivision y) and the disposal of the objections

114. C. 1787; Wanenmacher, *Canonical Evidence,* n. 219.
115. C. 1782; Wanenmacher, *Canonical Evidence,* n. 253.

against them and the presentation of their written reports are mentioned in footnote to ¶ 191 (under subdivisions t and u).[116]

203. The parties could be reminded at the time they are notified of the identity of the experts that they have a right to present material on which the experts may be questioned and that, depending on the cause, they may propose possible experts.[117]

204. The court should have a rule on the instruction to be given to the expert prior to the corporal inspection in cases where such an inspection is to be made.[118] This instruction should be drawn up with the greatest possible care. Some courts have more or less permanent instructions on impotence, insanity and non-consummation causes that have been prepared after much study and research and that may be varied in the individual case. Care should be taken that words used by the canon lawyer have the desired connotation to the expert. Attached to the instruction could be a report on the cause in so far as this is necessary for the examination and an instruction on how the report on the examination is to be made.

205. The constitution may desire to specify how the expert's

116. A tentative program for the session at which experts are to be examined would include: a) opening prayer; b) reading of decrees calling session and citing experts; c) introduction of first expert; d) reading of his written report and confirmation of this; e) delivery of questionnaire; f) sermon on oath and taking of oath; g) questioning of expert; h) reading back of testimony, corrections in it and taking of oaths for written report and for testimony; i) signing of testimony and departure; j) recording of opinion of the court on the expert and his testimony; k) decree on financial remuneration; l) repetition of this procedure (c-k) for each expert; m) questioning of matron, if she enters cause, on procedure during examination and especially on observance of rules of modesty; n) decree publishing report and testimony, if this is to be done — cf. Wanenmacher, *Canonical Evidence*, n. 319; o) decree ordering session for consideration of documents; p) decree ending session followed by signing of minutes and testimonies and closing prayer.
117. C. 1796; Wanenmacher, *Canonical Evidence*, n. 289.
118. *Instructio a.* 1923, Reg. 68; Wanenmacher, *Canonical Evidence*, n. 308; n. 317.

report is to be returned. Some courts give the experts a questionnaire to be filled out. The report must always be in writing for impotence only the oral examination in court, recorded and signed.[120]
and non-consummation causes[119] but for the others, the court may make its own rules. Some require written reports and others,

206. The questionnaire of the defender and the bond for the oral examination of the expert will be based on the above suggested report. The defender of the bond may be asked to remember that experts as a rule used guarded language and that the questions should aim at bringing forth a definite answer in unquestionable language.

207. The oath of the expert at the end of his oral examination should include his solemn affirmation of the truth of his written report.[121]

208. The opinion (*animadversiones*) of the court on the expert, which the constitution may suggest as a judicial commentary to be set down for the benefit of the court of appeal, could include both an opinion on the expert himself and an opinion on his testimony. The impression of the man, for example, can be prefaced with a report on his qualifications, his knowledge and skill, and on his character and religious life. The opinion on the value of the testimony should give reasons for the stand taken by the court.[122]

209. The constitution may demand a specific report on the means taken to prevent fraudulent substitution at the time of the

119. C. 1980 §§ 2-3.
120. Wanenmacher, *Canonical Evidence,* n. 312. This author also gives a possible outline for the report: I. Introduction: Full name; degrees; offices, etc., of experts; name of the curia and the judge hearing the cause; Full name and means of identification of the person examined; Points to be determined; Date and place of the inspection. II. Body of the report: Answers to questions of the court; Spontaneous observations of the expert; III. Conclusion (opinion of the expert); IV. Signatures; date and place of the report — *Canonical Evidence,* n. 313.
121. *Instructio a.* 1936, Art. 152.
122. *Instructio a.* 1936, Art. 154.

inspection by the expert. The Instruction for this precaution in non-consummation causes may well be applied, with proper changes, to other causes, for example, insanity causes, where an inspection must be made.[123]

210. The diocesan court might be reminded of the recent instruction of the Holy Office on the rules of modesty to be observed in corporal inspections.[124] Some diocesan courts to which experts are attached more or less permanently, may desire to indicate a definite place for such inspections, for example a particular Catholic hospital.

211. In many cases, the civil law testimony of experts, for example in an insanity cause, may be of value. Provision could be made requiring a court officer to read this testimony and make a report to the court on it.

212. The court would do well, prior to the examination, to come to some understanding on the costs of the examination with both the parties and the experts. As a rule, experts will have set fees for the labor involved in studying the instruction, making the examination, filling out the report and giving the oral testimony.[125]

Article 10. Commissions

213. The universal law allows the gathering of evidence outside the hall of sessions when necessary.[126] It makes few regulations however, on the procedure to be observed in such an event, leaving the details to the local legislator who best knows the conditions of his territory. And because of a certain confusion and a lack of uniformity in practice there would seem to be a need of at least some definite regulations.

214. In presenting the following material, this dissertation is making a clear distinction between formal trials, which require

123. S.C. Sacr., instr., 27 mart. 1929 — *AAS,* XXI (1929), 490.
124. S.C. Off., decr., 12 iun. 1942 — *AAS,* XXXIV (1942), 200; *The Jurist,* II (1942), 395.
125. C. 1805; Wanenmacher, *Canonical Evidence,* n. 328.

solemnities even in activities outside the hall of sessions, and informal processes which are devoid of those solemnities. The following paragraphs therefore, need not necessarily apply to a parallel method to be employed in the collection of evidence for informal processes.[127]

215. A commission may be defined as a delegation from a diocesan tribunal fulfilling a judicial function in a formal cause in some place other than the court room of the delegation tribunal which is judging the cause.

This definition emphasizes the delegated power of the commission. In itself it is not a court as such and therefore possesses only limited judisdiction over the particular cause. Therefore, when the "*turnus*" which is actually trying to cause itself goes outside its court room for a judicial act, for example to hear a person of dignity, it is not acting as a commission. The definition also emphasizes the place in which the function is discharged. An auditor, not actually judging a cause, hearing testimony in the hall of sessions where the cause is being tried, is not a commission. Again the judicial personnel of a distant court, even a collegiate body of several judges assembled *per se* for a session on one of its own causes and *per accidens,* as it were, hearing testimony in the name of another tribunal and hearing that testimony in its own hall, is a commission.

216. Commissions are twofold. Within the diocese of the court instructing the cause there is the so-called delegated commission[128] Outside the diocese and set up therefore by a second court in response to a request from the court judging the cause there is the technically described rogatory commission.[129]

217. The principle use of the delegated commission is to gather evidence at a place distant from the hall of sessions. Circumstances may also necessitate the court sending a commission to hear the

126. C. 1770 § 2.
127. Cf. ¶ 295 of this dissertation.
128. C. 1770 § 2 n. 4.
129. C. 1770 § 2 n. 3.

testimony of a person of dignity, of a person prevented from coming to the hall of sessions by state of life, for example a nun in a contemplative order, of a sick person or of an individual unwilling to come to the hall.[130] The following suggestions are made on rules for the delegated commission. They are derived from various sources and may possibly be of value to the individual tribunal.

218. A) A commission delegated in a formal trial except under extraordinary circumstances should be made up of at least two persons, the delegate and his notary.[131] In matrimonial and ordination causes, a third person is ordinarily to be present as a representative of the defender of the bond.[132] The universal law demands that the delegate and the defense representative be priests. The notary may be a trustworthy layman. "If the delegated priest cannot get another priest to associate with himself as defender of the bond, he must mention that fact in the record, and he must then ask questions or do the other necessary things himself. Similarly, if in partly settled or unsettled regions no one can be had to act as recorder, let the fact be noted in the record, and let the delegated judge himself draw up the record of the testimony he receives, with the proper entries."[133]

219. B) A delegated commission is different from a rogatory commission in the authority of the court hearing the cause. The rogatory commission is a request made of someone over whom the petitioner or first court has no authority. The delegated commission is a command from the bishop through his court.[134] The faculties to perform a judicial function are given to the delegated commission by judge. Ordinarily the priest delegated is given authority to associate with himself a notary and a defender although these may be

130. C. 1770 § 2 nn. 1 and 2.

131. C. 1770 § 2 n. 4; *Instructio a.* 1923, Reg. 24; *Instructio a.* 1931, Art. 15.

132. C. 1587; *Instructio a.* 1936, Art. 15.

133. *Instructio a.* 1923, Reg. 24 ¶ 4 (translation by Bouscaren, *The Canon Law Digest,* I, 772); *Instructio a.* 1931, Art. 15 ¶ 4.

134. ¶ 28 of this dissertation.

named directly by the court.[135] The commission is delegated to receive oaths of its own members and of witnesses, to hear certain witnesses and to call in *ex officio* witnesses if necessary, to add *ex officio* questions to those given in the questionnaire. The delegate or head of the commission may be permitted to subdelegate his commission although the constitution may not only withhold this faculty of subdelegation but may even forbid it except in case of real necessity, because as a rule the delegate is carefully chosen for his qualities of prudence, age and conscientious observance of instructions.

220. C) The constitution may choose to grant a general permission for all its auditors who hear testimony within the hall of session to go forth when necessary as a commission to fulfill an action outside the hall, possibly with the provision that the act and the reasons for it be recorded, for example, in the minutes of the session held outside.

221. D) The instructions accompanying the command and the faculties should include a summary of the cause, regulations on procedure, on secrecy and on the particular points destined for special investigation and finally the names and addresses of the witnesses to be heard. Accompanying this instruction will be the questionnaires from the defender of the bond acting in the cause.

222. E) The constitution may require that the commission proceed after the manner of sessions and that minutes (*acta sessionis*) be kept on each session. Thoroughness in mentioning all judicial activities during sessions makes the minutes complete and therefore saves much possible confusion.[136]

135. One middle west diocese has found it more efficient to set up an auditor, notary and defender in each deanery for collecting evidence. This more or less permanent delegated commission has its set place for hearing witnesses to which witnesses are requested to come to give their testimony. The great advantage of this stable provision is that the men so appointed grow accustomed to the procedure and the requirements and therefore return a more complete deposition

136. ¶ 150 of this dissertation.

and properly arranged session notes.

All sessions may be united into one depending on circumstances. The first session will be for the benefit of the commission itself. Oaths will therein be taken and the mandate, faculties and instructions of the delegating tribunal will be read. The second and subsequent sessions proceed with the actual work of the commission. In hearing witnesses the commission may be instructed to follow in so far as possible all universal and diocesan rules on identifications, oaths, questionings, character testimonials and animadversions.[137]

223. F) The Sacred Congregation of the Sacraments gives an authoritative suggestion on the oaths of the commission: "The priest so delegated must take the oath before the recorder to perform his duty well and faithfully and to keep secrecy; and the defender of the bond and the recorder must take a similar oath before the delegated priest. And the record must show that this has been done."[138]

224. G) Delegates could be reminded of the importance of character testimonials for witnesses heard since the court will have no other method of judging their reliability. Likewise the delegate should include his impression (*animadversiones delegati*) of each witness at the end of the deposition. This is especially important if the impression is based on something out of the ordinary.

225. H) The constitution would do well to specify that the instructions, faculties and questionnaires be forwarded to delegates and the completed commission be returned to the court both by registered mail if they are not delivered personally. The court itself should keep a record, possibly in the protocol book, of the sending and of the return of commissions.

226. I) Finally the constitution should make some rules on the finances of delegated commissions. For example, it could suggest that the delegate include his bill of costs with the completed commission in order that he and the others might be reimbursed for their expenses at least. As an alternative, the constitution might

137. ¶¶ 180-200 of this dissertation.
138. *Instructio a.* 1923, Reg. 24 ¶ 3; *Instructio a.* 1931, Art. 15 ¶ 3 (translation by Bouscaren, *The Canon Law Digest,* I, 772).

designate some officer of the court, the *officialis,* for example, as the judge of the costs.

227. The constitution may make regulations on how the diocesan court will dispatch requests to other courts for assistance in the form of rogatory commissions and on how it is to fulfill such requests coming to it. Naturally it cannot make any rules on how the second diocese is to fulfill requests. The constitution may urge that rogatories be used as infrequently as possible because of the too frequent unsatisfactory results.

228. A) The actual power or authority to fulfill a rogatory commission comes from the diocese in which the commission is fulfilled, although it commands the commission to act according to the instructions from the first court.[139] The commission as organized in the diocese *ad quam* is strictly a commission and not a court. Therefore even in matrimonial causes it is never necessary that three judges be employed as delegates although the court may deem it prudent that three delegates, in addition to a notary and a defense representative, sit in on some commission sessions. The request to the diocese *ad quam* may be for various judicial activities, for example, to cite and hear parties, witnesses and even experts, to make a judicial inspection, to carry out a decree and to force production of documents.[140]

229. B) The request, according to the custom of the Sacred Roman Rota, is addressed to the ordinary of the diocese although the envelope could actually be sent to the court itself.[141] The request made of the ordinary is that he appoint and delegate a com-

139. Roman Congregations and Courts send actual delegation because the Holy See has jurisdiction over the diocese *ad quam* whereas another diocesan court has not — *Normae a.* 1934, Art. 93 ¶ 1. Noval classifies rogatory letters sent to an equal court as simply *remissoriales,* to a superior court as *supplicatoriae* and to an inferior court as *imperativae* — *De Processibus* I, n. 104.

140. C. 1770 § 2 n. 3; c. 1570 § 2; *Instructio a.* 1923, Reg. 23; *Instructio a.* 1931, Art. 14.

141. *Normae a.* 1934, Art. 102; *Instructio a.* 1923, Reg. 23; *Instructio a.* 1931, Art. 14.

mission to fulfill the particular function, always indicating whether the request is for testimony required eventually in a solemn trial. The request may include the specific petitions that authority be given the commission to hear not only the witnesses mentioned but also *ex officio* witnesses and to develop points diligently by *ex officio* questions if necessary; that character testimonials be obtained; and finally that a record of these be drawn up and returned to the first diocese.

230. C) The information pertinent to the cause may be given with the request that it be kept secret. The instructions will be similar to those of a delegated commission.[142] It is often prudent to include a letter of introduction to the witness from the party requesting the testimony of the witness thereby insuring a more favorable reception of the citation. Some courts send letters of appreciation to witnesses after the commissions are returned. The usual information concerning the witnesses and the questionnaires from the defender of the bond will be included.

231. D) The constitution should make regulations on the reception of requests from other tribunals by the court, for example, that each request be recorded in the protocol book with the date received, that a specific officer, probably the secretary, be responsible for its custody, and that the *officialis* be empowered to appoint and delegate the commission.

232. E) The organization of the commission will depend on circumstances. If the judicial function can reasonably be fulfilled in the hall of sessions of the cooperating court that is the place where it should be executed.[143] In this case, the *officialis* may request that a "*turnus*" actively working on a cause of its own and therefore assembled at the hall of sessions fulfill the commission, but he should remember to delegate the authority to them. A commission gathering evidence outside the hall of sessions, for example, at a distant point in the diocese of the cooperating court, will be organized ordinarily as is the delegated commission, that is it will

142. ¶ 221 of this dissertation.
143. C. 1770 § 1.

be composed of a delegate, a notary and, in causes affecting the marriage bond and ordinations, a defense representative, and it will take the oaths in a similar manner.[144] The custom existing in some places of sending a single priest to receive the testimony of a witness in a formal trial is not to be praised and the constitution may forbid this for its own diocese except under most unusual circumstances which should be noted in the minutes. A judicial inspection, for example, a comparison of a document with an original, could probably be accomplished by a notary alone because of the nature of the particular action.[145]

233. F) The constitution may ask that the granting of the faculties to the rogatory commission fulfilling the function be in writing.[146]

234. G) The commission will fulfill the judicial function in the same manner as the delegated commission and the constitution may command that minutes be kept according to sessions by all such commissions carried out in its diocese.[147]

235. H) Some regulations could be made by the constitution on the return of the completed commission to the petitioning court. Some courts prefer to keep all original documents in their files and forward neatly arranged copies. Others retain the *acta processus* for their own files, for example, the request, the instruction, the information on the witnesses and the citations, and return the originals of the minutes, the depositions and the testimonials. Still others return all documents in their original form. Some courts return commissions in neatly bound portfolios with helpful indices and all should use registered mail to insure safe and undamaged delivery.[148]

144. ¶¶ 218 and 223 of this dissertation; *Instructio a.* 1923, Reg. 24 ¶ 1; *Instructio a.* 1931, Art. 15 ¶ 1.
145. C. 374 § 1 n. 3.
146. The Sacred Roman Rota gives the faculties in writing — *Normae a.* 1934, Art. 93.
147. ¶¶ 222-225 of this dissertation.
148. A return from a middle west diocese, for example, included the following: a) a letter announcing the return; b) an index; c) the request letter of the petitioning court; d) the constitution and delegation of the commission; e) citations of the witnesses with

236. I) The various letters of courtesy, the indices, the signed oaths of the officers of the court, while useful and even necessary at times for the completeness of the report of the commissions, need not be included in the transcriptions of the completed causes. They add nothing to the understanding of the cause and make the acts bulky and cumbersome.

237. J) The constitution should specify some arrangements for expenses in connection with rogatory commissions. It may, for example, rule that its court request the cooperating court to include with the returned commission a bill of expense; and again that its own court is to bear the expenses *in causis pauperum.*

Article 11.

The Session for Considering Documents, Presumptions and Indications

238. Documents, presumptions and indications will not as a rule be dealt with in a separate session but rather during sessions for other acts.

239. The constitution may choose to fix definite norms for drawing up original written documents and instruments in the diocese. No identical form is observed among diocesan *curiae.*[149] The following words may serve as a guide: "In practice there is a distinction made between the more solemn and the less solemn acts. The more solemn acts are authenticated by the signature of

proofs of the delivery of these citations; f) acts of the sessions, of which there were two; g) questionnaires from the petitioning court; h) answers of the witnesses; i) impressions of the witnesses; j) testimonial letters of credibility and character testimonials in question and answer form; k) testimonial on authenticity of copies made from originals. All were neatly bound.

149. Wernz-Vidal, *Ius Canonicum,* VI, n. 509, III; Willett, Robert, *The Probative Value of Documents in Ecclesiastical Trials,* (The Catholic University of America Canon Law Studies, n. 171, Washington, D.C.: The Catholic University of America Press, 1942) p. 50 (hereafter cited *The Probative Value of Documents*); Muniz suggests that fixed norms be established in provincial councils — *Procedimientos Eclesiasticos,* III, n. 364.

the ordinary and of the chancellor, or of another notary together with the affixing of the proper seal. The less solemn acts seem to have a sufficient mark of authentication in the signature of the ordinary or of a notary together with the affixed seal. Coronata however states that the minimum requirement for drawing up any public document in authentic form seems to be at least the signature of the author or of the notary."[150]

240. Because of the dispute on the point the constitution may wish definitely to grant to assistant pastors and possibly to other priests of the diocese not classified as ordinaries, pastors or notaries, the authority to issue authentic attestations and copies of records preserved in parochial books.[151]

241. Since "public civil documents are those which are considered as such by the laws of the various countries,"[152] the constitution may incorporate the civil law on this point of the state wherein its diocese is located, or it may give directions whereby such law may be found.[153]

242. An instruction directing court officers on where and how to obtain the more important civil documents in a particular locality would not be out of place.

243. The constitution may direct the consulting officer to give directions on the documents required during the trial. In marriage causes the defender of the bond must be interested in documents necessary for defense.[154] Special mention might be made in the rules of the need for consulting the pre-nuptial investigation records.[155]

244. The constitution may ask that all documents, if possible, be presented with the *libellus*, thereby to prevent delay and to make them available that parties and witnesses may be questioned on

150. Willett, *The Probative Value of Documents*, p. 50; Coronata, *Institutiones*, III, n. 1342.
151. C. 1813 § 1; Willett, *op. cit.*, p. 56; Coronata, *Institutiones*, III, n. 1342; Augustine, *Commentarium*, VII, p. 257.
152. C. 1813 § 2.
153. Willett, *op. cit.*, pp. 56-60.
154. C. 1968 § 2.
155. ¶¶ 68 and 135 of this dissertation.

them; that they be grouped in the acts after the *libellus*;[156] and that the minutes record both their reception into the trial at a session and the notification given the parties of the date of their examination.[157] The minutes should carefully record as to any document presented, its source, the recognition of its genuineness and authenticity, and the challenge made to it and the disposal of the challenge. The constitution may require mention of facts of special value, for example, that the letter was written *tempore non suspecto,* lest these be not apparent to the court of appeals. Naturally any absence of or any exemption of documents will be explained, as well as the presence of only parts of documents.

245. The constitution should demand that the diocesan court, in matrimonial causes especially, take necessary precautions to protect itself from possible law suits, especially from alienation of affection suits. The procedure to effect this may vary in individual causes and in some causes at least may extend to a refusal to undertake a cause unless the legal separation has taken place.[158]

246. As a precaution, the constitution may again demand that the *acta* carefully record all presumptions, especially personal presumptions, and all indications and circumstances present as confirmatory proof lest they be lost to the court of appeal.[159]

156. Some courts use the civil law enumeration of "Exhibit A," "Exhibit B," etc.

157. "When a document has been exhibited in court the interested party must be notified, and the proper time must be granted him for acquainting himself with the instrument with a view to refuting it if he be able or if he desire to do so; otherwise the trial is invalid" — Willett, *op. cit.,* p. 64; c. 1861 § 2.

158. For a treatment on the possibility of definitely requiring divorce papers, confer *The Jurist,* III (1943), 305, 306, Hannan, "Civil Divorce Requisite for Ecclesiastical Adjudication." Alford mentions that in some places civil divorces cannot be obtained — *Jus Matrimoniale Comparatum,* (New York: P. J. Kennedy & Sons, 1938), pp. 163-164.

159. Cc. 1825 — 1828; *Instructio a.* 1936, Arts. 170-174; Wanenmacher, *Canonical Evidence,* p. 237-362.

Article 12.

Publication of the Acts; Conclusio in Causa; the Discussion

247. In marriage causes especially the constitution may stress the responsibility of the judge and the defender of the bond to go over the acts carefully in quest of discordant facts, difficulties, conflicts, inconsistencies, obscurities and omissions before the *conclusio in causa.*[160]

248. The constitution, for the sake of order, may suggest a single formal court session to care for the publication and the *conclusio in causa.* Because of the practice, in vogue in many places, of having the procurator-advocates follow the instruction of the cause as it proceeds, they are as a rule familiar with the testi-

160. The following words, intended for causes being prepared for Rome but which are practical for all, may be a source of suggestions for the constitution: "Before the final conclusion of the process, the acts should be reviewed by the Judge as well as by the Defender of the Bond to discover whether the proofs are as complete as possible, that is, whether there exist any obscurities, contradictions, inconsistencies or omissions which can still be remedied... They should ... regard the acts with a certain sense of detachment as if they were reviewing them as strangers for the first time, unfamiliar with those details of persons and fact gained through the course of the oral hearings which often make significant, to those participating in the hearings themselves, the written record which to others, deprived of this advantage, remains perhaps obscure. This work of final review of the acts as a whole is thus a very important one, often disclosing the existence of gaps and conflicts in the testimony as well as a lack of clearness on important points, particularly in the dispositions of the parties and experts, or other defects which may have escaped the attention of the court... Where these exist, proper measures suited to the requirements of each case should be taken to remedy them, or at least, the acts should show that the court was conscious of these defects and had adopted every reasonable means to remedy them. It is important, too, that this final review be directed to the procedure or form of the process, and where it reveals the existence of any irregularities or deviations ... it should be examined whether the motives or reasons of these irregularities have been properly recorded in the acts" — Hickey, "De Processu Super Matrimonio Rato et non Consummato," — *The Jurist,* I (1941), 223-224.

monies and documents, and, as the instruction proceeds, bring in their counter measures. Hence after the formal publication they have nothing more to offer and the *conclusio* can be decreed. Present at the session should be the judge,[161] the advocate-procurators, the defender of the bond, the promoter of justice and the notary.[162]

249. The rule of the Sacred Roman Rota on new evidence after the *conclusio in causa* may be of help to some courts: "Fas erit tamen Ponenti novas admittere probationes, si agatur de causis, quae nunquam transeunt in rem iudicatam, aut de documentis nunc primum repertis aut de testibus qui antea ob legitimum impedimentum tempore utili induci non potuerunt. Sed proprio decreto id statuat Ponens, audita altera parte, cui congruum tempus adsignet ut super illis suas animadversiones conficere valeat; secus nullum erit iudicium."[163]

250. Because of contrary American civil law practices, some constitutions may desire to caution both sides to refrain from arguments in their briefs and animadversions based on sophistry, distortion, and misrepresentations.[164]

161. The auditor is sufficient — Wanenmacher, *op. cit.,* n. 577.

162. One definite advantage of such a formal session is the careful preservation of all happenings and their explanations, if needed, in the minutes of the sessions, especially since these events must be recorded. Cf. Wanenmacher, *op. cit.,* n. 577; *Instructio a.* 1923, Reg. 97 ¶ 2. The session might proceed thus: a) prayer; b) reading decree ordering session; c) formal decree of publication given orally by informing the procurators that the acts are at the hall of sessions and may be inspected — Wanenmacher, *op. cit.,* n. 577; d) declaration by advocate-procurators that they have no more to offer (recorded); e) report by defender of the bond (1) that he has reviewed the acts and found them sufficiently complete and (2) that he himself has no more to offer; f) report of the judge on the completeness of the acts; g) decree of *conclusio in causa;* h) decree ordering completion of briefs and animadversions by a certain time and limiting their length if necessary; i) decree ordering session for the sentence; j) decree closing session; k) signatures on minutes; l) prayer.

163. *Normae a.* 1934, Art. 121.

164. No standard form for the animadversions of the defender of the bond is given. The custom in non-consummation cases makes these

251. Following the private letter of the Sacred Congregation of Sacraments of January 5, 1937, on non-consummation causes, the constitution may demand that, while the defender of the bond may and even should assist the judge in reviewing the acts for possible defects even those telling against his position, in his animadversions he must limit himself to a defense of the bond, refraining from any admission that a favorable decision may be given to the plaintiff.[165]

252. The Sacred Roman Rota requires that if permission is granted to one party to extend the time for filing either the brief or the rebuttal beyond the accustomed length the other party must be notified that this privilege is granted to him also.[166] The Sacred Roman Rota likewise authorizes pecuniary fines for those negligent in preparing briefs.[167] The petition for extension of time for preparing briefs for the Sacred Roman Rota must be made not later than ten days before the time limit expires.[168]

253. Most courts in America require only one copy of briefs, rebuttals and animadversions.[169] At the tribunal offices, copies to fit in with the transcriptions of the acts are prepared and added immediately to these transcriptions.

254. The Sacred Roman Rota ordinarily does not have oral discussions. However the presiding judge may allow a "moderate discussion." If allowed, the parties must submit beforehand in writing points for discussion (*capita quaestionum*) to the presiding judge and to each other.[170]

255. Article 133 ¶ 3 of the *Normae* reads: Discussioni unus

rather short unless real difficulties are encountered. As a rule they are only comments on (1) the form of the process, (2) the merits of the cause, and (3) the presence of scandal. They need not contain any *species facti,* any summary of the evolution of the cause or any preamble details.

165. S. C. Sacr., 5 ian. 1937 — Bouscaren, *The Canon Law Digest,* II, 541.
166. *Normae a.* 1934, Art. 126; cf. c. 1865 ¶ 2.
167. *Normae a.* 1934, Art. 131.
168. *Normae a.* 1934, Art. 129 ¶ 2.
169. The S. R. Rota requires many copies. — *Normae a.* 1934, Art. 126 ¶ 1.
170. *Normae a.* 1934, Art. 132; cf. c. 1866 §§ 1-3.

etiam ex Tribunalis Notariis assistere debet, ut, Ponente decernente, disceptata referat in actis.[171]

Article 13. The Session for the Sentence

256. To avoid unnecessary delay at this point, the constitution may choose to give a maximum time limit to be allowed between the final defense and the session for the sentence for ordinary causes.[172] Time should be given by the court for composition of the review by the *ponens* as well as for consideration by the judges. Copies of the completed acts should be forwarded to the judge or judges immediately on completion of the last rebuttal.[173]

257. Only the judges may be present at this session if the court is collegiate, to the exclusion of even the notary.[174] Since minutes of the session will be kept, including the fact of the meeting, the names of those present, the place where and the time when held, the decision, excluding any mention of the *vota* or of the discussion, the presiding judge may be asked to designate one judge present, ordinarily the *ponens,* to record essential information lest it be lost.[175]

171. Cf. *Instructio a.* 1936, Art. 186; cf. c. 1866 ¶ 4.

172. "Three days should normally suffice to deliberate on an ordinary case and, except in more difficult marriage cases, the postponement should not exceed fifteen days" — Krol, *The Defendant,* p. 153, footnote 28; Coronata, *Institutiones,* n. 1399; Muniz, *Procedimentos Eclesiasticos,* III, n. 440; Roberti, *Schemata,* A. C. 347. A minimum of ten days is required for marriage causes — *Instructio a.* 1936, Art. 185.

173. Lemieux, *The Sentence,* p. 56. Ordinarily the notary or secretary will have had several copies made if the court is collegiate. Unless the trial unfolded quickly, these can be prepared with the successive steps. In this way, after the last rebuttal is in, they can be completed, indexed and forwarded to the judges in a very short time. The transcriptions are then ready to receive the minutes for the session of the sentence and the formal sentence and to be forwarded with little or no change to the court of appeals.

174. *Instructio a.* 1936, Art. 198; *Normae a.* 1934, Art. 137.

175. The following program is suggested if the trial is before a collegiate court: a) prayer; b) reading of decree ordering session; c) appointing of one judge as notary; d) reading of review by *ponens;*

258. As a precaution, the rules may warn the individual judge against informing others of his opinion either before or after the session of the sentence. If he is desirous of counsel, the constitution may order him to request a legally appointed judicial adviser. The secrecy of the *vota* and of the discussions binds perpetually and inviolably for matters not made public by the sentence.[176] The *vota*, with indications of changes of opinion and the reasons thereof, are sealed in an envelope and placed in the secret archives.[177] Connolly maintains this is to be a separate and distinct envelope under the curial seal.[178]

259. The constitution may desire to say something of the form of the *vota* of the judges. The *ponens* must review the cause as well as present his written opinion.[179] Properly prepared, much of the review of the *ponens* can be used in the first part of the formal sentence.[180] The review of the cause by the *ponens* will be

e) reading of his opinion with reasons by *ponens;* f) reading of his opinion with reasons by presiding judge; g) reading of his opinion with reasons by third judge (or by remaining judges if five are present according to precedence); h) oral discussion; i) final vote; j) recording of changes of opinion with reasons thereof on *vota* of judges changing; k) discussion of motives for formal sentence; l) discussion of expenses; m) decree ordering drafting of formal sentence; n) decree on time and place of formal publication (determined by *ponens* — *Instuctio a.* 1936, Art. 199); o) signing of minutes and of sentence by judges; p) decree closing session and prayer.

176. *Instructio a.* 1936, Art. 198 ¶ 2 and Art. 203 ¶ 2; *Normae a.* 1934, Art. 136; Lemieux, *The Sentence,* p. 63; Wernz-Vidal, *Ius Canonicum,* VI, n. 155; Connolly, *Appeals,* p. 97.

177. *Instructio a.* 1936, Art. 203; *Normae a.* 1934, Art. 138; Lemieux, *The Sentence,* pp. 56, 65 and 68; cf. ¶ 96 of this dissertation.

178. *Appeals,* p. 99.

179. *Normae a.* 1934, Art. 137.

180. "In the brief review, he [*the ponens*] points out the purpose and nature of the petition, the admissions and denials of the defendant, the concessions made by the parties, the proofs adduced and their value, the stand taken and the defense made by the contestants, what incidental questions arose and their solution, what questions remain to be settled and reasons for such, and any defects in the procedure which may exist" — Lemieux, *op. cit.,* pp. 56-57. The

objective and unbiased regardless of his opinion on the disposition of the cause. The actual *vota* of the *ponens* and of the other judges will be simply their opinions followed by motives in law and in fact, excluding any *species facti* and introductions. Very little time ordinarily should elapse between this session and the formal publication of the sentence because of the court's obligation to hasten trials in every reasonable way.[181]

260. The bishop may desire to remind his judges, through the constitution, of the recent allocution of the Holy Father to the Sacred Roman Rota on the moral certitude required in judicial processes.[182] "Between the extremes of absolute certainty and quasi-certainty lies moral certainty. It is such that it excludes any well founded or reasonable doubt, but not the possibility of the contrary. . . The judge may be satisfied with the lowest degree of moral certitude, that which excludes all reasonable doubt concerning the truth, provided that it is objective, and provided that the law or the unusual importance of the case do not require a higher degree."[183]

261. A commendable practice is to begin the formal sentence with the name of the bishop of the diocese as well as that of the reigning pope and the year of the reign of each. The Sacred Roman Rota does this for the reigning pope.[184] Any appropriate titles may be used for the divisions of the sentence and common use puts the

formal sentence will require an introduction of the identity of the tribunal and the participants, followed by a history or the evolution of the cause. This latter means the events leading to the institution of the petition; the object of the petition, with the objection of the respondent; a resume of the uncontroverted facts and of the doubts of the controversy and the gist of the final plea of the parties. Cf. Lemieux, *op. cit.,* p. 83.

181. C. 1876.

182. Address to the Sacred Roman Rota, Oct. 1, 1942 — *AAS,* XXXIV (1942), 338.

183. The quotation is from the summary of the allocution appearing in *The Jurist,* III (1943), 500-501; cf. also Bouscaren, *The Canon Law Digest,* II, 454-458.

184. *Normae a.* 1934, Art. 144.

185. Lemieux, *The Sentence,* pp. 83-84.

motives in law prior to those in fact although no special order is required.[186]

262. Included in the notification of the parties and their procurators of the sentence should be information on their right of appeal and on the method of making this appeal.[187] The useful time for making the appeal does not begin until the solemn publication.[188]

263. The constitution should make some provision requiring careful recording of the method, time and place of the solemn publication of the sentence, with proof that the parties, their advocates and procurators, and the defender were notified.[189] The signature of each judge on the solemn form of the sentence is proof that it was submitted to him for approval.[190] The notary also signs it and the seal of the court is affixed.

186. Roberti, *De Processibus,* n. 457; Lemieux, *op. cit.,* p. 83; *Normae a.* 1934, Art. 144 ¶ 2.
187. Some courts enclose a form letter on how to make an appeal, with advice to consult their advocate.
188. C. 1881; *Instructio a.* 1936, Art. 204 ¶ 4.
189. Even the contumacious respondent must be notified — *Instructio a.* 1936, Art. 204 ¶ 2.
190. *Instructio a.* 1936, Art. 200 ¶ 5; all judges sign the sentence regardless of their opinions and this is required for validity. Cf. P.C.I., dec., 14 iul. 1922 — *AAS,* XIV (1922), p. 529.

CHAPTER VII

APPEALS

264. The constitution should mention the name and address of its court of appeals. The Sacred Roman Rota ordinarily is the court of third instance and its address is: *Sacra Romana Rota; Palazzo della Dataria; Via della Dataria, 94; Roma, Italia.*

265. Because little is mentioned directly on these in the universal law, the constitution may desire to make a regulation on the form of the oral and written petitions of appeal to the court of first instance in formal trials.[1] The constitution can impress upon all that this action is part of a solemn trial, with its many technical formalities, and order that the oral petition be presented before the close of the session for the solemn publication.[2] It may also specify that while the petitioner needs but a word to express his wishes under these circumstances, the notary is to formulate the appeal with its proper solemnities[3] and that this is to be read back to the petitioner, approved by him and signed by him, by the judge and by the notary.[4] It would not be out of place to request at this time the reasons for the appeal which may or may not be inserted in the petition to the court of first instance but which must be inserted in the *libellus appellatorius.* The written petition must be addressed to the judge or to the collegiate court pronouncing the sentence.[5]

266. The constitution may demand that an officer of the court, the secretary, for example, or the *actuarius,* note the fact and date of appeal in the protocol book and that he at the same

1. C. 1882.
2. Connolly, *Appeals,* pp. 112-113.
3. C. 1882 § 1.
4. Connolly, *Appeals,* p. 114.
5. Connolly says the appeal is invalid if filed with anyone but the judge who pronounced the sentence that is impugned — *Appeals* p. 91; cf. also Bouix, *De Iudiciis,* II, 268; Wernz-Vidal, *Ius Canonicum,* VI, n. 610, note 67.

time notify the other party, his procurator and the defender of the bond and the promoter of justice if these enter into the trial.[6]

267. The *libellus appellatorius*, or formal petition to the court of appeals, is then prepared. The constitution may specify who prepares this and may choose to make clear that it must be drawn up according to the laws governing the drafting of an original *libellus*.[7] The motives in law and in fact for the appeal must be included although they need not be lengthy.[8] Hence the value of including them in the petition to the court *a quo*. If it is the defender of the bond who is making the appeal, these motives contain his defense of the bond made necessary by the sentence in favor of its dissolution.

268. Directions on forwarding the *libellus* to the court of appeal could be given. The *libellus* would naturally be accompanied by a letter from the court of first instance and must be accompanied by a copy of the petition to the court of first instance and a copy of the entire formal sentence.[9] As a rule these will be addressed to the ordinary of the diocese of second instance and forwarded by registered mail to the office of the court of second instance.

269. The constitution of a tribunal that acts as a court of appeals may require that an officer of the court, the secretary, for example, record the reception and its date in the protocol book, that he give it a protocol number and that he immediately inform the *officialis* of its presence.

270. The court of appeal investigates the right of the party to appeal, the observance of the required formalities in the petitions and the competence of the court. It then examines the motives for the appeal and issues its decree of acceptance or rejection. The constitution may direct an officer of the court, its secretary, for example, to forward this decree to the court of first instance, and if the cause was accepted, suggested names of procurators to be commissioned by the parties.

6. Connolly, *Appeals*, pp. 91-92.
7. Cc. 1706-1708; Connolly, *Appeals*, p. 153.
8. *Normae a.* 1934. Art. 157; Connolly, *Appeals*, p. 153.
9. C. 1884 § 1; Connolly, *Appeals*, p. 155.

271. The constitution may ask that the court of first instance record the acceptance of the appeal, notify all concerned, inform them, if necessary, of the time limit for prosecuting the appeal, and give directions on appointing the new procurators. Procurators acting at the court of second instance will greatly facilitate its procedure.[10] New procurators will generally be chosen because of the distance. The court of first instance will probably prepare the mandates of these procurators and the latter will be made out to specific persons because of the names included in the return from the court of second instance. The mandates will be signed by the parties and the notary.

272. The court will then forward the copies of the *acta*[11] with the mandates of the new procurators to the court of second instance. The court of first instance naturally will have learned how many transcriptions are desired by the court of appeal and will furnish this number.[12] If documents have been translated, the constitution may suggest that copies of the originals be included and, if to be sent to a foreign land, explanatory notes to elucidate "catch phrases," slang, peculiar idioms and colloquialisms. Registered mail ordinarily will be used.[13]

273. The secretary of the court of appeal will note the reception of the transcriptions and the constitution may choose to give some rules on the methods of procedure during the trial by the court of appeal.[14] The court of appeal will return its verdict to the court of first instance as quickly as possible and will include a bill or expense according to the schedule drawn up by the bishops of the province.[15]

10. *Instructio a.* 1936. Art. 213.
11. C. 1890; *Instructio a.* 1923, Reg. 101 ¶ 1; *Instructio a.* 1931, Art. 73; the judge *a quo ex officio* forwards the acts — Connolly, *Appeals,* p. 93.
12. Three copies, two of which are carbon copies, can be made almost as easily as one and this greatly facilitates the handling of the appeal in the higher court.
13. Connolly says the interested party may deliver them — *Appeals,* p. 101.
14. *Normae a.* 1934, Art 163.
15. Connolly, *Appeals,* p. 191.

274. The constitution may wish to instruct an officer of the court of first instance, the secretary for example, to inform the parties of the verdict, the expenses, their right to execute the sentence, for example, in matrimonial causes to marry, if the decisions were favorable, their rights of further appeal, for example if the decision of the court of first instance was reversed. A copy of the *acta* of the court of appeal should be carefully preserved with the *acta* of the original trial in the archive of the court of first instance and the protocol book should record the date of the completion of the appeal and the results.

275. For matrimonial causes, the constitution should include a regulation on the notification of the pastors of the parishes in the registers of which are recorded the invalid marriages and the baptisms of each of the parties concerning the ultimate outcome of the trials.[16] C. 1988 demands that the ordinary see to it that the pastors of these parishes are informed. He can do this by determining in his constitution the person who informs them, and the exact time. Possibly the secretary may be asked to do this and the rules may require that it be done at the time at which the parties are notified of the ultimate decision of the court. The 1936 Instruction asks that the ordinary be informed as soon as possible of the fulfillment of the obligation of informing the parishes.[17] It would seem that the constitution could demand that the report be made immediately to the *officialis* and mediately to the bishop with special mention of this fact in the annual or semi-annual report to him.

276. The 1923 Instruction gives a rule in preparing a non-consummation cause for Rome that may be of assistance in preparing causes for the Sacred Roman Rota: "Documents which are not in Latin, Italian or French must be literally translated into Latin. Likewise proceedings which are not recorded in Latin, Italian or French must be correctly translated into one of those languages. If an interpreter is to be used in making the translation,

16. *Instructio a.* 1936, Art. 225; *Instructio a.* 1923, Reg. 106; *Normae a.* 1934, Art. 153; Lemieux, *The Sentence,* p. 108.
17. *Instructio a.* 1936, Art. 225 ¶ 2.

he is to be chosen by the judge after hearing from the Defender of the bond, and he must, no less than the other officers of the court, take a twofold oath, to perform his work faithfully and to keep secrecy."[18]

18. *Instructio a.* 1923, Reg. 49; translation by Bouscaren, *The Canon Law Digest,* I, p. 778.

CHAPTER VIII

UNUSUAL CAUSES

ARTICLE V. CRIMINAL CAUSES

277. Criminal trials in diocesan courts are penal actions[1] for public offenses in the strict sense[2] that can possibly be proved with certainty through prosecution,[3] that are not excluded from the jurisdiction of the court by law or that the bishop does not choose to exclude because of other punishments.

Excluded by law are causes of the Holy Office;[4] occult crimes;[5] crimes of persons of great dignity including titular bishops;[6] crimes outlawed by prescription or condoned;[7] and crimes of pastors punishable through administrative procedure.[8]

The bishop may be satisfied at times with the types of punishment that may be given after the manner of a precept for crimes that are certain;[9] with *latae sententiae* punishments;[10] and with civil law punishments for laymen.[11]

In extraordinary cases and under certain definite circumstances the bishop may proceed with suspension *ex informata conscientia* even against *public* crimes.[12]

Finally the above classifications do not take into account the power of the bishop to punish through Canon 2222.

278. The bishop may choose to delegate the *officialis* for example, to receive denunciations made by clerics and laymen.[13]

1. C. 2210 § 1.
2. C. 2195; c. 2197 § 1.
3. C. 1946 § 2 n. 3; c. 2233 § 1.
4. C. 247 § 2; c. 1555 § 1.
5. C. 2197 n. 4; c. 2191 §§ 1 and 3.
6. C. 1557 § 1 n. 3; c. 2227 § 1.
7. C. 1702; c. 1703; c. 2233 § 1; c. 2240.
8. C. 1933 § 2; cc. 2168-2185.
9. C. 1933 § 4.
10. C. 2217 § 1 n. 2.
11. C. 1933 § 3.
12. C. 2191 § 3.
13. C. 1935.

The *officialis*, after the reception of a denunciation and if he deems it worthy of some belief, can then place the situation as soon as possible before the bishop possibly with its legal background and can assist the bishop in the subsequent procedure.

As a protection especially for clerics, the constitution may demand that ordinarily denunciations be in writing, signed and notarized.[14] The chancellor for example, may be asked to be present as notary especially since in some places the chancellors are notaries public and therefore give documents greater legal strength in civil courts if they are ever referred thereto, for example, in libel suits.

279. If in the judgment of the bishop and his council, for example, the denounced crime is neither notorious nor certain and the situation demands some action,[15] the investigator is to be chosen, appointed for the individual cause and given the oaths of office.[16] The *officialis* ordinarily will be judge or presiding judge of the cause and therefore should not be appointed investigator.[17]

280. Acts are to be kept of this investigation and these are to be preserved in the secret archives even if no trial develops.[18] The constitution may determine that the appointment of the notary to assist the investigator is to be reserved to the bishop or possibly that the chancellor is to act as notary.

281. The investigator with the assistance possibly of the promoter of justice presents the instructed acts to the bishop with his opinion on the situation.[19] The constitution may ask that this opinion include the legal background and especially a summary of the possible procedure mentioned in ¶ 277. The bishop may grant a special mandate to the *officialis* to receive these acts and make the subsequent decision on procedure.[20] The term "ordinary"

14. C. 1936.
15. C. 1942.
16. Cc. 1939-1941.
17. C. 1941.
18. C. 1945; c. 1946 § 2 nn. 1 and 2; Louis, *Diocesan Archives*, p. 71.
19. C. 1945; c. 1946 § 1.
20. C. 1946 § 2.

is used and therefore the vicar general could act here if necessary.[21] If the suspicion is of a crime technically termed public[22] the decision after the investigation may be that the suspicion is unfounded; that it is possibly well founded and that therefore the suspect bears watching; or that it is fairly certain or at least very probable and open to criminal action.[23]

282. The manner of summoning the suspect for the rebuke will depend on circumstances but care should be taken lest the court subject itself to a possible libel suit. This summoning is as a rule not yet the technical citation of a formal trial and therefore the solemnities need not be employed. For example, the summons may be a simple order to appear at the chancery office.

283. The decision to turn the acts over to the promoter of justice for the judicial accusation and subsequent prosecution through a trial rests with the bishop to the exclusion of the vicar general unless the bishop chooses to give this power in a special mandate to the *officialis*.[24] The formal judicial trial begins with this accusation and henceforth all formalities must be observed. The ordinary takes care that no further scandal comes to the diocese from the situation[25] and the *officialis* sees to it that justice is in no way impeded, for example, through intimidations or bribery.[26]

284. As has been partially noted in the above paragraphs, the universal law makes several restrictions of the power of the *officialis* in criminal causes.[27] The *officialis*, to act in these cases, needs a special mandate.[28] The bishop may choose to grant this power in the constitution or he may prefer to leave it as the universal law presents it. In any case it would be well to mention either

21. C. 1946 § 2.
22. ¶ 277 of this dissertation.
23. C. 1946 § 2 nn. 1-3.
24. C. 1954.
25. C. 1956.
26. C. 1957.
27. C. 1946 § 2; c. 1947; c. 1954; c. 1939; c. 1940; c. 1942 § 1.
28. C. 1946 § 2; Tobin, *De Officiali*, n. 252; Coronata, *Institutiones*, III, n. 1116.

the granting of the delegation through diocesan law or its continued reservation in order that the *officialis* may know definitely what his powers are if a situation arises.[29]

285. The bishop may reserve the appointing of the *"turnus"* for the trial to himself. Some criminal trials require only one judge; others require three judges[30] and still others require five judges.[31] Ordinarily the *officialis* is judge in trials of the first type and presiding judge in trials of the others unless the bishop chooses to reserve this power to himself.[32] The latter procedure is not recommended.[33] The associate judges of the *"turnus"* may be chosen from among the synodal judges or may be delegated judges.[34] The bishop may choose to appoint as delegated judges some of the older priests of the diocese or even priests from outside the diocese, especially in criminal causes of clerics.

Unless the bishop chooses others, the remaining officers are to be from the diocesan roster.[35] The bishop may choose to designate the chancellor as *actuarius* and may designate as advocate, if one is not chosen by the suspect, some especially well qualified priest who may or may not be of the *album.*[36]

286. Finally the constitution may rule that none of the rules on preliminary preparations is to apply in criminal causes.[37] Thus that nothing is to appear in ordinary record books, no protocol number is to be given and the chronological calendar is to be disregarded. Records are to be preserved at all times in the secret archive of the *officialis* during the trial[38] and in the diocesan secret archive after the trial.[39] The usual rules governing secret archives are

29. The investigator cannot be delegated *ad universitatem causarum* — C. 1941 § 1.
30. C. 1576 § 1 n. 1.
31. C. 1576 § 1 n. 2.
32. C. 1573 §§ 1 and 2; c. 1578.
33. C. 1578.
34. C. 1607 § 2.
35. C. 1607 § 2.
36. C. 1655.
37. Cf. ¶¶ 124-147 of this dissertation.
38. Cf. ¶ 95 of this dissertation.
39. Cf. ¶ 94 of this dissertation.

to be observed, especially the rule commanding destruction of documents by burning at proper times.[40]

Article B. Roman Causes

287. While it would seem that the unusual causes instructed for the Sacred Congregations of the Holy See do not belong in the constitution for a judicial tribunal acting with ordinary power, nevertheless the similarity of material and the employment of the same officers for their instruction makes mention of these at least desirable. Each individual ordinary will naturally use his own discretion as to whether these causes are to be included and also as to what material is to be employed. Most courts have their own existing customs and these will be excellent sources for the regulations of this portion of the constitution.

288. Each constitution can make its own rules on receiving these Roman causes, on their relationship to the consulting officers, on docketing and numbering them and on the preservation of permanent records of them.[41]

289. The bishop may determine in the constitution that the *officialis,* for example, represent him in the instruction of Roman causes but that he receive in every instance the prerequisite delegation where such is required in the various Instructions of the Holy See. In drawing up causes involving non-consummated marriages, the regulations of the Sacred Congregation of the Sacraments of May 7, 1923 and the Instruction of the Holy Office of June 12, 1942 must be carefully followed;[42] and ordination causes must follow the regulations of the Sacred Congregation of the Sacraments of June 9, 1931.[43]

290. The constitution could mention that the rule on forwarding the results of trials in matrimonial causes to the pastors

40. C. 379 § 1.
41. Cf. ¶¶ 124-147 of this dissertation.
42. S.C. Sacr., instr, 7 maii 1923 — *AAS,* XV (1923), XV, p. 389; S.C.S. Off., decretum, 12 iun. 1942 — *AAS,* XXXIV (1942), 200.
43. *AAS,* XXIII (1931), 457.

of the parishes in the registers of which are contained records of the marriage and of the baptisms applies with equal force to all Roman causes as well as to those pertaining to the ordinary competence of the court.[44] It may ask that an officer of the court, the secretary, for example, forward this information.

44. ¶275 of this dissertation; cf. also S.C. Sacr., instr., 29 iun. 1941, 11 c — *AAS,* XXXIII (1941), 297.

CHAPTER IX

INFORMAL CASES

Article 1. General Rules

291 Among the informal cases considered in this chapter, those dealing with marriages invalid because of lack of form, with the Pauline Privilege and with proof of death of a spouse definitely follow an administrative procedure. Some authors maintain that the summary cases of C. 1990 also follow this procedure.[1] As adminstrative cases, they would seem to have no place in a constitution for the judicial department of the diocese. However, because of the ever present possibility of a development of any one of them into a judicial cause, because of the employment as a rule of the officers of the judicial department for their instruction and because of the need of the technical knowledge of the judicial personnel in their consideration, the writer has included a chapter on them in this dissertation. The individual diocese is of course at liberty to include or exclude them in its constitution.

292. Each constitution makes its own rules on receiving informal cases, on their relationship to the consulting officers, on docketing and numbering them and on preservation of permanent records of them. Ordinarily rules on these things made for formal causes can be made to apply to informal cases.[2]

The constitution may require that a notary assist at all informal cases at least after the preliminary reception, that he keep minutes in one form or another, without of course the technical solemnities of formal causes, lest important information be lost and that he sign the documents and minutes.[3]

293. The need of precautions against possible civil law suits, especially against a technical alienation of affection charge, is to

1. Cf. ¶ 308 of this dissertation.
2. Cf. ¶¶ 92-106 and 124-142 of this dissertation.
3. C. 2142 requires the presence of a notary in cases considering the removal of pastors which follows an administrative procedure and which may therefore serve as a source of suggestions for the informal cases of this chapter. C. 2142 also rules, for example, that the *acta* of the administrative cases of removal of pastors be placed in the archives.

be observed in accepting informal cases. The comments presented in ¶ 245 of this dissertation should be considered at this point.

294. Needless to say the formalities of solemn trials do not apply in these cases. More will be said of this in Article 3 of this chapter. It can be mentioned here however that formalities in this dissertation are considered to be not only the technical activities required in a cause by human law as opposed to the natural law requirements but also the means by which these and all other activities are externalized. In these cases certain activities are necessary of their very nature but the manner of accomplishing them is not prescribed. Thus a decision in any of the cases is valid and licit by universal law if given orally. For the sake of public record the bishop will naturally require that the cases be presented to him in written form except possibly in an emergency. Such local rules on the external form to be employed in informal cases could be placed in the constitution.

295. There is a distinction between the formal depositions of a solemn trial and the informal depositions and affidavits of these cases. For example a single notary suffices for obtaining affidavits or informal depositions, whether in the hall of sessions or at a distant point, whether for cases within the diocese or in answer to a "rogatory" request from another diocese.[4] The notaries may be authorized by the constitution to receive the oaths of persons giving either affidavits or informal depositions. Even the regulation of Canon 1770 § 1 on the examination of witnesses in the hall of sessions does not apply by universal law to these cases since this is one of the formalities required only in solemn processes. However, diocesan law may require it when it is reasonably possible.

296. In informal procedures the competence of ordinary administration alone applies.[5] The bishop when he is within his territory has the authority to render the decision in these cases for any petitioner coming to him whether the petitioner have domicile, quasi-domicile or mere residence in the diocese. However prudence

4. The deposition mentioned above is a question and answer gathering of information and the affidavit is a simple statement.
5. C. 201 § 3.

may suggest that the officers of the tribunal be not allowed to accept petitions which could be instructed safely only where the individuals concerned are better known. The bishop may require for example, that permission be obtained from him before accepting the cases of *vagi*, of *peregrini* and even of *advenae*.[6]

297. The rules of "*ius accusandi matrimonium*," created for "causes", do not apply in these cases unless of course they change into formal causes.[7] The bishop however may wish to protect his officials and to guard against scandal by commanding that petitions of non-Catholics, of fallen-away Catholics, i.e. apostates, heretics and adherents of forbidden societies, and of public sinners for a declaration of freedom to marry be referred to him regardless of delegation received from him by his representatives.

298. The constitution may take precautions lest the limits of jurisdiction be overstepped in cases of Orientals of the various disciplines.

299. In those cases where the *officialis* or any other officer makes a decision in the name of the bishop, he may be required to sign himself as a delegate.

300. The constitution may mention here also that the rule on forwarding the results of trials in matrimonial causes to pastors of the parishes in the registers of which are contained records of the marriage and of the baptisms applies with equal force to all informal cases.[8] It may ask the secretary to forward this information lest it be neglected.

6. Cf. cc. 91, 92, 94 and 198; Kennedy, Edwin, *The Special Matrimonial Process in Cases of Evident Nullity,* (The Catholic University of America Canon Law Studies, n. 93, Washington, D.C.: The Catholic University of America, 1935), pp. 79-80 (hereafter cited *The Special Matrimonial Process*); Marx, The Declaration of Nullity, p. 67; Woeber, Edward, *The Interpellations,* (The Catholic University of America Canon Law Studies, n. 172, Washington, D.C.: The Catholic University of America Press, 1942), pp. 63-64.
7. Cc. 1970-1972; Kennedy, *op. cit.,* pp. 80-82; Marx, *op. cit.,* S.C.S. Off., 14 apr. 1931 — Bouscaren, *The Canon Law Digest,* II, 552; S.C.S. Off., resp. ad Epis. Harrisb., 20 apr. 1931 — Bouscaren, *op. cit.,* II, 552.

Article 2.

The Administrative Procedure of Lack of Form Cases

301. Very little direct universal law is given on the procedure to be observed in the declaration of nullity in lack of form processes.[9] The local lawmaker gives his own rules on forms and records, demanding much or little according to his judgment. It might be mentioned that, as an extreme, as far as the universal law is concerned, all the procedure could be oral from beginning to end. It becomes therefore, the duty of the local legislator to give practical prescriptions for these cases and even to make them binding if he deems this necessary by diocesan law.[10]

302. The bishop and the vicar general have the power *ex officio* to make the final decision in lack of form cases.[11] The constitution may choose to leave this power entirely in their hands. However, in many places, the *officialis* is considered to be in a better position to instruct these cases and is therefore given a general delegation to make the final decision.[12] The constitution may adopt this and make itself the instrument of giving this power to the *officialis*. The appropriateness of this delegation might be seen in the connection, even though it is remote, between these cases and the court, i.e. any one of them might become a formal trial cause.

8. ¶ 275 of this dissertation.
9. By lack of form is meant that defect in the marriage ceremony observed by a Catholic, bound in the particular instance by the Catholic form of marriage, arising precisely because it was celebrated before a justice of the peace or a non-Catholic minister. It is used in contradistinction to defective form which is taken in this work to mean a ceremony before a priest defective for example for lack of jurisdiction in the priest or for insufficient witnesses. This work does not enter into the controversy as to whether on occasions defective form cases may be cared for after the manner of lack of form cases.
10. Marx gives much good material and many excellent suggestions for such laws — *The Declaration of Nullity*. From parallel law arguments may be given as to what should be done, but a bishop, a true legislator, does not govern by application of parallel law but by direct law.
11. P.C.I., 16 oct. 1919 — *AAS,* XI (1919), 479; *Instructio a.* 1936, Art. 231 ¶ 1; Marx, *op cit.*, p. 69.
12. Marx, *op. cit.*, p. 69.

The common law places the power in the hands of the bishop and leaves it to him to employ it *per se* or *per alios* according to the circumstances and conditions of his diocese. The power may be delegated to the chancellor although he is not usually the recipient of habitual delegated jurisdiction.

303. The pastor is given a prominent place in the procedure of lack of form cases by the Pontifical Commission when it says that these cases are to be settled by him after consulting the ordinary.[13] The pastor can arrive at certitude in a case but must consult the ordinary as a safeguard. The response even seems to place the power of decision in the hands of the pastor.[14] The constitution might utilize these carefully chosen words mentioned in the footnote No. 13 by declaring that pastors, in the emergencies of C. 1044, are delegated, *ad cautelam* or at least to remove any subjective doubts, to make even the final decision in the case. This action might be considered a delegation of whatever power is reserved to the ordinary by the words of the decree *"consulto ordinario."* This power could be extended to assistant pastors for emergencies as a definite delegation.

304. The form of the petition is determined by the practical necessities of each situation. The constitution may of course ask for certain formalities for ordinary occasions.[15] The constitution, to simplify the procedure, may request that a filled out and notarized (by an ecclesiastical notary) questionnaire be attached to the petition answering in particular special questions pertaining directly to the case.[16] The parties could be asked to answer these questions under

13. "... resolvendi sunt... a parocho, consulto Ordinario..." — P.I.C., 16 oct. 1919, n 17 — *AAS*, XI (1919), 479

14. Marx says that the pastor is "competent to act in the cases of nullity of a marriage when the parties fail to observe the form. This is the law but the practise and custom are different" — *The Declaration of Nullity*, p. 74. He also says: "the assistant cannot grant a decree of nullity, even in the absence of the pastor, unless he has been delegated" — *op. cit.*, p. 74.

15. Marx presents the information ordinarily desired in this petition — *op. cit.*, pp. 75-76.

16. Marx, *op. cit.*, p. 77.

oath. The consulting officer, who is usually at least a notary if not a judge, could be deputized to receive the oath.

305. The constitution may require that ordinarily a memorandum or record be made of the proof that the petitioner was bound by the Catholic form at the time of the marriage. The main proof here is the baptismal record of the Catholic party, which generally gives the fact of baptism and the religion of the father and the mother. Because this certificate is the main proof also that the marriage was never validated, since the fact of validation is to be noted in the baptismal record according to C. 1103 § 2 and C. 470 § 2, the constitution should demand that the certificate be of a very recent date.[17] Added to this will be other proofs such as the record of confirmation and of first holy Communion, and the testimony of trustworthy witnesses.[18]

306. A second required memorandum, as a continuation of the record mentioned in ¶ 305, might be that of the proof of non-revalidation. Marx suggests especially the affidavits of at least two trustworthy Catholics and the supplementary oath. He declares that a search of the files of various chancery offices is "neither necessary nor practical" and, in substantiation of this, gives good, solid reasons.[19] However, since it is the practise of some courts, the bishop may insert this as a regulation in his constitution if he deems it necessary. When no positive evidence has been unearthed to raise a doubt and yet it is felt sufficient proof is not at hand, the constitution may simply demand the supplementary oath.[20]

307. Diocesan law may choose to rule on the form and disposal of the actual declaration by the authorities of the nullity of the marriage.[21] The omission of any and all formalities, even those

17. S.C. Sacr., instr., 29 iun. 1941, n. 4 c — *AAS,* XXXIII (1941), 297: Marx, *op. cit.,* pp. 79-82; p. 90.
18. Marx, *op. cit.,* p. 78.
19. *The Declaration of Nullity,* pp. 90-91.
20. Cf. S.C. Sacr., litt. priv., 20 maii 1920 — Bouscaren, *The Canon Law Digest,* II, 276.
21. Marx gives the elements that are natural to such a decree — *op. cit.,* p. 93.

required by diocesan law, does not in any way invalidate this decree. The constitution may ask that it be sent directly to the pastor rather than to the parties and may direct an officer of the court, the secretary, for example, to send notices to the pastors of the parishes in the registers of which are the records of marriage and baptism.[22]

ARTICLE 3 THE SUMMARY PROCEDURE OF CANON 1990

308. It is not the purpose of this work to enter into the controversy on the nature of this process. The individual constitution may of course take the stand advocated by the bishop. Rather this dissertation is concerned with what the universal law has left to the legislation of diocesan law concerning the process. The writer is of the opinion that, regardless of the nature of the procedure of C. 1990, the universal law has reduced the elements of these cases to almost the mere essentials of the natural law and has left to the local legislator to add to these essentials the practical formalities desirable in his community. Even granting that the process may be judicial, the Code designedly stripped it of all formalities. In other words C. 1990 introduces a significant change in law. The official interpretation of the Holy Office on this subject issued on June 5, 1889 uses the words: "hisce in casibus praetermissis solemnitatibus in Constitutione Apostolica *Dei Miseratione* requisitis. . ."[23] From this some authors have argued that only the special solemnities of the *Dei miseratione* could be omitted. But the Code deliberately leaves out the qualifying phrase "in Constitutione Apostolica *Dei miseratione*" and makes the "praetermissis solemnitatibus hucusque recensitis. . ." unqualified and absolute. It reduces the procedure to the essence of a procedure by natural law with an identification of the judge plus a retention of the positive ecclesiastical prescription of the presence of the defender of the bond. Citing the parties is not a formality but a requirement of the essence of the procedure. From this it is possible to conclude that even a judicial procedure here would require only citation of the parties in any

22. Marx, *op. cit.*, pp. 93-94.
23. *Fontes,* n. 1118.

form, certitude by the judge through the evidence presented, a decision or sentence expressed in any way and the presence of the defender of the bond who, as long as he fulfills his obligations according to his conscience, can express his opinion in any way. To extend this principle to its ultimate conclusion, a procedure fulfilling the requirements just mentioned, even if it were oral from beginning to end, would be both licit and valid by universal law.

309. It becomes the duty of the bishop to add the formalities desired over and above this universal law according to the conditions and circumstances of his locality. The Holy See, assuring itself that the essential certitude required can be guaranteed by the limited provisions given, wisely remembers that the varying conditions in diverse regions, for example, in Europe, the Americas and Asia, will dictate variety in formalities. Bishops, in drawing up local requirements in constitutions, can indeed be guided by parallel law but they have the liberty to employ or omit, to add to or to substract from the many traditional rules of procedure.

310. Because authors differ widely on the nature of the actual process of C. 1990, the constitution may determine the procedure to be followed in its diocese, i.e., that its officers are to consider it administrative or are to accept it as judicial. The material set forth in this article may be applied in its entirety, no matter which type of procedure is designated.

311. The bishop definitely has the power to make the declarations of nullity in these cases.[24] The mind of the Holy See, as expressed in the 1936 Instruction, seems to be that the decision be rendered ordinarily by him.[25] The *officialis* is told to instruct the case, as it were, and to refer it prepared to the ordinary.[26] Any departure from this procedure as far as the actual decision is concerned should not be countenanced by the constitution. Naturally the *vice-officialis* can instruct the case in the absence of the *officialis* and refer it to the ordinary.

24. C. 1990; *Instructio a.* 1936, Arts. 226 and 227.
25. Art. 227 ¶ 1.
26. Art. 226.

312. The Instruction also gives the procedure in those unusual situations where the ordinary is absent or impeded from acting.[27] A special mandate authorizing the *officialis* to render the sentence in these situations is to be given by the ordinary to him (the *officialis*) who is then to make the decision. The constitution may be the instrument employed by the ordinary to grant this special mandate. When setting forth the mandate once and for all the constitution may extend it to the *vice-officialis* whose office is similar in essence to that of the *officialis*.

313. The petition for a declaration of nullity in these cases, regardless of the procedure, is governed by diocesan law. None of the formalities of the *libellus* applies by universal law. The diocesan requirements, governed by the practical information needed, may adopt what formalities of the *libellus* it desires.

314. The non-Catholic may be a petitioner in these cases.[28]

315. Citation of the parties must be made. Again diocesan law alone governs the form of the citation since the Code allows the omission of universal formalities.[29] The citation naturally includes a hearing or at least an opportunity to be heard. The constitution may prescribe some formalities and may ask that a record be kept of the fact of citation.

316. For the hearing after the citation, the constitution may require a deposition by question and answer. Again by universal law no solemnities are in this matter. A simple interview in the presence of anyone of the officers suffices. The exclusion of judicial formalities implies that a simple affidavit before an ecclesiastical notary as well as a sworn deposition before a notary alone may be admitted in these cases. This is true also of any proof by witnesses that may be presented to supplement the proof by document. The constitution may specify that the interview with the respondent and

27. Art. 228.
28. S.C.S. Off., resp. ad Epis. Harrisb., 20 apr. 1931 — Bouscaren, *The Canon Law Digest,* II, 552; Kennedy, *The Special Matrimonial Process,* pp. 80-82.
29. C. 1990; Kennedy, *op. cit.,* p. 85.

the witnesses be conducted by the *officialis* and that the notary and even the defender of the bond be present.

317. The defender of the bond must be present in every case.[30] The constitution may particularize the meaning of intervention on his part. It may ask written animadversions or it may be satisfied to demand that he thoroughly investigate the case in every detail and offer written animadversions only when he has more than routine objections. It may ask that in all cases the fact of his presence be noted. The omission of specified solemnities for the intervention of the defender of the bond does not in any way lessen his deep responsibility in conscience to follow the details of every case as carefully as he would those of a formal trial cause. Only the external forms of his activities are left to his judgment or to the constitution.

318. The constitution may ask a memorandum of the proof that the impediment allegedly invalidating the marriage was existing at the time of the marriage. The omission of the solemnities in no way lessens the obligation of obtaining moral certitude concerning this.

319. A memorandum of the proof that there was granted no dispensation from the impediment would not be out of place. The constitution may give some regulations concerning the quest. For example if there is a positive reason for believing that a dispensation and revalidation were obtained in some place other than the place of the original contract, a search may be demanded in that place,[31] but reasons given by authors against the necessity, in investigating possible revalidation in lack of form case, of writing to even remotely possible places, for example only because of mere residence there for a time,[32] apply here also. It is not within the scope of this dissertation to enter into details as to the proofs required for the existence of individual impediments and the absence of dispensation from them.[33]

30. C. 1990.
31. Kennedy, *op. cit.*, pp. 93-94; Marx, *The Declaration of Nullity*, pp. 93-94.
32. Marx, *op. cit.*, pp. 90-91; Kennedy, *op. cit.*, pp. 93-94.
33. Cf. Interpretation of the Code Commission (P.C.I.) on the nature of proof — *AAS*, XXIII (1941) p. 353.

320. The 1936 Instruction asks that the sentence include the reasons in law and in fact.[34] Practical considerations alone should dictate any further requirements by diocesan law. The parties may be informed of the sentence in any way determined by local authorities.

321. The defender of the bond makes his decision before the ordinary makes his or at least at the same time so that when the sentence is rendered it can definitely state that the case is decided against the petitioner or is being appealed (which is rare) and therefore the party is not yet free to marry or is finished and the party may marry upon receipt of the decision. The ten days delay between the receipt of the decision and the celebration of the marriage required in solemn trials need not be observed. The *officialis* should take care that the decision include instructions on the freedom or non-freedom of the petitioner to marry.

Article 4. Pauline Privilege Cases

322. The competence of the diocesan authorities includes Pauline Privilege *cases* alone[35] to the exclusion of Pauline Privilege causes, either direct or indirect, which require solemn trials. The Holy Office alone is competent to care for these.[36]

323. The right to authorize the interpellations and to pass judgment on the case belongs to the ordinary of the place and this includes the vicar general.[37] The power may be delegated to the *officialis*[38] and included here is naturally all authority to expedite all matters pertaining to an ordinary case. This power might be

34. Art. 227 ¶ 1.
35. Cc. 1120-1124.
36. C. 1962; Woeber, *The Interpellations,* p. 74; Gregory, Donald, *The Pauline Privilege,* (The Catholic University of America Canon Law Studies, n. 68, Washington, D.C.: The Catholic University of America, 1931), p. 131.
37. C. 1122.
38. "Ad Officialem spectant non solum... causae contentiosae...sed etiam ... casus de applicatione Privilegii Paulini" — *Synodus Dioecesana Richmondiensis Tertia,* Stat. 35.

increased to include a delegation to dispense from the interpellations in case of emergencies when there is not time to refer the case to the Holy See or to the Apostolic Delegate.[39] Occasionally bishops may have obtained faculties to dispense in a limited number of cases other than emergencies.[40]

324. An individual rule may be given on the reception of these cases. For example, the consulting officer may be asked to obtain the necessary preliminary information on the identity of persons, competence, lack of baptisms, conversion, possibility of reconciliation; to inform the parties of documents needed; to obtain permission and delegation from the petitioner to make the interpellations; to assist in formulating the petition.[41]

325. The constitution may require of the petitioner both a written petition asking for the right to use the Pauline Privilege and a written delegation to make the interpellations.[42] No special formalities need be required in this petition or delegation although the signature of the pastor or of the consulting officer as well as of the party would not be out of place.

326. The constitution may ask that the notary be present when anything is done on the case after the preliminary reception of it and that he keep minutes lest some important information be not recorded. Possibly the bishop will be satisfied with memoranda of the various steps. By universal law the presence of the defender of the bond is not required but the constitution may ask this and he may be requested to present animadversions in writing, for example, if he feels them justified.

327. The procedure in proving the lack of baptism of the parties, the fact of conversion and a description of the moral

39. S.C.S Off., 11 aug., 1859 — *Fontes, n.* 954; Woeber, *op. cit.*, p. 129.
40. Woeber, *op. cit.*, p. 132.
41. Gregory suggests the following documents: marriage certificate; affidavits of lack of baptism; certificate of Catholic baptism; answers of the other party to the interpellations or proofs of questioning or dispensation; and a divorce certificate — *op. cit.*, p. 133.
42. Woeber, *op. cit.*, p. 63.

and physical departure of the other party with due emphasis on the the blameworthiness of the party who is responsible for the departure may be preserved in the form of minutes or in a memorandum.

328. The constitution may prefer that the other party be not cited as such but that a notary visit him personally and make the interpellations in a summary, non-judicial manner when this is possible. Citations may tend to irritate and they are not necessary in the extra-judicial form of questioning.[43] The bishop may of course prefer the summary judicial form of questioning.[44]

329. Care should be taken lest trouble be caused by asking the non-Catholic party, who has married again, if he or she will return to the first spouse. The court may be accused of alienation of affection by the second spouse. On occasions a dispensation from the interpellations should be obtained.

330 Authors recommend one month as the period granted the unbaptized party for deliberation.[45] The constitution may set this time with a delegation, possibly to the *officialis*, to shorten or to lengthen it.

331. No special form is required in the decision. Diocesan law may ask a short summary of the identity of the parties and of the facts and a specific statement on the right of the convert to marry a Catholic. This could be sent to the pastor of the parish where the convert's baptism is recorded as well as to the petitioner or the latter's pastor.[46]

Article 5. Cases Involving Proof of Death

332. If, during a pre-nuptial investigation, a former marriage, allegedly dissolved by the death of one spouse, is revealed, a declara-

43. Woeber, *op. cit.*, p. 78.
44. C. 1122; Woeber, *op. cit.*, pp. 75-78.
45. Woeber, *op. cit.*, pp. 79; 80; 99; Gregory, *op. cit.*, p. 138.
46. Gregory, *op. cit.*, pp. 97-99; 139.

tion of freedom must be given before proceeding to the second marriage.[47]

If the pastor has personal knowledge of the death of the first spouse, if the record of the death appears in the parish books, or if he has secured an authentic document certifying the death, he himself may give the declaration of freedom without recourse to the ordinary.[48]

A dispute exists concerning the procedure when the fact of death is known only through witnesses. The constitution should determine the procedure for its diocese. Most authors maintain that any proof of death less than personal knowledge or an authentic undisputed document must be submitted to the ordinary.[49] The constitution may adopt this as a rule. Or it may follow the minority opinion and allow the pastor to proceed if he has the testimony of two reliable eye-witnesses of the death or funeral.[50]

It is certain that unless there is at least the proof of two eye-witnesses, the pastor is severely bound in conscience to consult the ordinary.[51] The constitution would do well to incorporate this into diocesan law for the guidance of priests in parish work.[52]

333. The judicial department under the supervision of the *officialis* may be asked to instruct cases presented by pastors. Officers

47. C. 1069 § 2; c. 1031 § 1; S.C. Sacr., Instr., 29 iun., 1941, ¶ 4 c; ¶ 6 — *AAS*, XXXIII (1941), 297.
48. Rice, Patrick, *Proof of Death in Pre-nuptial Investigation,* (The Catholic University of America Canon Law Studies, n. 123, Washington, D.C.: The Catholic University of America Press, 1940), p. 55. According to Rice, this is the teaching of all authors.
49. Rice. *op. cit.,* p. 55.
50. Rice, *op. cit.,* pp. 55-56.
51 Rice, *op. cit.,* pp. 56-57.
52. An example of such a law may be found in the Provincial Council of Venice of 1925: "Quando agitur de feminis, quae praesumuntur viduae, quia scilicet earum mariti dicuntur obiisse, nec tamen de eorum morte ullum habeatur authenticum documentum, si novum petant matrimonium contrahere, certitudinis suffragia, quae haberi possint, undique pro viribus colligantur a parocho, et ad loci Ordinarium, cui in his casibus recurrendum est transmittantur." — d. 269, quoted by Cerato, *Matrimonium a Codice I.C. integre Desumptum* (4 ed., Patavii, Libr. Gregoriana edidit. typis seminarii, 1927), p. 99.

of this department are familiar with procedure work and furthermore these cases sometimes develop into solemn trial causes. Once instructed, the cases are to be presented to the bishop or the vicar general for decision. The *officialis* is not empowered by his office to give the declaration of freedom as long as the process remains administrative although the bishop may delegate him through the constitution to do this.[53]

334. Ordinarily these cases involving proof of death are administrative in nature and therefore follow the rules considered in this chapter on informal cases. Recourse from these administrative decisions should seldom be necessary but when made it must be to the Holy See.

The bishop may command that the more difficult cases, especially those based on presumptions only, be developed as judicial causes.[54] If this is done, these causes must follow all the rules of formal trials. Ordinarily one judge suffices although the bishop may refer them to a collegiate court. The *officialis* has power *ex officio* to render the sentence if judicial procedure is employed. The defender need not be present in this judicial procedure although he may be invited to participate by the constitution.[55] After the judicial sentence an appeal to the metropolitan court is not compulsory but may be employed.[56]

335. Mention might be made in the constitution of the power of the pastor to render the decision in danger of death. If there is sufficient reason and no time to consult the ordinary, the pastor who has neither personal knowledge nor an authentic document of the death may accept the oath of the living spouse as full proof providing the spouse has personal knowledge or other definite proof of the death and there is no positive motive to doubt the truth of the sworn statement.[57]

53. Rice, *op. cit.,* p. 48.
54. Rice, *op. cit.,* pp. 51-52.
55. Rice, *op. cit.,* p. 52; Ayrinhac-Lydon, *Marriage Legislation in the New Code of Canon Law,* (New York: Benziger, 1932), p. 135.
56. Rice, *op cit.,* p. 52.
57. Rice, *op. cit.,* pp. 58-59.

336. In instructing the case or cause proving death, the directions of May 13, 1868, must be followed.[58]

337. Even when the case remains administrative, care should be taken to preserve carefully all the acts because, among other reasons, of the possibility of recourse to the Holy See. If the case continues as administrative, this is not required for validity and judicial forms need not be observed.

58. S.C.S. Off. Instr., 13 maii 1868 — *Fontes,* n. 1002; S.C. Sacr., 18 nov. 1920 — *AAS,* XIV (1922), 96; SC. Sacr., 1 iul. 1929, n. 48 — *AAS,* XXI (1929), 360; Rice *op. cit.,* pp. 41-42.

CHAPTER X

JUDICIAL EXPENSES

338. The universal law prescribes that the bishops of each province are to draw up a schedule or list of fees of various kinds to be charged parties desirous of the services of the diocesan tribunal.[1] The constitution could incorporate the schedule as prepared by the bishops. The law seems to call for a detailed schedule for individual judicial acts, for example, preparing the *libellus* or preparing a defense. The tendency in the United States, while keeping fees far below even necessary expenses, has been to combine these into an average sum for ordinary causes.

339. Because causes and cases vary widely in the labor necessary for their instruction, the custom of some places of giving a possible minimum and a possible maximum for causes and cases seems most appropriate.[2] While the law does not make mention of all the following, the schedule drawn up at the provincial meeting of the bishops, or their schedule augmented by items introduced by the individual ordinary, may include fees and expenses for them: A) Solemn trials in the diocesan court;[3] cases mentioned in C. 1990;[4] lack of form cases;[5] Pauline Privilege cases; Roman Causes;[6]

1. C. 1909; *Instructio a.* 1936, Art. 233: The archbishops and bishops of the Province of Quebec, Montreal and Ottawa for example promulgated on February 2, 1937 a detailed schedule that is exemplary of the desires of universal law. Of such schedules in the United States, mention might be made of that of the Province of Portland — *Acta et Decreta Concilii Provincialis Portlandensis in Oregon Quarti,* Art. 152 ¶ 1.
2. An example of this may be seen in the schedule prepared for the Sacred Roman Rota advocates and procurators — *Tariff of Fees of the Tribunal of the Sacred Roman Rota* of May 26, 1939 — *AAS,* XXXI (1929), 622; also printed in pamphlet form by the Polygot Vatican Press (hereafter cited *The Tariff of* 1939).
3. For example the Portland Schedule, *op. cit.,* n. 152 ¶ 1.
4. Portland Schedule, *op. cit.,* n. 153.
5. Cf. Marx, *The Declaration of Nullity,* p. 108.
6. That is, diocesan expenses for preparing such causes since the fees charged by Roman courts will be made known in rescripts from these offices.

appeals to the court of second instance;[7] appeals to the court of third instance.[8]

B) Fees for special activities such as translations of documents and completed *acta;* transcriptions of completed *acta;* inspection and attestation of correctness of translations and transcriptions; transcriptions of individual documents from records and archives;[9] rogatory and delegated commissions.

C) Fees for procurators and advocates;[10] fees for experts, both as to services and expenses, according to customs prevailing in civil courts;[11] fees for witnesses which may be for expenses only.[12]

341. Approval by the Holy See is not needed for this schedule unless it is drawn up in a provincial council.[13]

342. In places where the bishops of the province have not yet drawn up the schedule, the constitution would do well to instruct its court or possibly the *officialis* on procedure until the schedule is ready.

343. The Rota allows the presiding judge of the "*turnus*" to draw up the details of expenses.[14] The constitution may employ its presiding judge for the same office though he must act within the schedule of the bishops,[15] and though the collegiate tribunal must enter into discussions of these expenses and of the question of gratuitous patronage.[16] The *officialis* or the presiding judge may be empowered to reduce or increase expenses for unusual situations.[17]

344. The constitution may determine that the procurator

7. C. 1888; for example, Portland Schedule, *op. cit.*, n. 152 ¶ 2.
8. This is generally the Sacred Roman Rota and therefore only the expenses incurred by the diocesan courts would be listed here.
9. All referred to in C. 1909 § 1; cf. also *Instructio a.* 1936 Art. 233.
10. C. 1909 § 1; cf. for example *The Tariff of* 1939.
11. C. 1805; *Instructio a.* 1936, Art. 234 ¶ 2.
12. C. 1787.
13. C. 1909; c. 291 § 1.
14. *The Tariff of* 1939, Art. 4 ¶ 2.
15. *Instructio a.* 1936, Art. 235.
16. *Instructio a.* 1936, Art 236 ¶ 1; Art. 237 ¶ 1.
17. Notanda of *The Tariff of* 1939, ¶ 3.

shall inform the party of the expenses of the court and that he shall act as intermediary to arrange for their payment.[18] The party should be furnished with a receipt or an account of all money paid.[19]

345. The constitution should designate the person who is to act as the recorder of funds received and disbursed. If the court has a treasurer this duty naturally falls to him. The annual report to the Holy See requires an account of taxes and fees for each case, of *honoraria* of advocates and experts and of provisions for gratuitous service.[20] The bishop may ask a similar or even more detailed account in the report made to him.

346. The universal law suggests a deposit to be made by the plaintiff before the trial begins.[21] The Sacred Roman Rota requires a preliminary deposit of 200 Italian liras and allows the presiding judge to increase this if preliminary questions are to be resolved before the introduction of the principal suit.[22] The expenses of the trial are set by the decree of the "*concordantia dubii,*" half of which are to be paid immediately and the other half before the printing of the pleadings.[23] Diocesan law may make its own specifications, for example, that half the expenses be deposited when the trial begins and the other half before the appeal is permitted.[24] Like the Sacred Roman Rota it may wish to enforce its decrees on expenses by ordering the suspension of the cause *ipso facto* when specific time limits are passed without the required deposits being made.[25]

347. Exemptions and reductions for solemn trials must be made only by a procedure following the solemnities of law.[26] The

18. *The Tariff of* 1939, Art. 4 ¶ 5.
19. *The Tariff of* 1939, Art. 4 ¶ 7.
20. S.C. Sacr., litt., 1 iul. 1932, n. I — *AAS,* XXIV (1932), 272.
21. C. 1631; c. 1909 § 2; *Instructio a.* 1936, Art 235.
22. *The Tariff of* 1939, Art 2 ¶ 1.
23. *The Tariff of* 1939, Art. 2 ¶ 3.
24. C. 1913; c. 1873 § 1 n. 4; *Instructio a.* 1936, Art. 236.
25. *The Tariff of* 1939, Art. 2 ¶ 4.
26 Cc. 1914-1916; *Instructio a.* 1936, Art. 236-240; *Normae a.* 1934, Arts. 176-177.

constitution may urge its officers to be careful lest deserving parties be denied complete justice because of financial problems. It should also insure secrecy for the document on economic conditions.[27] Each diocese may make its own rules on exemptions and reductions of expenses for cases of C. 1990 and for lack of form cases. In many places, because of predominantly non-Catholic populations, care must be taken lest the Church be accused of mercenary aims.

348. In many places the judges, the auditors, the promoter of justice and the defender of the bond perform their tribunal labor without remuneration.[28] While some may feel that this is preferable to remuneration based on the individual cause lest these officers be in any way influenced thereby, nevertheless it would seem only just that some, at least general, remuneration be made, possibly from diocesan funds, for the work accomplished. The norms for the tribunals of the Philippine Islands recommend salaries but declare they should be moderate because "judges and officers for the most part already have some ecclesiastical benefice."[29]

349. Notaries, procurators, advocates and messengers receive remuneration in some places at least. The secretary of the court, if one is employed, will naturally receive a salary adjusted to recompense received from his position in the diocese. The advocates and procurators should not receive more than the remuneration for the procurators and advocates of the Sacred Roman Rota.[30]

27. *Instructio a.* 1936, Art. 238.
28. Doheny, *Canonical Procedure,* p. 378.
29. S.C. Sacr., *Normae,* 28 apr. 1941, Art. 17 and 18 — *AAS,* XXXIII (1941), 367.
30. Norms for the Philippine Islands, Art. 20 — *AAS,* XXXIII (1941), 367.

APPENDIX

A TENTATIVE CONSTITUTION

TITLE I

INTRODUCTORY RULES

(Numbers after individual rules refer to paragraphs in the commentary portion of the dissertation).

ARTICLE 1: The diocesan (archdiocesan) court of ...., exercising jurisdiction in the first instance over the diocese (archdiocese) of .... (and in the second instance over the dioceses of ...., ..., and ....) is an ecclesiastical tribunal of one or more judges and of other lawfully appointed officers, endowed with ordinary power to adjudicate in formal trial contentious and criminal causes within its competence and under the supervision of the ordinary. ¶ 26

ART. 2: The following constitution, as supplementary law to the regulations of the supreme authority of the Church, was promulgated by the Most Reverend Ordinary and is binding as diocesan law upon all officers, advocates and procurators of the tribunal, upon all priests engaged in the sacred minstry in the diocese and upon all persons over whom the ordinary exercises jurisdiction. ¶ 27

ART. 3: The hall of sessions of this court is located at .... and therein all activities of solemn procedure shall be conducted unless the law of this constitution in individual cases allows otherwise.

ART. 4: The diocesan tribunal acts in the name of the bishop in judicial matters and in those administrative procedures enumerated in this constitution. Its commands and requests are therefore to be considered as commands and requests of the ordinary. The tribunal in turn is at all times subject to the supervision of the bishop. ¶ 28

ART. 5: In the absence of the bishop, the vicar general is authorized to act as adviser to the *officialis*. Under these circumstances and in an emergency, he is hereby authorized to name and constitute an *officialis* or a *vice-officialis* and to represent the bishop in causes and cases reserved to him. ¶ 30.

TITLE II

ORGANIZATION OF THE COURT

ART. 6: Officers of the tribunal must observe the solemnities and formalities of formal trials as well as the prescriptions of this constitution. If for any cause they depart from them mention of this and the reasons for it must be made in the records. ¶ 32

ART. 7: The *officialis* enjoys precedence over all clerics of the diocese except the vicar general and is endowed with all rights, powers and duties enumerated for him in the universal law. ¶ 33

ART. 8: The *officialis* as delegated moderator of the judicial department is given the following duties and powers:

1) To take care that all officers diligently fulfill their duties; ¶ 36
2) To name the officers of all "*turni*" employing in proper order those listed on the diocesan roster; ¶ 39
3) To appoint for individual causes and to name to "*turni*" in case of necessity priests not of the roster for all positions except that of judge; ¶ 38
4) To subdelegate to the *vice-officialis* his authority to approve advocates and procurators for individual causes and likewise his power to constitute notaries;
5) To substitute another for any officer, including the presiding judge, of any "*turnus*" hearing any cause including those reserved to the ordinary; ¶ 40
6) To change the chronological order of the calendar in individual instances and for a good cause; ¶ 43
7) To choose, constitute and substitute guardians (*tutores* and *curatores*) for minors, for those lacking the use of reason and

for moral persons and either to approve or to substitute others for guardians named by civil authorities; ¶ 44

8) To receive requests for rogatory commissions from other dioceses and to constitute and delegate the desired commissions; ¶ 45
9) To name for any "*turnus*" auditors, even priests not of the roster, and judicial advisers, even priests not of this diocese; ¶ 46
10) To punish, not only as presiding judge but also as delegated moderator, any and every neglect of duty and every act of disrespect, even those not mentioned in law, on the part of officers and of party representatives in sufficient measure to keep order in court and to obtain full cooperation from all concerned. ¶ 37

ART. 9: The *officialis* as presiding judge is empowered to preside at all causes, contentious or criminal, whether of clerics or of laymen, coming to this diocesan court by any title whatsoever with the exception of those instituted by non-Catholics, apostate and renegade Catholics and public sinners. In these latter cases permission is to be obtained before presenting their causes to the Holy See or before admitting them to the tribunal. ¶ 47

ART. 10: As presiding judge the *officialis* is given the following special powers and authority:

1) To receive the oaths and professions of faith of all officers named to the roster or to the "*turnus*" by the bishop or by any other authority; ¶ 48
2) To choose and to delegate commissions to fulfill judicial acts within this diocese for causes presided over by himself and to appoint notaries, even priests not of the roster, and procurators, even priests and Catholic laymen not of the *album*, to facilitate the delivery of citations and the collection of evidence in emergencies. ¶¶ 49-50

ART. 11: The *officialis* is empowered to apportion causes requiring a single judge between himself and the *vice-officialis* according to the circumstances of the individual cause; ¶ 51

ART. 12: The constitution herewith imposes or reimposes the following obligations on the *officialis*: ¶ 53

1) To make himself available at definite times for consultation by priests and laymen on possible causes and cases; ¶ 53 A
2) To determine the order of the court calendar;
3) To shorten trials as much as justice and charity will allow by refusing useless and delaying petitions, by keeping time limits as short as possible and by adopting any other measures he deems opportune; ¶ 53 B
4) To check personally all mandates; ¶ 53 C
5) To supervise the attempts at reconciliation and to approve the conditions if attempts are successful; ¶ 53 D
6) To supervise the recording of facts in causes and cases, calling attention to unusual but pertinent matters to be recorded and even at times by wording what is to be written; ¶ 53 E & F
7) Before closing a cause to go over the acts carefully to see if any matter is missing, incomplete, contradictory or ambiguous; ¶ 53 G
8) To prepare a short animadversion of his impression of any party, witness or expert heard by him; ¶ 53 H
9) To care for all rogatory and other requests coming to the diocese from other tribunals. ¶ 53 I

ART. 13: The *vice-officialis* is granted the faculties and delegations contained in Article 9 and 10 and is to act either as presiding judge or as single judge in accordance with assignments given him by the *officialis*. As judge or presiding judge, he is to fulfill the duties mentioned in Article 12 ¶¶ 3-8. ¶¶ 54-57

ART. 14: 1) The synodal judges are to be divided into senior and junior judges according to their years in office and in the priesthood. Each "*turnus*" will be made up of one senior and one junior judge beginning with the oldest in one group and the youngest in the other and proceeding in turn (1 and 12; 2 and 11; etc.) according to notifications from the *officialis* or the secretary. ¶ 59

2) All judges are by diocesan law designated as auditors with all rights of auditors for every cause in which they participate; ¶ 61

3) The secretary of the court is requested to note in the annual report to the bishop the date of appointment and the number of years since that date of each judge lest any judge inadvertently continue beyond his ten year assignment without reappointment. ¶ 62

ART. 15: 1) The presiding judge of a *"turnus"* for any good reason may request an auditor to gather evidence for a cause. This auditor will be chosen by the *officialis* and the latter may designate a priest not of the roster when circumstances warrant this; ¶ 63

2) Unless circumstances warrant a change, the *officialis* is required to designate auditors of the roster *"per turnum;* ¶ 63

3) Auditors, both permanent and temporary, are permitted to collect testimony outside the hall of sessions for a reasonable cause, observing if possible all other solemnities. Mention of the fact and the reasons for it must be made in the acts; ¶ 63

4) Auditors are delegated to appoint commissions to collect testimony at distant points for causes heard in the diocese; ¶ 63

5) Except for urgent reasons auditors are not to be used to gather testimony of parties in causes; ¶ 174

6) Auditors will fulfill the commands of Article 12 ¶¶ 6-8; ¶ 64

ART. 16: The *vice-officialis,* all judges and the secretary may be chosen by the individual judge as *assessores* for any cause. The *officialis* is authorized to approve for individual causes other priests even those not of the roster as judicial advisers. ¶¶ 65-66

ART. 17: 1) The defenders of the bond will accept duties in causes and cases in accordance with appointments by the *officialis.* The latter is required to appoint them in turn. When a defender not of the roster is designated by the *officialis,* reasons for this are to be noted in the acts; ¶ 67

2) The defender of the bond in a cause shall investigate the competence of the diocesan tribunal most closely when the basis is quasi-domicile; he shall obtain, if possible, copies of the pre-nuptial investigations; he shall never resort to sophistry, misrepresentations or sharp practices in his animadversions; he shall confine himself to arguments in support of the bond and at no time express himself in favor of dissolution of it; ¶ 68

3) The *officialis* will choose the substitute defender of the bond in case the defender originally appointed must withdraw; ¶ 67

4) The promoter of justice may be designated as substitute for the defender of the bond and any defender may, according to the judgment of the *officialis,* be appointed substitute for the promoter. ¶ 69

ART. 18: Since but one permanent promoter of justice is appointed in this diocese, he is required to serve in the capacity of this office on all required occasions. If circumstances prevent his acting, a substitute will be named by the *officialis.* ¶ 69

ART. 19: The tribunal shall employ a permanent priest-secretary to be named by the bishop. The secretary shall be *ex officio* first vice chancellor of the diocese. It will be his duty:

1) To assist the *officialis* in all his judicial and administrative activities;
2) To care for all correspondence of the court;
3) To care for the permanent records of appointments by placing them in the register of the roster and to note the day and hour of the reception and fulfillment of causes, cases and commissions in the protocol book;
4) To be present at and to record in the register of the roster the oaths of all permanent officers;
5) To prepare the annual reports of the diocesan tribunal for the Holy See and for the bishop;
6) To fulfill other duties given to him by the bishop or by the *officialis,* such as notifying officers of their appointments to the "*turni.*" ¶¶ 70-71

ART. 20: 1) Notaries will be named for individual causes by the *officialis* and this designation will be in turn, exclusive of the chancellors and the secretary, unless a good reason prompts a change in this prescribed procedure in an individual cause. No notary, not even the chancellor, shall act as *actuarius* without designation by the proper authority; ¶ 72

2) The *actuarius* of the cause, besides discharging the duties mentioned in the universal law, will care for the portfolio, keep all records and documents therein, notify officers of the time and place of sessions if necessary, and carefully keep the minutes of each sessions even when a stenographer is employed to set down the testimony being heard. ¶ 73

ART. 21: The archivist of the court will be the first vice-chancellor of the diocese (the secretary). His duties will be:

1) To take care that no peril come to the archives from theft, fire or water;
2) To put completed and suspended causes and cases in the archives at the command of the presiding judge;
3) To make indices of all archive material in accordance with the system employed by the court. ¶ 74

Art. 22: The secretary will be librarian. His duties in this field will be :

1) To care for the books of the libarary;
2) To preserve and ultimately to have bound all official magazines subscribed for by the court;
3) To purchase new books under the direction of the *officialis;*
4) To keep an index of all books and magazines;
5) To record the borrowing of books and magazines. ¶ 75

Art. 23: The secretary shall also be treasurer. As treasurer his duties will be:

1) To have the schedule of fees and taxes at hand and to assist the presiding judge in computing expenses;
2) To keep records of moneys due to the court;
3) To receive the fees of the court;
4) To enter all financial transactions in the ledger;
5) To distribute moneys of the court under the directions of the *officialis.*

Art. 24: The *actuarius* is required to act as *apparitor* or bailiff for the cause on which he is serving. As such, his duties are:

1) To receive parties, witnesses and experts and to direct them to the proper waiting room;
2) To introduce these to the hall of sessions at the designated time and under the directions of the presiding judge;
3) To direct their departure from the hall and to take care lest those already heard have communication with those about to be heard. ¶ 77

Art. 25: The messenger, when appointed, shall take care:

1) To deliver documents to persons and places according to directions;

2) To give assurance to summoned persons that no great inconvenience will be encountered by appearance at court and especially that no information offered will be brought into civil courts or in any way used against the one volunteering it;
3) To record the fact, time and place of the delivery and to sign this record.

ART. 26: The court stenographer will be chosen with special attention to the obligation of secrecy. The duties of the stenographer will be:

1) To make copies of documents and transcriptions of causes and cases according to directions received;
2) To take care that all writings and transcriptions are executed without defects and without mistakes; to hand papers over to be signed only after they have been examined carefully for such errors. ¶ 79

TITLE III

RULES FOR THE ROSTER AND FOR THE "*TURNUS*"

ART. 27: 1) All permanent appointments to the roster, including those of minor officers, are reserved to the bishop; ¶ 80

2) These permanent appointments, made in writing, shall be preserved with the dates thereof in the register for the roster; ¶ 81

3) The terms of the *officialis*, the *vice-officialis* and the judges shall continue from synod to synod or, in the absence of synod within the required period, for ten years; the terms of all other officers shall be for three years; ¶ 82

4) All officers, including those in minor positions, shall take the oaths of office, of secrecy and against Modernism as well as make the profession of faith and the fact with the dates of such permanent oaths and professions shall be preserved in the register for the roster. ¶ 83

ART. 28: 1) The *officialis* shall make appointments of all officers of all "*turni*" except those of criminal causes which are reserved to the ordinary; ¶ 87

2) Substitutions of officers to all "*turni*" are to be made by the *officialis;* ¶ 89

3) Substitute officers shall always designate themselves as such. ¶ 89

ART. 29: 1) Records of appointments to "*turni*" and of substitutions thereto are to be preserved in the protocol book and are to appear, with dates of original appointments to the roster, in the minutes of the first session of the individual causes; ¶ 90

2) Oaths of officers appointed for individual causes shall be taken at the first session and shall be recorded in the minutes of that session;

3) Appointments of the *auditor* and the *ponens* shall be preserved in the protocol.

TITLE IV

REGULATIONS ON EQUIPMENT, TIMES, PLACE AND ANNUAL REPORTS

ART. 30: 1) The tribunal library will be a distinct section of the library of the diocesan curia located near the hall of sessions in the chancery building;

2) The *officialis* will see to the purchase of essential source books, commentaries, both pre-code and post-code, canon law magazines and civil law books from appropriations to be made by the bishop.

3) A card index of all books and magazines shall be made;

4) Any book or magazine removed from the library must be signed for and returned within one week. ¶ 92

ART. 31: 1) The court will have the following archives:

a) A general stationary archive, which will be a portion of the diocesan stationary archives;
b) A current archive for non-secret pending causes and cases;
c) A secret archive, which will be a portion of the diocesan secret archives;
d) A current secret archive under the care of the *officialis* for pending secret causes and cases and for the *vota* of judges;

e) An *instruenda* archive or file for the records of all consultations. ¶¶ 93-99

2 All secret documents shall be sealed in envelopes before being placed in the secret archives; ¶¶ 94 and 96

3) Indices of files and archives shall be according to the card system and shall be cross referenced from cards under the protocol number:

a) under the name of the plaintiff;
b) under the name of the respondent;
c) under the type of cause or case. ¶ 100

4) At the end of each month the secretary will bring up to date the short inventories of all causes and cases in the protocol book; ¶ 101

5) The secretary will be in charge of all archives except those that are secret and access to them must be through him or through the *officialis*. Removal of documents beyond the hall of sessions requires permission of the *officialis* and those removing them must sign for them. ¶ 103

ART. 32: 1) Individual portfolios will be marked with the names of the parties and the protocol number;

2) The seal of this court will be distinct from that of the diocese and a distinct seal will be used for causes of second instance. A rubber stamp seal may be employed for less important documents. ¶ 104

ART. 33: The record books of the court will include:

1) The register for the permanent appointments to the roster;
2) The protocol book for essential information on causes, cases and commissions;
3) A date book for sessions and appointments;
4) A minute book in looseleaf form;
5) A court ritual in loose leaf form into which will be gathered the formulas of all necessary oaths and professions of faith;
6) A ledger book for finances;
7) A source book for private replies from the Holy See;
8) The Book of Gospels;
9) A loose leaf book for preserving communications from the ordinary. ¶ 105

ART. 34: 1) The court will have a solemn opening each year on the first Tuesday after Labor Day with the celebration of Mass attended by all officers of the roster. The books will be closed on the last day of July and all ordinary activities suspended during the subsequent month;

2) Following the Mass of the opening of the court, an official inspection of appointments will be made, new officers will take their oaths and instructions will be given for the year by the moderator;

3) The annual report to the bishop will be completed by the last day of July as well as all inventories and indices;

4) At least one consulting officer will remain on duty at the appointed hours during the summer vacation;

5) The *officialis* is authorized to suspend all court work during the early days of Holy Week and during the week prior to Christmas;

6) Reasons for judicial activities on Sundays and Holydays must be noted in the minutes of the cause. ¶¶ 107-108

ART. 35: 1) At least one consulting officer must be available at the chancery during the morning hours of each week day;

2) The *officialis* will arrange the schedule by which the consulting officers will fulfill ¶ 1 of this Article;

3) The *officialis* will list several hours each week when he is available for consultation on more serious problems and he will post this schedule on the bulletin board in the hall of sessions;

4) The *officialis* will set definite hours and definite days for the meetings of the various "*turni*" in order that the officers may know well in advance when they are expected to be present and he will post this schedule on the bulletin board. ¶¶ 109-110

ART. 36: The hall of sessions will have at least two waiting rooms lest there be discussions between witnesses heard and those about to be heard.

2) The secretary will endeavor to furnish the hall so as to add dignity to the proceedings and will watch carefully that the hall and all equipment are kept in repair. ¶ 110

ART. 37: 1) Officers and party representatives, if they are priests, are required to appear always in full clerical dress during sessions, to refrain from anything that under the circumstances would take from the respect due to the court and to keep proper silence during sessions. The presiding judge will watch that his court maintain a high level of dignity;

2) Each court session will open and close with a prayer;

3) The court in session will be addressed as "the reverend court." ¶¶ 111-112

ART. 38: 1) The annual report to the bishop must contain:

a) The number of causes and cases handled during the year, the present status of each and an explanation for the continuance of any cause or case beyond the duration of a year's time;
b) The number of rogatory commissions handled during the year;
c) A complete financial memorandum;
d) The state of the roster including especially the dates of all appointments and the need, if any, of new appointments;
e) The state of the *album* of procurators and advocates;
f) A report on the recordings in matrimonial and baptismal records of the results of trials and of case procedures;

2) The annual report to the Holy See must be submitted to the bishop for his approval. ¶¶ 113-114

TITLE V

THE PARTIES AND THEIR REPRESENTATIVES

ART. 39: 1) In determining the right of persons to stand in court, officers are encouraged to give the law as broad an interpretation as recognized authors permit;

2) Lest scandal inadvertently arise, the ordinary must be consulted when there arises a question of applying to the Holy See for permission to admit non-Catholics and apostate Catholics as petitioners in court or of admitting other renegade Catholics and public sinners as petitioners in any cause or case.

3) Likewise the ordinary must be consulted before admitting minors or ecclesiastical moral persons as plaintiffs or before citing them as respondents. ¶¶ 115-116

ART. 40: The diocesan list (*album*) of procurators and advocates will be preserved by the secretary in the register for the roster and a report on it must be made each year to the bishop;

2) Permanent approval of advocates and procurators will be made by the bishop alone but delegation is granted to the *officialis* to approve them for individual causes;

3) The *officialis* is given authority to judge whether necessity dictates a relaxation of the universal law regarding degrees and other legal qualifications for procurators and advocates;

4) Advocates and procurators are bound to observe not only universal law but also prescriptions of this constitution when acting in this court. Approval of their appointments and their work is under the supervision of the *officialis* at all times;

5) Permanent procurators and advocates shall be required to take the oaths of office and of secrecy and to make the profession of faith. ¶¶ 117, 118, 122.

ART. 41: It will be the duty of the secretary to inspect mandates given by parties to their representatives, to notarize them if necessary and to place them in the acts. ¶ 119

ART. 42: Advocates and procurators are encouraged to request permission to be present at the various sessions of the trials in which they participate and the presiding judges are urged to grant these requests whenever reasonably possible. ¶ 121.

ART. 43: Fees payable to procurators and advocates will be governed by the diocesan schedule. ¶ 123

TITLE VI

JUDICIAL PROCEDURE

CHAPTER 1.

THE PRELIMINARY RECEPTION OF CAUSES

ART. 44: 1) The notaries of the court and the advocates of the *album* will act as consulting officers and will make themselves available according to the schedule for this work; (Article 35)

2) Prior to the introduction of a cause or a case, the petitioner and his adviser must discuss its possibilities with a consulting officer. ¶ 125

Art. 45: 1) Laymen are requested to present their causes and cases to the consulting officer through clerical advisers, that is, through priests engaged in active ministry in this diocese and especially through their pastors;

2) Clerical advisers shall not promise or give any assurance to the interested parties of a favorable decision at any time previous to the final curial decision; ¶ 128

3) Clerical advisers should make brief investigations of causes and cases before presenting them to the consulting officer. They will limit these investigations ordinarily to an interrogation of the parties and will be careful lest they influence either parties or witnesses and thereby prejudice the cause or case; ¶ 127

4) Ordinarily no affidavits or testimonies are to be gathered unless requested by the court. Exceptions to this rule exist when death, departure or prejudice may prevent the interviewing of the individuals concerned by the court. ¶ 127

Art. 46: 1) The consulting officer is asked to make inquires concerning a possible reconciliation and to pursue diligently the realization of this reconciliation either *per se* or *per alios* if a reasonable possibility presents itself; ¶ 129

2) Inquiries are to be made by the consulting officer concerning competence of the court and the right of the party to plead or petition in the respective cause or case and parties are to be informed of the fact if the information is unfavorable. Special attention is to be paid to the culpability of the petitioner in marriage causes and cases; ¶ 137

3) If he deems it necessary, the consulting officer may institute a brief non-judicial inquiry into the respective cause or case but he is to limit this investigation to the parties and to individuals who volunteer information without questioning; ¶ 127

4) The consulting officer must gather information on why the petition is being presented in court and on possible scandal arising from its acceptance;

5) Consulting officers, if they are certain no cause or case is present, may urge petitioners to desist from requesting the assistance of the court. If such a party insists, a petition must be allowed. ¶¶ 129, 130 and 137

ART. 47: Instructions and information are to be given the petitioner by the consulting officer on the following points:

a) On the choice of a procurator and an advocate from the diocesan list and on the composition of the necessary mandates; ¶ 130
b) On the composition of the *libellus* and on the information to be placed therein; ¶ 131
c) On the *articuli* or points for the questioning of the respondent;
d) On the list of witnesses and their addresses and on the *articuli* for the questioning of them to be presented with this list, both of which are ordinarily to accompany the *libellus*; ¶ 133
e) On letters of introduction to witnesses and on releases from professional secrecy; ¶ 133
f) On the *"informationes parochi;"* ¶ 134
g) On the documents to be presented; ¶ 135
h) On the need for identification;
i) On judicial expenses and fees and on deposits required; ¶ 135
j) On the petition for gratuitous patronage, if this is desired, and on the reasons and proofs to be presented therewith. ¶ 136

ART. 48: The consulting officer will submit the following written or oral reports and the following documents to the court when they are ready:

a) A memorandum of the interview;
b) The *libellus* with the necessary mandates;
c) A memorandum on the attempts at reconciliation;
d) A memorandum on the competence of the court and on the rights of the parties to plead or petition;
e) A memorandum on his investigation concerning the respective cause or case with his recommendation;
f) A memorandum on why the petition was presented and on possible scandal;
g) The list of witnesses, *articuli* for the questioning of them, introductory letters and releases from secrecy;

h) The necessary documents;
i) The required deposit for expenses or the petition for gratuitous patronage or reduction of fees with the reasons for these and the proofs of their need;
j) The *"informationes parochi;"*

ART. 49: The *"informationes parochi"* will be a letter from the pastor of the party or from a priest who is familiar with the circumstances, containing his information on the respective cause or case, his opinion on the character of the parties, a report in marriage causes especially on the possibility of a reconciliation of the parties, a judgment as to the presence of possible scandal, an explanation of the reason for which the cause or case is being presented and a list of names of possible *ex officio* witnesses for character and proof. ¶ 134

ART. 50: A brief summary of all consultations including those not resulting in further action is to be placed in the *instruenda* file under the name of the person interviewed with a cross reference to it under the name or names of other interested persons. ¶ 139

ART. 51: 1) The consulting officer will present the respective cause or case to the secretary of the court when it is ready for consideration and the secretary will enter its reception in the protocol book, with the day and hour of its reception;

2) A protocol number will be given it according to the diocesan system and the petition and its accompanying documents will be placed in a portfolio and entered in the current archives;

3) Mere consultations left in the *instruenda* archive need not receive protocol numbers. ¶ 140

ART. 52: The diocesan protocol system will follow a system of consecutive numbering for all causes and cases docketed. ¶ 141

ART. 53: All documents deposited with the court are considered as belonging to the tribunal for the duration of the trial and are not to be removed from the hall of sessions while the cause or case endures. ¶ 142

ART. 54: 1) Being informed of the docketing by the secretary, the *officialis* will issue a decree constituting the *"turnus"* if it is a cause requiring this action or will otherwise arrange for its adjudication. In the decree constituting the "*turnus*" he will also set the date and time for the first session and order the assembling of the court and the citing of the defender of the bond and the promoter of justice; ¶¶ 143-147

2) The secretary will then notify all officers appointed to the "*turnus*" and present the citation to the defender of the bond. Accompanying the notifications of the judges and the citation of the defender of the bond will be copies of the *libellus* enabling these officers to review the legal background of the respective cause prior to the session; ¶¶ 144-145

3) The secretary will then inform the plaintiff of the names of the officers and of the date of the session with instructions on his right to raise exceptions to the persons of the judges and a request that these exceptions be presented before the session convenes. ¶ 146

Chapter 2.

The Acts, Sessions and Decrees

Art. 55: 1) In formal trials, officers will fulfill all solemnities required by universal law;

2) The presiding judge and the notary will be especially watchful that the acts record every pertinent detail with such clarity that the judges of the courts of appeal may have a complete understanding of every situation;

3) Special care shall be taken of the minutes of the sessions that they record not merely what is said at the sessions but also actions, explanations, presumptions, and all other pertinent facts that occur. Most decrees need be mentioned only and not necessarily copied in full;

4) It is the duty of the presiding judge to dictate if necessary entries for the minutes lest valuable information be lost;

5) In completed acts, the minutes will introduce the material of each session and explain it. ¶¶ 149; 150; 161.

Art. 56: 1) The *actuarius* will preserve the acts under two divisions, *acta causae* and *acta processus*. In the latter division he is requested to separate essential from non-essential papers;

2) In making transcriptions of the acts, non-essential papers of the *acta processus* need not be included and the essential papers of the *acta processus* will be placed in a group after the *acta causae;*

3) As documents accumulate, they are to be placed in the portfolio of original documents. Three copies will be made immediately for the convenience of the officers of the court and entered into separate portfolios in proper order. These transcriptions are to be available to the judges and the defender at all times during the trial. ¶¶ 151; 152; 155.

ART. 57: 1) The *actuarius* will sign and seal each page of the original documents and will stamp the *"concordat cum originali"* and sign each page of the first transcription; ¶¶ 154; 155

2) Original documents will receive their own pagination. In making transcriptions however a straight pagination of all papers is to be used without reference to the pagination of the originals; ¶ 157

3) As the cause draws to a close, the *actuarius* will prepare an index for the transcriptions according to their pagination. ¶ 156

ART. 58: 1) All material of the trial should be mentioned at a session lest a necessary explanation be omitted in the minutes;

2) Individual judicial acts should be completed if possible in a single session and when this is impossible an explanation should be given in the minutes. ¶¶ 159-160

ART. 59: The presiding judge directs the course of the trial through decrees. Ordinary directing decrees during a session may be given orally and mere record of the fact in the minutes suffices. More important decrees making decisions relevant to the cause should be accompanied by reasons in law and in fact. ¶ 162

CHAPTER 3.

INDIVIDUAL SESSIONS

ART. 60: 1) This constitution commands that all judges be present at the session for the *libellus* and recommends the presence of the defender; ¶ 163

2) The presiding judge should see that reports on all previous activities be presented at the first session. The consulting officer should be present to make his reports, many of which may be made orally;

3) If the basis of competence in a marriage cause is quasi-domicile, the Instruction of December 23, 1929 is to be carefully observed. ¶ 165

ART. 61: 1) In matrimonial causes, the respondent shall be cited through a priest-messenger if possible. If a messenger cannot be employed, registered mail is to be used; ¶¶ 168; 170

2) The priest-messenger will explain the seriousness of the situation and will stress the absence of legal entanglements, publicity, obligations, embarrassments, etc. He may also at this time present the names of the officers serving on the "*turnus*" and explain the party's right of objections to the plaintiff and the officers. ¶ 169

ART. 62: 1) Ordinarily full solemnities are to be observed in hearing the respondent. The following is only a possible emergency measure in extreme necessity:

2) In difficult cases, rather than lose valuable testimony and to avoid, if possible, a declaration of contumacy, the *officialis* is authorized to designate the priest-messenger as a notary to interview the party under oath and even, upon the completion of this latter office, to allow him to be designated procurator by the otherwise disobedient party;

3) The interview by the messenger-notary will touch on all things necessary for the joinder of issue and even for the trial if he deems this expedient, on possible witnesses and on questions to be asked the plaintiff;

4) The messenger-procurator will have the party sign the mandate and will represent the party at the joinder of issue thus leaving the way open for the introduction of the respondent's testimony in the trial. ¶ 171

ART. 63: In cases of obstinacy, the presiding judge is urged to employ other methods of winning cooperation such as the intervention of a close friend of the party or of a person of dignity. ¶ 172

ART. 64: Following the decree on the joinder of issue, the court will immediately consider judicial expenses or gratuitous patronage and make its decision. The petition for gratuitous patronage ordinarily should be accompanied by a letter from some responsible person, the pastor, for example, attesting the inability of the plaintiff to bear expenses and his worthiness to receive gratuitous consideration. ¶ 178

ART. 65: 1) The session for the hearing of the parties should be joined, if this can be arranged, with that of the joinder of issue; ¶ 179

2) All judges as well as the defender of the bond and the promoter of justice are requested to be present at the hearing of the parties if possible.

ART. 66: 1) In questioning parties, witnesses and experts, the presiding judge should not only break up difficult and complex questions and insist on answers to every point, but should also develop important points by *ex officio* questions and even at times probe for new information bearing on the question. Individuals are to be encouraged to develop their answers on vital issues; ¶ 181

2) Associate judges and the defender of the bond will ordinarily write their *ex officio* questions and present them to the presiding judge to be asked at the conclusion of the main questioning. ¶ 182

ART. 67: 1) The *articuli* (points of questioning) are to be forwarded by the defender of the bond after his questions have been formulated, to the presiding judge who is to review them prior to the session for questioning and to develop his own thoughts on them;

2) The presiding judge may add questions desired by the parties if these have been overlooked by the defender of the bond. ¶ 183

ART. 68: Defenders of the bond and promoters of justice, in drawing up their questionnaires, are to remember the American tendency toward brief answers to questions in court and develop their questions accordingly. ¶ 184

ART. 69: 1) The *actuarius* will record all answers word for word unless the presiding judge desires to edit them and therefore they will be recorded in the first person;

2) *Ex officio* questions will be designated as such with mention of the source of each question. ¶ 185

ART.70: 1) Judges will endeavor to make the oath of parties, witnesses and experts as solemn as possible and therefore a form other than that used in the civil court is urged;

2) Prior to giving the oath after the testimony, the judge will explain the secrecy desired when he considers an explanation will be useful. ¶ 187

ART. 71: 1) Parties requesting witnesses will secure the consent of these witnesses to come to court and will provide letters of introduction when needed as well as points for questioning and releases from secrecy of those who would be bound to secrecy by professional consultation; ¶ 192

2) When witnesses have been requested and are not heard, an explanation of this should appear in the acts; ¶ 194

3) The acts will clearly state for whom each individual witness is testifying, the nature of the witness (whether he is a witness to the merits of the cause or to character), any unusual dignity possessed by him and any point that would detract from the value of his testimony. ¶ 195

ART. 72: 1) Careful record should be kept of the consideration of all objections to witnesses; ¶ 197

2) Publication of testimony is to be made ordinarily by informing the parties that the testimony may be consulted at the hall of sessions. ¶ 201

ART. 73: At the time they are notified of the identity of experts, parties may be informed of their right of objection and their right of presenting points upon which questions may be based (*articuli*). ¶ 203

ART. 74: 1) The court is urged to make and preserve permanent instructions for experts upon types of causes frequently heard;

2) The presiding judge shall decide what material of the trial shall be conveyed to experts that they may have a proper understanding of results desired;

3) To insure completeness of testimony, experts may be asked to make their reports in the form of answers to definite questions;

4) During the oral testimony judges will remember the dangers of varied connotations of words among experts and authors and the hesitancy of experts to be definitely certain in their responses. ¶¶ 204-206

ART. 75: The animadversions of the court on each expert will review his qualifications and his character as well as the impression he made and the court's opinion of the testimony. ¶ 208

ART. 76: In matrimonial causes, all examinations by experts will be prefaced by an account of precautions taken to prevent fraudulent substitutions. ¶ 209

ART. 77: In causes previously reviewed by experts in civil courts, a review of expert testimonies then given may be made by an ecclesiastical court officer. ¶ 211

ART. 78: Fees for experts should be agreed upon prior to the examination. ¶ 212

ART. 79: 1) Constitution of delegated commissions must be recorded in the acts of the session decreeing such commissions and reasons should be given why such are employed; ¶¶ 213-217

2) Delegated commissions in all causes (not necessarily cases) shall be made up of at least two persons, an auditor and a notary, and in matrimonial causes, when reasonably possible, of a third, the defense representative; ¶ 218

3) Each deanery will have a permanent commission composed of three priests familiar with procedural law and this commission will be called upon when possible to collect testimony in that territory; ¶ 219, footnote 135

4) Members of permanent delegated commissions will take a permanent oath of office.

ART. 80: 1) Faculties of delegated commissions include the authority to name substitute notaries and defense representatives, to receive oaths of officers and of witnesses, to call *ex officio* witnesses and to add *ex officio* questions. Auditors of these commissions may not subdelegate their office without permission; ¶ 219

2) Instructions to commissions should briefly summarize the causes, give instructions on procedure, on secrecy, on special results desired, on witnesses to be heard and on questions to be asked; ¶ 221

3) Commissions should not reveal to respondents and witnesses the instruction given to them by the tribunal on the causes when there is danger that this will antagonize the respondents or witnesses;

4) Letters of introduction to witnesses should be sent to commissions when these are useful;

5) Commissions will proceed after the manner of sessions and will take special care in preserving minutes of all activities, unusual circumstances and other pertinent facts. ¶ 222

ART. 81: 1) Commissions will add character testimonies and animadversions to each completed testimony on the merits of the cause; ¶ 224

2) Commissions are to be returned in person or by registered mail. ¶ 225

ART. 82: Officers of commissions are entitled to reimbursement for expenses at least and an estimate of these shall be included with the returned commission. ¶ 226

ART. 83: 1) Rogatory commissions will be addressed to the ordinary of the diocese to which they are sent and shall be carefully recorded in the minutes of the sessions decreeing the requests;

2) The ordinary of the second diocese shall be requested to constitute and delegate a commission for a solemn trial according to the instructions enclosed and to delegate this commission also to ask *ex officio* questions and to cite and hear *ex officio* witnesses if such can be found;

3) The usual instructions, questionnaires, letters of introduction, etc., of Article 80 ¶¶ 2-4 shall be included. ¶¶ 229-230

4) The judge *ad quem* shall be requested to return a bill of expenses along with the completed commission. ¶ 237

ART. 84: 1) Rogatory requests received from other dioceses shall be recorded in the protocol book by the secretary and shall be given to the *officialis* to constitute and delegate the proper commissions;

2) Rogatory commissions for causes (not necessarily for cases)

shall fulfill all solemnities of formal hearings including sessions at the hall of sessions if possible, and the presence of a full commission at each session;

3) Permanent deanery commissions shall be employed to fulfill rogatory requests at a distance from the hall of sessions when possible. ¶¶ 231-232

ART. 85: The regulations of Article 80 ¶¶ 1 and 5 and of Articles 81 and 82 apply to rogatory commissions also. ¶ 234

ART. 86: Rogatory commissions returned from this diocese to the diocese *a qua* shall be divided into *acta causae* and *acta processus,* with an index, a concluding *votum episcopi,* which the *officialis* is delegated to prepare and sign, expressing an opinion on the cause from the viewpoint of the testimony gathered, and shall be neatly bound in a portfolio. ¶ 235

ART. 87: Commissions of all kinds shall be formally introduced to the trial upon their return by presentation at a session and shall be published in the same manner as other testimonies.

ART. 88: 1) Assistant pastors are granted the authority to issue authentic copies of records preserved in parochial books; ¶ 240

2) Documents for trials ordinarily should be presented with the *libellus* and no document is to be placed in the acts without its authenticity and value being considered at a session;

3) For more important documents affecting the essence of a cause the parties or their representatives will be notified when these are to be introduced in order that they may prepare objections to them; ¶ 244

4) Special circumstances of documents must be carefully recorded in the minutes.

ART. 89: It will be the special duty of the presiding judge to see to the recording of presumptions, indications and circumstances entering into a trial. ¶ 246

ART. 90: Before concluding the cause, the judge or the auditor and the defender of the bond, if he enters the cause, will carefully study the acts to detect discrepancies, difficulties, conflicts, inconsistencies, obscurities and omissions and either have these corrected or explained.

ART. 91: Formal publication and the conclusion ordinarily should be accomplished in one session. ¶ 248

ART. 92: 1) Advocates and defenders in their briefs and animadversions will refrain from all sophistries, distortions and misrepresentations. ¶ 250

2) The defender must at no time express himself in favor of dissolution of the bond; ¶ 251

3) Copies of briefs, animadversions and rebuttals are to be given to the *actuarius* who will have necessary transcriptions made for the portfolios; ¶ 253

4) Equal opportunities must be given to both sides to present rebuttals and oral discussions. ¶¶ 252-254

ART. 93: 1) Copies of the acts will be presented to the judges within three days of the reception of the last rebuttal;

2) Ten days, dated from the reception of the completed transcriptions, shall be the ordinary time allowed the judges to review the cause, the *ponens* to prepare his written review and all judges to prepare their written *vota*. ¶ 256

ART. 94: 1) The presiding judge will appoint the *ponens* to keep essential minutes of the session for the sentence; ¶ 257

2) The review of the trial by the *ponens* shall be so well prepared that it may be used extensively in the formal sentence; ¶ 259

3) Each judge will give reasons in law and in fact for his decision and will prepare his *votum* with sufficient care that it, with necessary additions, could be used in the formal sentence. ¶ 259

ART. 95: Judges are warned to refrain from expressing their opinion to any but their associate judges on the "*turnus*" and to duly authorized judicial advisers either before or after the sentence. ¶ 258

ART. 96: Judges, in reaching their decision, will be mindful of the words on the nature of certitude addressed to the Sacred Roman Rota by His Holiness, Pope Pius XII contained in volume XXXIV (1942) of the *Acta Apostolicae Sedis* (p. 338). ¶ 260

ART. 97: The formal sentence will include in its preamble the name and year of reign of the Holy Father and of the bishop. ¶ 261

Art. 98: 1) The solemn publication of the sentence will take place at a session when possible with the minutes recording the time and place, the fact of appeal and other pertinent facts. ¶ 263

2) The date of the solemn publication of the sentence will be recorded in the protocol book;

3) Parties and their representatives, when notified of the decision, are to be informed of their right of appeal and are to be given instructions on how this appeal is to be made. ¶ 262

TITLE VII

APPEALS

Art. 99: The court of second instance is the tribunal of the archdiocese of ...., located at ...., ...; the court of third instance is the Sacred Roman Rota, *Palazzo della Dataria; Via della Dataria,* 94; *Roma, Italia.* ¶ 264

Art. 100: 1) Oral petitions of appeal for *causes* must be made during the session for the solemn publication of the sentence and must then be drawn up by the *actuarius* in solemn form and signed. The written petitions may be made at any time within the prescribed period.

2) This formal petition contains the statement of identities of the parties, of the judge *a quo* and of the judge *ad quem,* the definitive portion of the sentence, the dates of sentence and appeal and signatures. ¶ 265

Art. 101: The secretary will note the appeal and its date in the protocol book and notify all concerned. ¶ 266

Art. 102: The advocate, or defender of the bond if he appeals, draws up the *libellus appellatorius* according to the laws of the original *libellus* with motives in law and in fact for the appeal. ¶ 267

Art. 103: 1) The secretary will then forward the petition, the *libellus appellatorius* and a letter of courtesy to the ordinary of the court of appeal; ¶ 268

2) Upon receipt of the decree of the second court accepting the appeal, the secretary will note the fact and date in the protocol book, will notify all concerned, giving informtion on the time limits set to prosecute the action, will arrange for the signing of mandates of procurators for the court of appeal and will forward these mandates and the transcriptions of the acts to the latter court; ¶¶ 271-272

3) Translations should be accompanied by copies in the original and care should be taken that idioms, colloquialisms, etc., are explained in the appeal to the Sacred Roman Rota; ¶ 272

4) The secretary will take all necessary precautions that the material of the appeal be safely delivered to the court of appeal. ¶ 272

ART. 104: On receipt of the sentence on the appeal, the secretary will enter this with the date in the protocol book, will place copies of all documents on appeal in the portfolio for the permanent record, will inform all concerned of the decision and their consequent rights and will forward information to all parishes concerned, if necessary. ¶¶ 274-275

TITLE VIII

UNUSUAL CAUSES

CHAPTER 1.

CRIMINAL CAUSES

ART. 105: 1) The *officialis* is hereby delegated to receive denunciations against clerics;

2) Denunciations are ordinarily to be disregarded unless completed in writing before the *officialis* and the chancellor, signed and notarized;

3) The *officialis* will present trustworthy denunciations to the bishop with a brief summary of the legal background. ¶¶ 277-278

ART. 106: 1) Delegation of the investigator is reserved to the ordinary;

2) The investigator will report to the ordinary for instructions and for the oath; ¶ 279

Art. 107: 1) The investigation will be conducted most secretly;

2) Acts of the investigation will be drawn up by the chancellor or, in his absence, by the investigator unless the ordinary appoints another notary;

3) The completed investigation, with its legal background, will be presented to the bishop for further instructions. ¶¶ 280-281

Art. 108: At the decision of the bishop the suspect will be ordered to appear before the bishop to present his viewpoint and to receive admonitions. ¶ 282

Art. 109: 1) On the decision of the bishop alone the acts of the investigation will be given to the promoter of justice for formal accusation;

2) Precautions against further scandal and against the impeding of justice will be carried out by the *officialis* under instructions from the bishop. ¶ 283

Art. 110: 1) The *officialis* will act as judge or as presiding judge in all criminal causes unless other arrangements are made by the ordinary;

2) To the ordinary is reserved the appointment of the "*turnus*" when this is necessary;

3) The chancellor will act as *actuarius* in all criminal trials;

4) The advocate of the suspect will be chosen by the bishop if the suspect neglects to choose a priest worthy of approval. ¶¶ 284-285

Art. 111: 1) Ordinary rules of preliminary reception and docketing of causes and of the court calendar are to be disregarded in criminal causes;

2) Acts of the investigation and of the trial are to be preserved while the cause is pending in the secret archive of the *officialis*. Upon completion or interruption of the cause, they are to be sealed in an envelope and placed in the diocesan secret archives. ¶ 286

CHAPTER 2.

ROMAN CAUSES

ART. 112: Roman Causes will be received, docketed and preserved according to the rules of Title VI, Chapter 1. ¶ 288

ART. 113: The *officialis* will supervise the instruction of all Roman causes and will carefully fulfill all prescriptions of the Holy See both as to procedure and as to procurement of required subdelegations and signatures from the ordinary. ¶ 289

ART. 114: The rules of this constitution on formal causes and on the preservation of records will be observed in all cases where these are helpful to the instruction of Roman causes. ¶ 290

TITLE IX

INFORMAL CASES

CHAPTER 1.

GENERAL RULES

ART. 115: 1) Informal cases will be received and docketed according to rules of Title VI, Chapter 1, *mutatis mutandis;*

2) The *officialis* will direct the instruction of all informal cases;

3) A notary shall assist in this instruction and will keep informal records of all essential and useful information. ¶ 292

ART. 116: Unless the *officialis* rules otherwise in individual cases civil divorce papers should be exhibited before procedure will commence on any marriage case. The court is not to urge the divorce but only to inform the petitioner of its rule. ¶ 293

ART. 117: Where it is reasonably possible depositions and affidavits for informal cases should be taken at the hall of sessions by a judge (auditor) and the notary. Otherwise a notary will be competent to gather them and any notary so deputed is authorized by this constitution to receive them under oath;

2) Requests for information, testimony and affidavits sent to another diocese will always indicate the informal nature of the process thus permitting the diocese *ad quam* to dispatch a single authorized priest instead of a full commission to fulfill the request. ¶ 295

ART. 118: Cases will not be accepted by the *officialis* unless the ordinary has at least voluntary jurisdiction over the petitioner under some title. Permission of the ordinary must be obtained when the basis is quasi-domicile of *advenae* or mere residence in the cases of *vagi* and *peregrini;* ¶ 296

2) Permission to admit non-Catholics, apostate and renegade Catholics, Catholics adhering to forbidden societies, and public sinners as petitioners must be obtained from the ordinary; ¶ 297

3) A brief record of all useful information shall be kept of the basis of competence and of the investigation into the worthiness of the parties to petition for consideration. ¶ 296-297

ART. 119: The rule on forwarding the results of trials in matrimonial causes to pastors of parishes in the registers of which are the records of the marriage and of the baptisms (Art. 104) applies with equal force to decisions in all informal cases. ¶ 300

ART. 120: All acts in informal cases will be permanently preserved in the tribunal archives after the manner of acts in formal causes.

CHAPTER 2.

LACK OF FORM CASES

ART. 121: 1) The *officialis* is delegated to make the final decision in all lack of form cases except those of non-Catholic and of unworthy Catholic petitioners which are reserved to the ordinary. In the absence of the *officialis,* the *vice-officialis* will instruct these cases and refer them to the bishop or to the vicar general for the decisions; ¶ 302

2) Pastors and assistant pastors are delegated to make a summary investigation and the final decision in lack of form cases

in the emergencies of C. 1044 but they are requested to inform the *officialis* as soon as possible of their procedure. ¶ 303

ART. 122: 1) The form of all documents (petitions, memoranda and decisions) will be determined by practical considerations and these documents will preserve all necessary and useful information; ¶¶ 304-307

2) Memoranda of the proofs of the binding force of the Catholic form of marriage in the case and of the non-revalidation shall be made lest valuable information be lost; ¶¶ 305-306

3) The recently executed certificate of baptism and the testimony of two trustworthy Catholics, or, if these are not to be had, the supplementary oath, shall be deemed sufficient proof of non-revalidation unless some positive evidence gives rise to a contrary suspicion. ¶ 306

ART. 123: This constitution recommends that the defender of the bond review each case when possible prior to the decision.

CHAPTER 3.

THE INFORMAL CASES OF C. 1990

ART. 124: 1) The *officialis* will supervise the instruction of the informal cases of C. 1990 and will refer them in completed form to the bishop for the decisions; ¶ 311

2) A special mandate is hereby given to the *officialis* authorizing him to render the sentence when the bishop is absent or impeded from acting; ¶ 312

3) In the absence of the *officialis* the *vice-officialis* will instruct the cases and refer them to the bishop for decision;

4) In instructing these cases the officers are to consider the procedure as administrative. ¶ 310

ART. 125: 1) Forms of petitions, citations, depositions, memoranda, animadversions and sentences, will be determined by practical considerations only and will endeavor to preserve all necessary and useful information; ¶¶ 309, 313 and 315

2) A record shall be kept of the presence of the defender of

the bond in each case and in those cases where the defender considers animadversions necessary or useful he shall make them in writing; ¶ 317

3) The cited parties shall be interviewed, when possible, by the *officialis* himself in the presence of a notary and the defender of the bond. The form of the interview will be dictated by practical circumstances. ¶¶ 315-316

ART. 126: 1) Memoranda of the proof of the existence of the impediment and of the non-revalidation shall be made lest information be lost; ¶¶ 318-319

2) Proof of non-revalidation will be determined by circumstances but ordinarily will consist in recently executed certificates of baptisms, in the answer of the chancery of the place of marriage asserting that no dispensation was obtained and in the sworn testimony of two trustworthy Catholics, or, if two such Catholics with knowledge of the facts are not to be had, in the supplementary oath, unless positive evidence gives rise to a suspicion that truth is being concealed. ¶ 319

ART. 127: 1) The sentence will include a statement of the identities of the parties and of the judge, a simple statement of the decision and a brief summary of the reasons in law and in fact for the decision.

2) The secretary will inform the petitioner of the decision and its consequences and also forward this information, if he deems it useful, to the respondent of the marriage in question. ¶ 320

ART. 128: Careful record will be kept of the appeal, if any, and the usual precautions for the safe transmission of the acts to the court of appeal will be observed;

2) Practical necessities will dictate the form of the petition for appeal and it will include whatever reasons the party or the defender of the bond feel will strengthen the case before the judge of the court of appeal;

3) The court of appeal is to be requested to include a bill of expenses when returning its decision.

CHAPTER 4.

PAULINE PRIVILEGE CASES

ART. 129: The *officialis* will prepare all Pauline Privilege cases and refer the completed acts, with his recommendations, to the ordinary for final judgment. In his absence, the *vice-officialis* will instruct them and present them to the ordinary. ¶ 323

ART. 130: 1) It will be the duty of the consulting officer to gather preliminary information on identities, competence, lack of baptisms, conversion and possibility of reconciliation, to inform the parties of documents needed and to obtain permission and written delegation from the petitioner to make the interpellations; ¶¶ 324-325

2) The case will be presented to the *officialis* in a written petition, the form of which will be decided by necessities; ¶ 325

3) Memoranda of the various steps will be made by the notary, especially on proofs of lack of baptisms, on the nature of the moral or physical departure of the non-baptized spouse and on the responsibility for this departure. ¶ 326

ART. 131: 1) The interpellations are to be made in a summary, non-judicial manner and, if possible, by a personal visit of an authorized notary; ¶ 328

2) If the departing spouse is married again or is about to be married, special care will be taken lest the interpellations be misinterpreted by the second couple. If this possibility is probably present, a dispensation from the interpellations is to be obtained. ¶ 329

ART. 132: One month's time is to be given to the unbaptized party for deliberation. The *officialis* is authorized to shorten or lengthen this period in particular cases. ¶ 330

ART. 133: Practical considerations will determine the form of the decision permitting the second marriage and the manner of transmitting this to those concerned. ¶ 331

Chapter 5.

Cases Involving Proof of Death

Art. 134: 1) If, during a pre-nuptial investigation, a former marriage, allegedly dissolved by the death of one spouse, is revealed, a declaration of freedom must be given before proceeding to the second marriage.

2) If a priest of the parish has personal knowledge of the death of the spouse, if the record of the death appear in the books or if an authentic document certifying the death has been obtained, the pastor may give the declaration of freedom.

3) If the proof of the death of the spouse is less than that mentioned in ¶ 2 of this Article, the case must be referred to the ordinary for the declaration of freedom. ¶ 332

Art. 135: 1) The officers of the diocesan tribunal, under the direction of the *officialis* and with the cooperation of the pastors, will prepare all cases coming to the chancery of proof of death according to the Instruction of the Sacred Congregation of the Holy Office of May 13, 1868.

2) The *officialis* is required to develop the more difficult cases of proof of death as judicial causes.

3) All cases, developed after the manner of administrative procedure, will be referred by the *officialis* to the ordinary for final decision. The *officialis* will present his recommendations with the prepared case. ¶¶ 333-334

Art. 136: Pastors and assistant pastors are delegated to make a summary investigation and the final decision in all proof of death cases in the emergencies of C. 1044 but they are requested to inform the *officialis* as soon as possible of their decisions. ¶ 335

Art. 137: A careful record must be kept of all information and of all procedure in proof of death cases and these acts will be preserved in the diocesan archives after the manner of acts in formal causes. ¶ 337

TITLE X

JUDICIAL EXPENSES

ART. 138: The provincial schedule of judicial fees and taxes as well as the bishop's arrangements on salaries and remunerations for officers is fully incorporated into this constitution. ¶¶ 338-341; 348-349

ART. 139: The procurator in solemn trials and the pastor or priest adviser in all other cases will arrange for the payment of fees and taxes and will furnish the party with a signed receipt and a short account of the expenditure of all money paid. ¶ 344

ART. 140: All income and all expenditures will be carefully noted in the finance ledger by the treasurer and a detailed report on these as well as on gratuitous services will be included in the annual report to the bishop. ¶ 345

ART. 141: 1) A deposit of one-half of the estimated judicial expenses is to be made by the petitioner prior to the joinder of issues and the remainder prior to the appeal; ¶ 346

2) Fees for informal cases are payable upon receipt of the rescript announcing the decision.

CONCLUSIONS

A constitution for his court is one of the best methods a bishop can employ to assure himself of an efficient judicial department.

The mind of the Church, as expressed in universal law, is that each court develop its own set of rules. This is seen both in direct references in the universal law to local laws and in presumptions of their presence.

The Roman tribunals have set an example and a high standard in the development of distinctive rules of court.

The granting of special powers, delegations and responsibilities to court officers can be accomplished and preserved most satisfactorily through a permanent constitution. By means of this lasting record not only are the needed powers made available but also doubts and hesitancies are removed and recourse to probable interpretations is eliminated. New offices and other progressive improvements arising from local customs and needs are made stable through constitutional law.

Practically every society and organization has its own by-laws and rules governing its *"modus operandi"* and its equipment lest its procedure becomes careless and slipshod and consequently inefficient. Few have more important purposes than the diocesan tribunal. Hence it is to be concluded that the local ecclesiastical court should be at least equally concerned about its orderly conducting of business and the background thereto.

Even though the centuries have developed rules of ecclesiastical judicial procedure to a wonderful perfection, nevertheless there remains a vast field for local legislation concerning it. Phases of it, for example, the preliminary reception of causes, of their nature are practically untouched by universal law and still other phases require distinct legislation because of peculiar conditions in individual countries.

Finally, the various informal processes, freed by the universal law of most procedural rules that they may be thereby better adapted to the conditions and circumstances of each territory, require direction according to these conditions and circumstances.

BIBLIOGRAPHY

Sources

Acta Apostolicae Sedis, Commentarium Officiale, Romae, 1909—.

Acta et Decreta Concilii Plenarii Baltimorensis Tertii, A.D. MDCCCLXXXIV, Baltimore: John Murphy, 1886.

Acta et Decreta Sacrorum Conciliorum Recentiorum, Collectio Lacensis, 7 vols., Friburgi Brisgoviae: Herder & Co., 1870-1890.

Acta et Decreta Concilii Provincialis Portlandensis in Oregon Quarti, Portland, Oregon, 1932.

Acta Sanctae Sedis, 41 vols., Romae, 1865-1908.

Benedicti XIV Bullarium, 3 vols. in 4, Prati, 1845-1847.

Canones et Decreta Sacrosancti Oecumenici Concilii Tridentini, Romae: Ex typis Polyglottis S.C. de Propaganda Fide, 1904.

Codex Iuris Canonici Pii X Pontificis Maximi iussu digestus Benedicti Papae XV auctoritate promulgatus, Praefatione, Fontium annotatione et Indice Analytico-Alphabetico ab Emo. Petro Card. Gasparri Auctus, Romae, Typis Polyglottis Vaticanis, 1917. Reimpressio, 1929.

Codicis Iuris Canonici Fontes cura Emi. Petri Card. Gasparri editi, 9 vols., Romae (Civitate Vaticana): Typis Polyglottis Vaticanis, 1923-1939. (Vols. VII-IX ed. cura et studio Emi. Justiniani Card. Seredi.)

Collectanae S. Congregationis de Propaganda Fide, 2 vols., Romae: Typographia Polyglotta S.C. de Propaganda Fide, 1907.

Concilii Plenarii Baltimorensis II., in Ecclesia Metropolitana Baltimorensi, a die VII ad diem XXI Octobris, A.D. MDCCCLXVI, et a Sede Apostolica Recogniti, Acta et Decreta, ed. altera, Baltimorae: Ioannes Murphy, 1894.

Corpus Iuris Canonici, 2. ed.; Lipsiensis (Friedberg), 2 vols., Lipsiae, 1879-1881.

Didascalia et Constitutiones Apostolorum, ed. Franciscus X. Funk, 2 vols., Paderborn, 1905.

Harduin, Jean, *Acta Conciliorum et Epistolae Decretales ac Constitutiones Summorum Pontificum,* 12 vols., Parisiis, 1715.

Instructio Austriaca Josephi Cardinalis Rauscher, 4 maii 1855— Analecta Iuris Pont., II (1857) 2546-2562.

Liber Synodalis Fargensis, Milwaukee: Bruce, 1941.

Mansi, J. D., *Sacrorum Conciliorum Nova et Amplissima Collectio,* 53 vols., in 59, Parisiis, 1901-1927.

S. Romanae Rotae Decisiones seu Sententiae quae ... prodierunt anno 1909-1941, 24 vols., Romae: Typis Vaticanis, 1912-1941.

Synodus Dioecesana Spokanensis Prima, Spokane, 1939.

Statuta Archidioecesis Sancti Francisci in Synodo Secunda, San Francisco, 1936.

Synodus Dioecesana Spokanensis Prima, Spokane, 1939.

Synodus Dioecesana Harrisburgensis Octava, Philadelphia: Dolphin Press, 1928.

Synodus Dioecesana Richmondiensis Tertia, Richmond, 1932.

Theodosiani Libri XVI cum Constitutionibus Sirmondianis, ediderunt Th. Mommsen et Paulus M. Meyer, adsumpto apparatu P. Krueger, 3 vols., Berolini, 1905.

Authors

Alford, C. B., *Jus Matrimoniale Comparatum,* New York: P. J. Kennedy & Sons, 1938.

Ayrinhac, H. A., *Administrative Legislation in the New Code of Canon Law, New Yorks Longsmans,* Green, 1930.

————————, *Constitution of the Church in the New Code of Canon Law,* New York: Longsmans, Green, 1930.

Ayrinhac, *Marriage Legislation in the New Code of Canon Law,* revised by P. J. Lydon, New York: Benziger, 1936.

————————, *Penal Legislation in the New Code of Canon Law,* revised by P. J. Lydon, New York: Benziger, 1936.

(Bachofen), Charles Augustine, *A Commentary on the New Code of Canon Law,* 8 vols., Vol. VII, *Ecclesiastical Trials,* 3 ed., 1930; Vol. VIII, *Penal Code,* 3. ed., 1931, St. Louis: Herber.

Bassibey, LAbbe R., *Le Mariage devant les Tribuneaux Ecclesiastiques,* Paris: Librairie Religieuse H. Oudin, 1899.

Beste, Udalricus, *Introductio in Codicem, Collegeville, Minn.*: St. John's Abbey Press, 1938.

Bouix, D., *Tractatus de Iudiciis Ecclesiasticis,* 2 vols., Parisiis, 1855.

Bouscaren, T. L., *The Canon Law Digest,* Milwaukee: Bruce Publishing Co., Vols. I-II, 1934 and 1943.

Canavan, Walter, *The Profession of Faith,* The Catholic University of America Canon Law Studies, n. 151, Washington, D.C.: The Catholic University of America Press, 1942.

Cappello, Felix, *Praxis Processualis,* Torino-Romae: Marietti, 1940.

Chelodi, Ioannes, *Ius Poenale,* 4. ed., recognita et aucta a Vigilio Dalpiaz, Tridenti: Ardesi, 1935.

Cicognani, Amleto, *Canon Law,* 2. ed., authorized English version by J. O'Hara and F. Brennan, Philadelphia: Dolphin Press, 1935.

Connelly, Thomas, *Appeals,* The Catholic University of America Canon Law Studies, n. 79, Washington, D.C.: The Catholic University of America, 1932.

Coronata, Matthaeus Conte a., *Institutiones Iuris Canonici,* 5 vols., Taurini: Marietti, Vols. I-II, 2. ed., 1939; Vols. III-IV-V, 1933-1935-1936.

D'Angelo, S., *La Curia Diocesana a Norma del Codice di Diritto Canonico,* Giarre (Sicilia): Casa Editrice D. Pietro Lisi, 1922.

Devoti, Ionnes, *Institutionum Canonicarum* Libri IV, 4. ed. Romana, Leodii, 1874.

Digest of the United States Supreme Court Reports, 11 Vols., Rochester, N. Y.: The Lawyers Co-operative Publishing Company, 1939; Vol. XI, *Court Rules.*

Dillon, Robert, *Common Law Marriages,* The Catholic University of America Canon Law Studies, n. 153, Washington, D. C.: The Catholic University of American Press, 1942.

Doheny, William, *Canonical Procedure in Matrimonial Cases,* Milwaukee: Bruce Publishing Co., 1938.

————————, *Practical Manual for Marriage Cases,* Milwaukee: Bruce Publishing Co., 1938.

Donovan, James, *The Pastor's Obligation in Pre-nuptial Investigation,* The Catholic University of America Canon Law Studies, n. 115, Washington, D. C.: The Catholic University of America, 1938.

Dugan, Henry, *The Judiciary Department of the Diocesan Curia,* The Catholic University of America Canon Law Studies, n. 26, Washington, D. C.: The Catholic University of America, 1925.

Feeney, Thomas, *Restitutio in Integrum,* The Catholic University of America Canon Law Studies, n. 129, Washington, D. C.: The Catholic University of America Press, 1941.

Fournier, Edouard, *Les Origines du Vicaire General,* Paris: Auguste Picard, 1922.

————————, *Le Vicaire General au Moyen-age,* Paris: Chez L'Auteur, 1923.

Fournier, Paul, *Les Officialites au Moyen-Age,* Paris, 1880.

Gasparri, Petrus, *Tractatus Canonicus de Matrimonio,* 3. ed., 2 vols., 1904.

Gregory, Donald, *The Pauline Privilege,* The Catholic University of America Canon Law Studies, n. 68, Washington, D. C.: The Catholic University of America, 1931.

Glynn, Joseph, *The Promoter of Justice,* The Catholic University of America Canon Law Studies, n. 101, Washington, D. C.: The Catholic University of America, 1936.

Hogan, James, *Judicial Advocates and Procurators,* The Catholic University of America Canon Law Studies, n. 133, Washington, D. C.: The Catholic University of America Press, 1941.

Hughes, James, *Witnesses in Criminal Trials of Clerics,* The Catholic University of America Canon Law Studies, n. 106, Washington, D. C.: The Catholic University of America, 1937.

Kay, Thomas, *Competence in Matrimonial Procedure,* The Catholic University of America Canon Law Studies, n. 53, Washington, D. C.: The Catholic University of America, 1929.

Kealy, John, *The Introductory Libellus in Church Court Procedure,* The Catholic University of America Canon Law Studies, n. 108, Washington, D.C.: The Catholic University of America, 1937.

Kennedy, Edwin, *The Special Matrimonial Process in Cases of Evident Nullity,* The Catholic University of America Canon Law Studies, n. 93, Washington, D. C.: The Catholic University of America, 1935.

Koeniger, Albert, *Katholisches Kirchenrecht,* Freiburg in Breisgau: Herder, 1926.

Krol, John, *The Defendant in Contentious Trials,* The Catholic University of America Canon Law Studies, n. 146, Washington, D. C.: The Catholic University of America Press, 1942.

Lega, M—Bartoccetti, V., *Commentarius in Iudicia Ecclesiastica iuxta Codicem Iuris Canonici,* 3 vols., Romae: Anonima Libraria Cattolica Italiana, 1938-1941.

Lemieux, Delisle, *The Sentence in Ecclesiastical Procedure,* The Catholic University of America Canon Law Studies, n. 87, Washington, D. C.: The Catholic University of America, 1934.

Marx, Adolph, *The Declaration of Nullity of Marriages Contracted Outside the Church,* The Catholic University of America Canon Law Studies, n. 182, Washington, D. C.: The Catholic University of America Press, 1943.

Moriarity, Eugene, *Oaths in Ecclesiastical Courts,* The Catholic University of America Canon Law Studies, n. 110, Washington, D. C.: The Catholic University of America, 1937.

Mothon, Joseph, *Institutions Canoniques,* 3 vols., Paris: Desclee de *Brouwer,* 1924; Vol. III, *Formulaire et Table Analytique.*

Muniz, T., *Procedimientos Ecclesiasticos,* 2. ed., 3 vols., Sevilla: Lib. de Sobrino de Izquierdo, 1926.

Motry, Hubert L., *Diocesan Faculties According to the Code of Canon Law,* The Catholic University of America Canon Law Studies, n. 16, Washington, D. C.: The Catholic University of America, 1922.

Louis, W. F., *Diocesan Archives,* The Catholic University of America Canon Law Studies, n. 137, Washington, D. C.: The Catholic University of America Press, 1941.

Noval, Ioseph, *Commentarium Codicis Iuris Canonici, Liber IV, De Processibus, Pars. I, De Iudiciis,* Augustae Taurinorum-Romae, 1920.

Official Catholic Directory, The, New York: P. J. Kennedy, 1822-1943; 1943 Edition.

Ottaviani, Alaphridus, *Institutiones Iuris Publici Ecclesiastici* 2. ed., 2 vols., Romae: Typis Polyglottis Vaticanis, 1935-1936.

Prince, John, *The Diocesan Chancellor,* The Catholic University of

America Canon Law Studies, n. 167, Washington, D.C.: The Catholic University of America Press, 1942.

Reiffenstuel, Anacletus, *Ius Canonicum Universum,* 4 vols., Venetiis, 1735.

Rice, Patrick, *Proof of Death in Pre-nuptial Investigation,* The Catholic University of America Canon Law Studies, n. 123, Washington, D. C.: The Catholic University of America Press, 1940.

Roberti, Franciscus, *De Processibus,* 2 vols., Romae: apud Aedes Facultatis Iuridicae ad S. Apollinaris, 1926.

Schmalzgrueber, Franciscus, *Ius Ecclesiasticum Universum,* 5 vols, in 12, Romae, 1843-1845.

Schmidt, John, *The Principles of Authentic Interpretation in Canon 17 of the Code of Canon Law,* The Catholic University of America Canon Law Studies, n. 141, Washington, D. C.: The Catholic University of America Press, 1941.

Smith, S. B., *Elements of Ecclesiastical Law,* 5. ed., 3 vols.; Vol. II, *Ecclesiastical Trials,* New York: Benziger Bros., 1892.

——————, *New Procedure in Criminal and Disciplinary Causes of Ecclesiastics in the United States,* 2 ed., New York, Benziger Bros., 1888.

Tobin, Thomas, *De Officiali Curiae Dioecesanae,* Romae: apud Aedes Pontificiae Universitatis Gregorianae, 1936.

Van Hove, A., *Commentarium Lavaniense in Codicem Iuris Canonici,* Vol. I, Tom. I, *Prolegomena,* Mechliniae: H. Dessain, 1928.

United States Code, The, 50 Titles, St. Paul, Minn.: West Publishing Co.

Vermeersch, A. —Creusen, J., *Epitome Iuris Canonici,* 3 vols., Mechliniae-Romae: H. Dessain, Vol. I, 6. ed., 1937; Vols. II-III, 5. ed., 1934-1936 .

Wanenmacher, F., *Canonical Evidence in Marriage Cases,* Philadelphia: Dolphin Press, 1935.

Wernz, Franciscus, *Ius Decretalium,* 2. ed., 6 vols., Romae: 1908-1913.

Wernz, F.—Vidal, P., *Ius Canonicum,* 7 tomes in 8 vols., Romae: apud Aedes Universitatis Gregorianae, Vol. VI, *De Processibus,* 1927.

Whalen, D., *The Value of Testimonial Evidence in Matrimonial Procedure,* The Catholic University of America Canon Law Studies, n. 99, Washington, D. C.: The Catholic University of America, 1935.

Willett, Robert, *The Probative Value of Documents in Ecclesiastical Trials,* The Catholic University of America Canon Law Studies, n. 171, Washington, D. C.: The Catholic University of America Press, 1942.

Woeber, Edward, *The Interpellations,* The Catholic University of America Canon Law Studies, n. 172, Washington, D. C.: The Catholic University of America Press, 1942.

Woywod, Stanislaus, *A Practical Commentary on the Code of Canon Law,* 6. ed., 2 vols., New York: Wagner, 1941.

Periodicals

Analecta Iuris Pontifici, Romae, 1855-1868; Parisiis, 1869-1891.
Apollinaris, Romae, 1928—.
Homiletic and Pastoral Review, The, New York, 1900—.
Jurist, The, Washington, D. C., 1941 —
Jus Pontificium, Romae, 1921 —

ABBREVIATIONS

AAS — *Acta Apostolicae Sedis.*

Fontes — *Codicis Iuris Canonici Fontes.*

Instructio a. 1936 — Instruction on procedure in matrimonial causes, S. C. de Sacr., 15 aug. 1936.

Instructio a. 1923 — Instruction on procedure in causes involving non-consummated marriages, S. C. de Sacr., 7 maii, 1923.

Instructio a. 1931 — Instruction on procedure in causes involving the sacrament and obligations of Holy Orders, S. C. de Sacr., 9 iun. 1923.

Normae a. 1934 — *Normae S. Romanae Rotae Tribunalis,* 22 iun. 1934.

P.C.I. — Pontificia Commissio Interpretationis.

S.C.C. — Sacra Congregatio Concilii.

S.C.S. — Sacra Congregatio de Disciplina Sacramentorum.

S.C. de Prop. Fide — Sacra Congregatio de Propaganda Fide.

ALPHABETICAL INDEX

(Numbers of index refer to paragraph numbers unless prefixed by the word "page")

A

Abatement, 15
Acceptance of causes, 130
  Cf. reception
Accusation, judicial, 283
Acta, sessionis,
  Cf. minutes
  causae, 151, 152
  processus, 151, 152, 183, 235
Actions, penal, 277, 281
Actor, cf. plaintiff, parties
Acts, cost of, 339
  and court of appeal, 272, 274
  definition, 148
  forwarded to judges, 256
  index of, 156
  pagination of, 157
  preserving essential facts, 64, 170, 246, 255
  of proof of death, 337
  publication of, 248
  removal of, 148
  reviewing of, 251, 247
  rules on preservation, 151, 152
  safeguarding appointments, 62
  supervision by judge, 53
  cf. documents, minutes, transcriptions
Actuarius,
  and citations, 145
  choice of, 72
  as bailiff, 77
  and appeal, 266
  and minutes, 150, 151
  special duties, 73
  and seal, 154
  signs acts, 154
  and transcriptions, 155
  recording answers, 185
  in criminal causes, 285
  in informal cases, 292, 295, 304, 316, 326, 328
  cf. notary
Addressing the court, 112
Advenae, 296
Adviser, clerical, 125-128
  judicial, 38, 46, 65-66, 258
Advocate, approval of, 42
  authorization, 117
  one with parties, 31
  qualifications, 118
  list of, 117, 131, 285
  choice of, 131
  recording appointments of, 117
  mandate of, 119, 142
  oath of, 121, 122
  duties of, 120
  and *libellus,* 132
  at sessions, 111, 121, 248
  right of objection, 146
  and sentence, 262-263
  in criminal causes, 285
  fees of, 123, 339, 349
Affidavit, 295, 306, 316
Album, cf. list, advocate, procurator
Alienation, of affection, 245, 293, 329
Animadversions,
  of the judge, 17, 53 H, 186, 208
  of auditor, 64, 186, 222, 224
  of defender, 68 G, 250, 251, 317, 326
Answers in court, 182
  recorded, 185
  edited, 185, 182
Apostates,
  as plaintiffs, 47, 116, 297
Apparitor,
  cf. bailiff
Appeal,
  need of rules for, 18
  against rejection of *libellus,* 167
  against sentence, 164-276
  court of, 264
  reasons for, 265, 267
  petition to court, 265
  reception of, 273
  procedure for, 273
  sentence of, 273
  record of, 266, 271, 274
  expense of, 273, 339, 346
  in cases of C 1990, 321
  in proof of death causes, 334
  cf. *libellus appellatorius*
Appointments,
  by vicar general, 30, 35, 67
  by *officialis,* 35, 38, 50 D, 67 72
  "per turnum", 15, 59
  in writing, 81
  record of, 71 C
  checking, 107

Appreciation, letters of, 198, 230
Archives, general, 93, 97
current, 98, 140
secret, 93, 94, 258, 280, 286
special secret, 95, 96, 280, 286
instruenda, 99, 139, 140
of chancery, 11
need of rules for, 18
care of, 74
indices for, 74, 94, 107
access to, 103
use of, 274
Archivist, 74
Articuli, 133, 168, 183
Attendance at sessions, 111, 121
Auditor, use of, 15, 22, 31, 63, 64
appointment, 38, 46, 63, 143
term of office, 63
oath of, 83, 223
and *libellus,* 163
and joinder of issue, 175
and examinations, 180, 181
and *articuli,* 183
animadversions of, 64, 186, 224, 222
and commissions, 63, 171, 218, 220, 223, 228, 232
and *officialis,* 38, 46
for criminal causes, 63
remuneration of, 348
Austrian Instruction, 3
Author of documents, 239

B

Bailiff, 38, 76, 83
Baptism, certificate of, 305
lack of, 324, 327
Bishop, relation of, to constitution, cf. Forward; also ¶¶ 10, 16, 23 (footnote 17), 25
as presiding judge, 47, 86
as moderator, 29
represented by court, 28
appointing officers, 34, 38, 60, 70, 80
appointing *turni,* 87
appointing advocates and procurators, 117
reservation of causes to, 116
name of, on sentence, 261
and expenses, 338, 339
and criminal causes, 277-286
power of, to punish, 277
and denunciations, 278
and Roman causes, 289
and informal cases, 294, 296, 302, 308, 309, 311, 323
Blanks, 106
Books, parochial, 240
of court, 105
Brief, of parties, 250, 252, 253

C

Calendar of court, 43, 286
Cases, informal, 291-337
of lack of form, 52, 116, 291, 307-310, 339
of Pauline Privilege, 52, 291, 322-331, 339
of proof of death, 52, 291, 332-337
of C. 1990, 52, 116, 291, 308-321, 339
of removal of pastors, 277
nature of, 294, 308, 310
expenses of, 338
Catholics, unworthy, as plaintiffs, 47, 116
in informal cases, 297
Causes, nature of, 26 (footnote 3)
criminal, 277-286
of Holy Office, 277
Roman, 287-290
ordination, 23, 289
non-consummation, 23, 204, 251, 276, 289
Pauline Privilege, 322, 339
proof of death, 334
reception of, 140, 124-139, 287, 288
recording of, 71 B, 286, 288
acceptance of, 130
review of, 256
index of, 156
expenses of, 339
preservation of, 92-101
Certificates, 28, 240, 305, 324, 327
Certitude in sentence, 260, 308
Chancellor, oath of, 83
as *actuarius,* 72
as archivist, 74, 97, 103
and documents, 239
and criminal causes, 278, 280, 285
and lack of form cases, 302
Chancery office, 282, 306
Character witnesses, 134, 222, 224, 229
Citation, of defender, 145
of promoter, 145
of plaintiff, 167
of respondent, 15, 17, 168-172, 235
of witness, 230, 235
of suspect, 282
by priest-messenger, 78, 168-171

by registered mail, 170
by newspaper, 170
in cases of C. 1990, 308, 315, 316
in Pauline Privilege cases, 328
record of delivery of, 169
Civil law documents, 241
Civil law trials reviewed, 153
Closing of court season, 107
College of S. R. Rota, 23, 31
Colloquialisms, 272
Commissions,
in Austrian Instruction, 3
uniform practise for, 19
definition of, 215
in general, 213, 237
of formal trials, 214
of informal cases, 214, 295
delegated, 216-226
use of, 217
personnel of, 218
oaths of, 219
instruction for, 221
rogatory, 216, 227-237
dispatching requests, 227, 229
authority of, 228, 229, 232, 233
composition of, 228, 232
reception of, 45, 227, 231
purpose of, 228, 229
instruction for, 230
return of, 235
care of, 53 I, 71 D
authorization of, 49, 63, 138, 220
authority of, 219
procedure for, 222, 234
mentioned in minutes, 150, 200
introduced at a session, 159, 200
record of, 71 D, 225, 229, 231, 339
to respondent, 171
expenses of, 226, 237, 340 B
notary as, 171
for informal cases, 295
Communion, certificate of, 305
Competence, 137, 165
of quasi-domicile, 68 B, 165
in informal cases, 296, 324
of court of second instance, 270
Conclusio in causa, 247-249
Conclusions, page 178
Confirmation, certificate of, 305
Constitutions of Tribunals of the Holy See, 5, 7
Constitution for diocesan courts,
necessity of, 8, 13-20
scope of, 9-11, 26
relation of, to bishop, 10, 16, 23 (footnote 12), 25, 28
relation of, to curia, 11
relation of, to clergy, 12, 25
sources of, 21-25
adoption of, 25, 27
Constitution, tentative, pages 143-177
Consultation, 18
record of, 99
set hours for, 22, 53, 107, 109, 125
during vacations, 107
pre-*libellus*, 125-139
Consulting officer,
rules for, 129-139, 243
set hours for, 109, 125
during vacation, 107
recording information, 153
and competence, 165
and Roman causes, 288
and informal cases, 292, 304
and expenses, 199
Contumacy, 171, 172, 173
Conversion, 324, 327
Copies,
of records, 240
of briefs, 253
in original language, 272
carbon, 155
cf. transcriptions
Correspondence of courts, 71 B
Costs, cf. expenses
Court of appeals, 268-272
constitution of, 269
address of, 264
procedure of, 273
Crimes, public, 277, 281
occult, 277
notorious, 279
certain, 277, 279
of persons of dignity, 277
of pastors, 277
outlawed, 277
condoned, 277
Criminal causes, 52, 60, 63, 148, 277-286
Crucifix, 110
Culpability of plaintiff, 165, 327
Curatores, cf. guardians
Cursor, cf. messenger
Customs, 14, 21-24, 180, 232, 287

D

Death, proof of, 332-337
Decision,
private, 128
in informal cases, 294, 302, 307, 308, 312, 320, 331, 335
cf. sentence
Declaration,

of freedom, 332
cf. decision
Decree, value of, 162
manner of, 162
mentioned in minutes, 150
fulfillment of, 228
Defective form cases, 301 (footnote 9)
Defender of the bond, 31, 67-68
appointment of, 67, 38, 80
number of, 67
relation to *turni*, 67
substitution for, 40, 67
oath of, 83, 223
special duties, 68
citation of, 145
and *libellus*, 163
and joinder of issue, 175, 176
and gratuitous patronage, 178
and *articuli*, 183
and questionnaires, 184, 189, 206, 230
and commissions, 218, 223, 228, 230, 232
and documents, 243
reviewing acts, 247, 251
and *conclusio*, 248
animadversions of, 251, 250, 317
and appeal, 266
and interpreter, 276
and informal cases, 317, 321, 326, 334
remuneration of, 348
Definition, of constitution, 6
of court, 26
Delegate, of commission, 218, 224, 228, 232
cf. auditor
Delegates, signature of, 299
Delegation of powers,
in constitution, 16, 22
to vicar general, 30
to *officialis*, 34-48, 60, 117, 231, 278, 281, 289, 302, 303, 323, 329, 330, 333
to auditor, 61
in criminal causes, 278, 281, 330
in Pauline Privilege cases, 323, 329
for interpellations, 325
in lack of form cases, 302, 303
in proof of death cases, 333
in cases of C. 1990, 311
for Roman causes, 289
Departure of party, 327
Deposit, for expenses, 135, 199, 346
Deposition, 235, 295, 316
formal and informal, 295
Diocesan paper, 170
Discussion, oral, 250-255
on sentence, 257-258
Dispensation, 10, 27
in cases of C. 1990, 319
in Pauline Privilege cases, 323, 329
Documents,
civil, 241, 242, 278
norms for execution of, 24, 239
information on, 135, 243
reception of, 142, 71 D, 244
ownership of, 142
restored to parties, 148
pagination of, 157
production of, 228, 244
comparison of, 232
of commissions, 235
session for,, 238-244
in acts, 244
of informal cases, 292, 316, 324, 332
absence of, 244
exemption of, 244
translation of, 272, 276
destruction of, 286
cf. letter
Docketing,
manner of, 140-143
of Roman causes, 288
of criminal causes, 286
of informal cases, 292
Domicile, 296
cf. competence

E

Edict, summons by, 170
Etiquette in court, 112
Evaluation of testimony, 3
Evidence, at preliminary inquiry, 127
gathered by commissions, 217
Examinations in court,
in general, 180-182
of parties, 189-190
of witnesses, 191-201
of experts, 202-212
by commissions, 217, 229
in informal cases, 295
Execution of sentence, 274
Exemption, from expenses, 347
of documents, 244
Expenses, 135, 178, 338-347
of witnesses, 198
of examinations, 212
of commissions, 226, 237
of court of appeal, 273, 274
cf. fees, taxes

Experts, 189 (footnote), 202-212, 228, 339, 191 (footnote)
Explanation of phrases, 272

F

Faculties, of commission, 219, 222
Fees,
of advocates and procurators, 123
of experts, 212
of commissions, 226
listing of, 178, 338
cf. taxes, expenses
File, 99, 235, 306
cf. archive
Filing, 97, 100, 139
Finances, report on, 114
cf. fees, taxes, expenses
Fines, 37, 120, 252
Formalities, nature of, 294
for cases of C. 1990, 308, 309, 313, 315, 316
Form of marriage, Catholic, 305
Format, cf. portfolio
Folder, cf. portfolio
Forms, 106
Formula of doubt, 175, 176
Freedom to marry, 321
Funeral, witness of, 332

G

Gospels, Book of, 105 I, 110
Guardians, 44

H

Hall of sessions, 18, 57, 110
for commissions, 232
for informal cases, 295
Hearing,
parties, 189-190, 316
witnesses, 191-201, 17
experts, 205-207
Heretics, as plaintiffs, 47, 116, 297
Holidays, 18, 107
Holydays, 108

I

Identification of parties, 135, 222, 324
Idioms, explanation of, 272
Illness, cf. sickness
Impediment in cases of C. 1990, 318
Inpotence, 204
Impression, cf. animadversions
Index,
of acts, 156
of commissions, 235, 236
Indications, 238, 246
Informationes parochi, 134, 178
Inquiry, pre-*libellus*, 127
Insanity, 204
Inspection, corporal, 204, 209, 210, 339
judicial, 228, 232
Instruction, of experts, 204
of commissions, 218, 219, 222, 234, 235
of proof of death cases, 336
Instruenda file, cf. archive
Instruments, 239
cf. documents
Interpellations, 323, 324, 325, 328
Interpreter, 276
Interpretation of laws, 27
Interrogatories, cf. questionnaires
Introduction for witnesses, 133, 192, 230
Investigator, 279-281
Inventory, 100, 101, 107

J

Joiner of issue, 172, 174-179
Judges, 31
honorary, 19, 59
appointment, 19, 62, 114
number, 22
power, 22
single, 51
term, 82
oath, 83
delegated, 38, 60, 285
designation to *turnus*, 39, 58, 59
substitution of, 40
duties, 88
and *vice-officialis*, 58
as auditors, 22, 61, 63
as advisors, 65
decision on *libellus*, 163
and joinder of issue, 175
and examinations, 180-185, 189
receiving oaths, 187
animadversions of, 17, 53 H, 186, 208
and commissions, 228
reviewing acts, 247, 251
and *conclusio*, 248
as notary, 257
and sentence, 257-260
and appeal, 265
and interpreter, 276

determining fees, 123, 178
in criminal causes, 279, 285
in cases of C. 1990, 308
remuneration of, 348
cf. presiding judge, *turnus*
Jurisdiction of court, 18
Jus accusandi, 115, 116, 137, 297
cf. parties

L

Lack of form cases, 52, 291, 301-307
Language, 57, 272, 276
Latin for minutes, 161
Law suits, civil, 245, 278, 282, 293
Letter,
of pastor, 134, 178
of introduction, 133, 192, 230
of appreciation, 198, 230
of courtesy, 236
of special value, 244
with *libellus appellatorius,* 268
Libel suits, 278, 245, 282, 293, 329
Libellus,
instruction on, 132
length of, 132
acceptance or rejection, 134
presentation, 140
reception of, 140, 142
sent to judges, 144
session for, 163-173
and cases of C. 1990, 313
decision on given to parties, 167
read at joinder of issue, 175
fee for, 338
Libellus Appellatorius, 265-270
Librarian, 75, 80, 81
Library, 11, 17, 75, 92
List, of fees, 338
cf. advocates and procurators
cf. witnesses

M

Mail, registered, 170, 225, 235, 272, 268
Mandates,
of vicar general, 30
of *officialis,* 4, 283, 284, 312
of officers, 143
of advocates and procurators, 119, 131, 142, 271, 272
of commissions, 219, 222
checking of, 53 C
Memoranda,
of non-judicial information, 153
of civil trials, 153
of former ecclesiastical trials, 153
in lack of form cases, 305, 306
in cases of C. 1990, 318, 319
in Pauline Privilege cases, 326,327
Messenger, 38, 50, 78, 83, 168-171, 349
Minors, 116
Minutes of sessions, 73, 149, 150, 151, 160, 161, 177, 222, 234, 235, 244, 257, 292, 326, 327
Moderator of the court, 29
delegated, 35-37
Modesty, rules of, 210
Moral persons, 42, 116
Non-Catholic, as plaintiff, 47, 116
in informal cases, 297, 314, 329, 330
Non-consummation causes, 204, 276, 289
Non-consummated marriages, 23, 251, 289
Notary, 31
appointment of, 38, 50, 72, 80
substitution of, 40
list of, 72
oath of, 83, 223
as secretary, 70-71
as messenger, 171
and documents, 239
and joinder of issue, 175
and commissions, 218, 228, 232
and copies of records, 240
and discussion, 255
and *conclusio,* 248
and sentence, 257
and appeal, 265, 271
and criminal causes, 278, 280
and informal cases, 292, 295, 304, 316, 326, 328
remuneration of, 349
cf. *actuarius*
Notary public, 278
Notification of officers, 144-145
of sentence, 262
of pastors concerning sentence, 275, 290, 300, 331
Number, protocol, 97, 99, 102, 140, 141, 142, 286, 288, 292

O

Oaths,
of office, 83
of secrecy, 83, 187
against modernism, 83
of truthfulness, 187
supplementary, 306
as proof of death, 335

of auditors, 63
of special officers, 91
of advocates and procurators, 121, 122
of experts, 207
of commissions, 219, 222, 223, 236
of interpreter, 276
of investigator, 279
reception of, 48, 107
recorded, 71 E, 83, 150
copies of, 105 H
form in court, 187
in informal cases, 295, 304, 306
unnecessary, 19
not at preliminary inquiry, 127
Officers,
oath of, 83
names sent to parties, 146
objections to, 168, 146
for joinder of issue, 174
for commissions, 231
for criminal causes, 285
for informal cases, 291, 333
Officialis
history of, 2
and delegated powers, 16, 23, 34-52, 4
office of, 23 (footnote 13)
as delegated moderator, 29
right of, to delegate, 30 (footnote 13)
appointment, 34 (footnote 17), 80, 83
precedence, 33
special duties, 53, 109
as presiding judge, 47
as single judge, 51, 334
and *turni*, 58, 87, 143
and substitutions, 89
appointing auditors, 63
appointing defender, 67
appointing advocates and procurators, 117, 118, 120, 131
appointing commissions, 231, 232
assisted by secretary, 71 A
and library, 75
and treasury, 76
receiving oaths, 91
and archives, 103, 95
consultations, 109
supervising acts, 149
and competence, 165
informed of appeal, 269
and notification of pastors, 275
and criminal causes, 278, 279, 281, 283, 284, 285
and Roman causes, 289
and informal cases, 299, 302, 311, 312, 316
and expenses, 226, 342, 343
cf. also judge and presiding judge
Offenses, public, 277, 281
occult, 277
Opening of court season, 17, 107
Ordinary,
and documents, 239
and copies of records, 240
and notification of pastors, 275
and criminal investigations, 281, 283
and Roman causes, 287
and lack of form cases, 303
and cases of C. 1990, 311, 312, 321
and Pauline Privilege cases, 323
and proof of death cases, 332, 335
and judicial expenses, 339
Ordination causes, 289
Orientals as plaintiffs, 116, 298

P

Pagination,
of acts, 152, 157
of transcriptions, 152
Parties,
right of, to stand in court, 115, 137, 270
non-Catholics as, 116, 314 139
pre-*libellus* consultation of, 125-
identification of, 135, 164
objection of, to officers, 146
and rejection of *libellus,* 167
culpability of, 166, 327
and joinder of issue, 175, 176
and *articuli,* 183
examination of, 189-190, 228
presenting witnesses, 133, 192, 230
and experts, 203
and commissions, 228
and documents, 243
and discussion, 254
at sessions, 111
and expenses, 346
names of, on portfolio, 102, 142
notified of sentence, 262, 263
and petition of appeal, 265, 266, 274
and sentence of appeal, 274
and cases of C. 1990, 314, 315, 320
cf. also petitioner, plaintiff
Pastors,
as advisers, 125
as conciliators, 129

as procurators, 138
letters of, 134, 178
and copies of records, 240
crimes of, 277
and informal cases, 303, 325, 331, 332, 333, 335
cf. priests
Pastors, assistant,
and parish records, 240
and lack of form cases, 303
Patronage, gratuitous, 69 B, 134, 136, 178
Pauline Privilege cases, 52, 291, 322-331
causes, 322
Penal actions, 277, 281
Penances, 37
Peregrini, 296
Per turnum appointment, 41, 59
Petition, cf. *libellus*
cf. *libellus appellatorius*
of appeal, 265, 268
in informal cases, 296, 297, 304, 313, 324, 325
Petitioner, cf. plaintiff, parties
in informal cases, 296, 305, 308, 314, 321, 325
Plaintiff, cf. parties
examined first, 190
and witnesses, 191
Ponens,
when appointed, 143
as auditor, 61
reviewing cause, 256, 259
as notary, 257
Portfolio, 73, 102, 142, 151, 152
for commissions, 235
Positiones, cf. *articuli*
Power of court, 28
Prayer at sessions, 112
Precedence, 33, 84
Precept,
punishment by, 277
as summons, 282
Preliminary care of causes, 12, 15, 124-147, 286
of cases, 292, 324
Pre-nuptial investigation, 17, 28, 68 C, 243, 332
Pre-ordination oath, 17, 68 C
Prescription, 277
Presiding judge, cf. *officialis,* judge
bishop as, 86
and citations, 145
and respondent, 172
and joinder of issue, 175, 176
and examinations, 181
issuing decrees, 162
supervising acts, 149, 150
words preserved, 150
and *conclusio,* 249
and discussion, 254
and expenses, 343
in criminal causes, 279, 285
Presumptions, 238, 246, 334
Priests,
as advisers, 125-128
as delegated judges, 285
as conciliators, 129
as messengers, 78, 168
as special procurators, 171
as delegates on commissions, 218, 232
and parish records, 240, 275, 290, 300, 307
cf. pastors
Procedure, administrative, 277, 291-337, 308, 334
Procurator,
office of, 31
approval of, 42, 117, 138
appointment of, 50, 131
qualifications of, 118
mandate of, 119, 142
list of, 117, 131
recording appointments of, 117
duties of, 120
oaths of, 121, 122
at sessions, 111, 121, 248
priest-messenger as, 171
and joinder of issue, 175
and articuli, 183
notified of sentence, 262-263
and appeal, 265-266, 270, 271
fees and expenses, 123, 344, 339, 349
special, 116
Profession of faith, 48, 83
Promotor of justice,
office of, 31
appointment of, 38, 80
substitution of, 40
number of, 69
special duties, 69
oath of, 83
at consultation, 138
citation of, 145
and culpability, 165
and questionnaires, 184
and witnesses, 191, 206
and gratuitous patronage, 178
and conclusio, 248
and appeal, 266
and criminal causes, 281, 283

remuneration of, 348
Promulgation, 25, 27
Proof of death cases, 52, 291, 332-337
Proofs, not in *libellus*, 132
Protection of court, 245, 278, 282, 293, 329
Protocol book, cf. record
Public offenses, 277, 281
Publication of acts, 248
of sentence, 259, 261, 262, 263
Punishments, 14, 15, 37, 120, 173, 277

Q

Quasi-domicile, 68 B
in informal cases, 296
Questionnaires,
rules for, 17, 19, 184
sources of, 133
supplemented, 181
presented in court, 184
for experts, 205, 206
of commissions, 221, 225, 230
for lack of form cases, 304
Questions,
by judge, 181, 183
ex officio, 19, 181, 229
presented by others in court, 182
nature of, 184
based on testimony, 189
by commissions, 222

R

Rebuke, 282
Rebuttal, 252
Reception of causes, 140, 286, 288
of cases, 292, 324
of commissions, 227, 231
Reconciliations of parties, 3, 53 D, 129, 134, 324
Record books,
need of, 18
and annual reports, 105, 113
register of the roster, 71 C, 81, 83, 85, 105 A
protocol book, 43, 71 D, 90, 105 B, 140, 225, 231, 274, 265, 269 286
ledger book, 76, 105 E
date book, 105 C
minute book, 105 D
source book, 105 F
communication book, 105 G
Record of causes, 100
of consultation, 137, 139
of reconciliation, 129, 153
of citations, 169, 170, 315
of commissions, 225, 229, 231
of documents, 244
of appeal, 266, 269, 271, 274
of sentence, 114
of Roman causes, 288
of criminal causes, 280, 286
of death, 332
of informal cases, 292, 294, 301, 305, 306
cf. acts
Records, copies of, 240
Recorder, 223
cf. notary, *actuarius*
Recourse, 334, 337
Reduction of expenses, 347
Registers, of baptism, 275, 290, 300, 305, 307, 331
of marriages, 275, 290, 300, 307
Rejection of causes, 130, 137
Religious, as plaintiffs, 116
Remuneration, of officers, 348, 349
Report, annual
to bishop, 10, 62, 71 G, 107, 114, 275
as safeguard of appointments, 62
to Holy See, 71 G, 113
Requests, 235
cf. commissions
Reservation of causes, 47 A, 116
Resignation of officers, 85
Residence, as basis of competence, 296, 319
Respondent,
citation of, 15, 17, 78, 168, 315, 172, 235
procurator of, 117
objections of, to officers, 168
list of witnesses of, 168
articuli of, 168
obligation of, 168, 171
and joinder of issue, 171, 175
contumacy of, 171, 172
examination of, 189-190
cf. parties
Return receipt of citation, 170
Revalidation, proof of, 305, 306, 319
Review of cause, 256, 259
Ritual, 105 H
Rogatories, cf. commission
Roman causes, 52, 287, 290
Roster, 31, 40, 46, 48, 50, 80

S

Scandal, presence of, 134, 283
Schedule,
  of fees, 123, 338
  for consultations, 22, 53, 107, 109, 125
  for sessions, 109
Scope, of constitution, 9
Seal, 18, 71 E, 104, 154, 239, 258
Secrecy,
  special, 121, 134
  of judges, 258
  of commissions, 221, 223
  of interpreter, 276
  for finances, 347
Secretary of court,
  appointment, 70, 80
  duties of, 71
  as archivist, 74, 103
  as notary, 72
  as librarian, 75
  as treasurer, 76
  and annual report, 114
  checking mandates, 119
  docketing causes, 140
  notifying officers, 144
  and citations, 145
  and *articuli*, 183
  and commissions, 231
  and appeals, 266, 269, 270, 273, 274
  notifying pastors of sentences, 275, 290, 300, 307
  remuneration of, 349
Sentence,
  session for, 256-263
  composition of, 259, 261
  solemn publication of, 259-263
  moral certitude of, 260
  of court of appeal, 273
  execution of, 274
  in cases of C. 1990, 308, 312, 320, 321
  cf. decision
Separation, legal, 245
Sequestration of witnesses, 196
Sickness, 30, 40, 89
Signature, by stamp, 154
Slang, 272
Societies, Canon Law, 17, 23
Solemnities,
  nature of, 294
  reason for non-observance, 32
  cf. formalities
Stamp, 104, 154, 155
  cf. seal
Stenographer, 11, 79
Substitutes, 89
Substitution,
  of officers, 16, 40, 89
  fraudulent, of parties, 209
Summons, 282
  cf. citation
Suspect, 282, 285
Suspension, *ex informata conscientia*, 277
Suspension of cause, 346
Suspicion, 16, 30, 40, 89, 281
Synodal laws, 4, 7, 12, 17, 24, 25, 62, 124

T

Tables for court, 110
Taxes,
  Need of legislation for, 14, 15, 22
  information on, 135
  recording of, 76
  reduction of, 136
  consideration of, 136
  cf. expenses, fees
Term of offices, 82
Testimonials, character, 222, 224, 229, 235
Testimony,
  private, 127, 200
  signed in court, 188
  communication of, to parties, 201
  in civil court, 211
  and commissions, 217
  and informal cases, 295
Time,
  need of rules for, 14, 18, 22
  for consultations, 53, 107, 125
  of reception of causes, 140
  to pursue cause, 167
  for rebuttal, 252
  before sentence, 256
  to prosecute appeal, 271
Transcriptions, of causes
  made by, 79
  use of, 152, 236
  number of, 152, 155
  pagination of, 152, 157
  attestation of, 155
  of briefs, 253
  forwarded to judges, 256
  for court of appeal, 272
  of criminal causes, 285
  cf. acts, minutes, documents
Translations, 272, 276, 339
Treasurer, 76
Turnus,
  nature of, 23 (footnote 13) 31, 59

need of rules for, 19
and vicar general, 30
and *officialis,* 35, 38-41, 46, 48, 58
and judges, 59
unusual, 57
rules of, 86-91
constitution of, 143
as commission, 232
for criminal causes, 285
cf. judges
Tutores, cf. guardians

V

Vacation,
for laws, 25
for court officers, 107
Vagi, 296
Vicar General, 30, 35, 87, 103, 281, 283, 302, 323, 333
Vice-chancellor,
as notary, 72
as archivist, 74, 97
as secretary, 70
oath of, 83
Vice-officialis,
appointment of, 30, 35, 80
and *officialis,* 36, 46, 57
and *turni,* 39, 57, 87, 143
as single judge, 50
use of, 54
powers of, 55, 56
and judges, 58
oath of, 83
Vota of judges,
nature of, 259
form of, 259
secrecy of, 258, 257
disposal of, 96, 258
Votum episcopi, 45

W

Witness stand, 110
Witnesses,
at preliminary inquiry, 127
list of, 133, 221, 230, 235
petition for use of, 133
articuli for, 133, 168, 183
character, 134, 222, 224, 229
not interfered with, 191
for respondent, 168
examination of, 191-201, 222, 228, 229
consent of secured, 192
order of examination, 193
non-appearance of, 194
exemption of, 194
exclusion of, 194
distinction between, 195
special qualities of, 195
sequestration of, 196
objections to, 197
reimbursement of, 198, 339
ex officio, 229
introduction for, 133, 192, 230
and documents, 243
in cases of C. 1990, 316
and proof of death, 332

BIOGRAPHICAL NOTE

William Edward Vaughan was born in Salt Lake City, Utah, on November 3, 1908. His early education was received in the public and parochial schools of Salt Lake City. In September, 1927, he entered St. Patrick's Seminary at Menlo Park, California. Ordained in the Cathedral of the Madeleine, Salt Lake City, on June 10, 1933, he was appointed assistant pastor of St. Joseph's Parish, Ogden, Utah. In October, 1935, he was made pastor of Our Lady of Lourdes Church, Magna, Utah, in which capacity he served for four years. In the fall of 1939, he was transferred to the College of St. Mary of the Wasatch, Salt Lake City, as chaplain and teacher of philosophy. From 1938 until 1941 he was editor of the Intermountain Catholic Edition of the Register. In September, 1941, he enrolled in the School of Canon Law at the Catholic University of America, where he received the Baccalaureate in Canon Law in May, 1942, and the Licentiate in Canon Law in May, 1943.

CANON LAW STUDIES *

1. FRERICKS, REV. CELESTINE A., C.PP.S., J.C.D., Religious Congregations in Their External Relations, 121 pp., 1916.
2. GALLIHER, REV. DANIEL M., O.P., J.C.D., Canonical Elections, 117 pp., 1917.
3. BORKOWSKI, REV. AURELIUS L., O.F.M., J.C.D., De Confraternitatibus Ecclesiasticis, 136 pp., 1918.
4. CASTILLO, REV. CAYO, J.C.D., Disertacion Historico-Canonica sobre la Potestad del Cabildo en Sede Vacante o Impedida del Vicario Capitular, 99 pp., 1919 (1918).
5. KUBELBECK, REV. WILLIAM J., S.T.B., J.C.D., The Sacred Penitentiaria and Its Relation to Faculties of Ordinaries and Priests, 129 pp., 1918.
6. PETROVITS, REV. JOSEPH, J.C., S.T.D., J.C.D., The New Church Law on Matrimony, X-461 pp., 1919.
7. HICKEY, REV. JOHN J., S.T.B., J.C.D., Irregularities and Simple Impediments in the New Code of Canon Law, 100 pp., 1920.
8. KLEKOTKA, REV. PETER J., S.T.B., J.C.D., Diocesan Consultors, 179 pp., 1920.
9. WANENMACHER, REV. FRANCIS, J.C.D., The Evidence in Ecclesiastical Procedure Affecting the Marriage Bond, 1920 (Printed 1935).
10. GOLDEN, REV. HENRY FRANCIS, J.C.D., Parochial Benefices in the New Code, IV-119 pp., 1921 (Printed 1925).
11. KOUDELKA, REV. CHARLES J., J.C.D., Pastors, Their Rights and Duties According to the New Code of Canon Law, 211 pp., 1921.
12. MELO, REV. ANTONIUS, O.F.M., J.C.D., De Exemptione Regularium, X-188 pp., 1921.
13. SCHAAF, REV. VALENTINE THEODORE, O.F.M., S.T.B., J.C.D., The Cloister, X-180 pp., 1921.
14. BURKE, REV. THOMAS JOSEPH, S.T.D., J.C.D., Competence in Ecclesiastical Tribunals, IV-117 pp., 1922.
15. LEECH, REV. GEORGE LEO, J.C.D., A Comparative Study of the Constitution "Apostolicae Sedis" and the "Codex Juris Canonici," 179 pp., 1922.
16. MOTRY, REV. HUBERT LOUIS, S.T.D., J.C.D., Diocesan Faculties According to the Code of Canon Law, II-167 pp., 1922.
17. MURPHY, REV. GEORGE LAWRENCE, J.C.D., Delinquencies and Penalties in the Administration and the Reception of the Sacraments, IV-121 pp., 1923.

* Below n. 100 only the following numbers are still available: Nn. 3, 4, 9, 25, 34, 57, and 75. Beginning with n. 100 only the following are available: Nn. 100-111 inclusive, and n. 113.

18. O'Reilly, Rev. John Anthony, S.T.B., J.C.D., Ecclesiastical Sepulture in the New Code of Canon Law, II-129 pp., 1923.
19. Michalicka, Rev. Wenceslas Cyrill, O.S.B., J.C.D., Judicial Procedure in Dismissal of Clerical Exempt Religious, 107 pp., 1923.
20. Dargin, Rev. Edward Vincent, S.T.B., J.C.D., Reserved Cases According to the Code of Canon Law, IV-103 pp., 1924.
21. Godfrey, Rev. John A., S.T.B., J.C.D., The Right of Patronage According to the Code of Canon Law, 153 pp., 1924.
22. Hagedorn, Rev. Francis Edward, J.C.D., General Legislation on Indulgences, II-154 pp., 1924.
23. King, Rev. James Ignatius, J.C.D., The Administration of the Sacraments to Dying Non-Catholics, V-141 pp., 1924.
24. Winslow, Rev. Francis Joseph, O.F.M., J.C.D., Vicars and Prefects Apostolic, IV-149 pp., 1924.
25. Correa, Rev. Jose Servelion, S.T.L., J.C.D., La Potestad Legislativa de la Iglesia Catolica, IV-127 pp., 1925.
26. Dugan, Rev. Henry Francis, A.M., J.C.D., The Judiciary Department of the Diocesan Curia, 87 pp., 1925.
27. Keller, Rev. Charles Frederick, S.T.B., J.C.D., Mass Stipends, 167 pp., 1925.
28. Paschange, Rev. John Linus, J.C.D., The Sacramentals According to the Code of Canon Law, 129 pp., 1925.
29. Piontek, Rev. Cyrillus, O.F.M., S.T.B., J.C.D., De Indulto Exclaustrationis necnon Saecularizationis, XIII-289 pp., 1925.
30. Kearney, Rev. Richard Joseph, S.T.B., J.C.D., Sponsors at Baptism According to the Code of Canon Law, IV-127 pp., 1925.
31. Bartlett, Rev. Chester Joseph, A.M., LL.B., J.C.D., The Tenure of Parochial Property in the United States of America, V-108 pp., 1926.
32. Kilker, Rev. Adrian Jerome, J.C.D., Extreme Unction, V-425 pp., 1926.
33. McCormick, Rev. Robert Emmett, J.C.D., Confessors of Religious, VIII-266 pp., 1926.
34. Miller, Rev. Newton Thomas, J.C.D., Founded Masses According to the Code of Canon Law, VII-93 pp., 1926.
35. Roelker, Rev. Edward G., S.T.D., J.C.D., Principles of Privilege According to the Code of Canon Law, XI-166 pp., 1926.
36. Bakalarczyk, Rev. Richardus, M.I.C., J.U.D., De Novitiatu, VIII-208 pp., 1927.
37. Pizzuti, Rev. Lawrence, O.F.M., J.U.L., De Parochis Religiosis, 1927. (Not Printed).
38. Bliley, Rev. Nicholas Martin, O.S.B., J.C.D., Altars According to the Code of Canon Law, XIX-132 pp., 1927.

39. BROWN, MR. BRENDAN FRANCIS, A.B., LL.M., J.U.D., The Canonical Juristic Personality with Special Reference to its Status in the United States of America, V-212 pp., 1927.
40. CAVANAUGH, REV. WILLIAM THOMAS, C.P., J.U.D., The Reservation of the Blessed Sacrament, VIII-101 pp., 1927.
41. DOHENY, REV. WILLIAM J., C.S.C., A.B., J.U.D., Church Property: Modes of Acquisition, X-118 pp., 1927.
42. FELDHAUS, REV. ALOYSIUS H., C.PP.S., J.C.D., Oratories, IX-141 pp., 1927.
43. KELLY, REV. JAMES PATRICK, A.B., J.C.D., The Jurisdiction of the Simple Confessor, X-208 pp., 1927.
44. NEUBERGER, REV. NICHOLAS J., J.C.D., Canon 6 or the Relation of the Codex Juris Canonici to the Preceding Legislation, V-95 pp., 1927.
45. O'KEEFE, REV. GERALD MICHAEL, J.C.D., Matrimonial Dispensations, Powers of Bishops, Priests, and Confessors, VIII-232 pp., 1927.
46. QUIGLEY, REV. JOSEPH A. M., A.B., J.C.D., Condemned Societies, 139 pp., 1927.
47. ZAPLOTNIK, REV. JOHANNES LEO, J.C.D., De Vicariis Foraneis, X-142 pp., 1927.
48. DUSKIE, REV. JOHN ALOYSIUS, A.B., J.C.D., The Canonical Status of the Orientals in the United States, VIII-196 pp., 1928.
49. HYLAND, REV. FRANCIS EDWARD, J.C.D., Excommunication, Its Nature, Historical Development and Effects, VIII-181 pp., 1928.
50. REINMAN, REV. GERALD JOSEPH, O.M.C., J.C.D., The Third Order Secular of Saint Francis, 201 pp., 1928.
51. SCHENK, REV. FRANCIS J., J.C.D., The Matrimonial Impediments of Mixed Religion and Disparity of Cult, XVI-318 pp., 1929.
52. COADY, REV. JOHN JOSEPH, S.T.D., J.U.D., A.M., The Appointment of Pastors, VIII-150 pp., 1929
53. KAY, REV. THOMAS HENRY, J.C.D., Competence in Matrimonial Procedure, VIII-164 pp., 1929.
54. TURNER, REV. SIDNEY JOSEPH, C.P., J.U.D., The Vow of Poverty, XLIX-217 pp., 1929.
55. KEARNEY, REV. RAYMOND A., A.B., S.T.D., J.C.D., The Principles of Delegation, VII-149 pp., 1929.
56. CONRAN, REV. EDWARD JAMES, A.B., J.C.D., The Interdict, V-163 pp., 1930.
57. O'NEILL, REV. WILLIAM H., J.C.D., Papal Rescripts of Favor, VII-218 pp., 1930.
58. BASTNAGEL, REV. CLEMENT VINCENT, J.U.D., The Appointment of Parochial Adjutants and Assistants, XV-257 pp., 1930.
59. FERRY, REV. WILLIAM A., A.B., J.C.D., Stole Fees, V-136 pp., 1930.
60. COSTELLO, REV. JOHN MICHAEL, A.B., J.C.D., Domicile and Quasi-Domicile, VII-201 pp., 1930.

61. Kremer, Rev. Michael Nicholas, A.B., S.T.B., J.C.D., Church Support in the United States, VI-136 pp., 1930.
62. Angulo, Rev. Luis, C.M., J.C.D., Legislation de la Iglesia sobre la Intencion en la application de la Santa Misa, VII-104 pp., 1931.
63. Frey, Rev. Wolfgang Norbert, O.S.B., A.B., J.C.D., The Act of Religious Profession, VIII-174 pp., 1931.
64. Roberts, Rev. James Brendan, A.B., J.C.D., The Banns of Marriage XIV-140 pp., 1931.
65. Ryder, Rev. Raymond Aloysius, A.B., J.C.D., Simony, IX-151 pp., 1931.
66. Campagna, Rev. Angelo, Ph.D., J.U.D., Il Vicario Generale del Vescovo, VII-205 pp., 1931.
67. Cox, Rev. Joseph Godfrey, A.B., J.C.D., The Administration of Seminaries, VI-124 pp., 1931.
68. Gregory, Rev. Donald J., J.U.D., The Pauline Privilege, XV-165 pp., 1931.
69. Donohue, Rev. John F., J.C.D., The Impediment of Crime, VII-110 pp., 1931.
70. Dooley, Rev. Eugene A., O.M.I., J.C.D., Church Law on Sacred Relics, IX-143 pp., 1931.
71. Orth, Rev. Clement Raymond, O.M.C., J.C.D., The Approbation of Religious Institutes, 171 pp., 1931.
72. Pernicone, Rev. Joseph M., A.B., J.C.D., The Ecclesiastical Prohibition of Books, XII-267 pp., 1932.
73. Clinton, Rev. Connell, A.B., J.C.D., The Paschal Precept, IX-108 pp., 1932.
74. Donnelly, Rev. Francis B., A.M., S.T.L., J.C.D., The Diocesan Synod, VIII-125 pp, 1932.
75. Torrente, Rev. Camilo, C.M.F., J.C.D., Las Processiones Sagradas, V-145 pp., 1932.
76. Murphy, Rev. Edwin J., C.PP.S., J.C.D., Suspension Ex Informata Conscientia, XI-122 pp., 1932.
77. MacKenzie, Rev. Eric F., A.M., S.T.L., J.C.D., The Delict of Heresy in its Commission, Penalization, Absolution, VII-124 pp., 1932.
78. Lyons, Rev. Avitus E., S.T.B., J.C.D., The Collegiate Tribunal of First Instance, XI-147 pp., 1932.
79. Connolly, Rev. Thomas A., J.C.D., Appeals, XI-195 pp., 1932.
80. Sangmeister, Rev. Joseph V., A.B., J.C.D., Force and Fear as Precluding Matrimonial Consent, V-211 pp., 1932.
81. Jaeger, Rev. Leo A., A.B., J.C.D., The Administration of Vacant and Quasi-Vacant Episcopal Sees in the United States, IX-229 pp., 1932.
82. Rimlinger, Rev. Herbert T., J.C.D., Error Invalidating Matrimonial Consent, VII-79 pp., 1932.

83. BARRETT, REV. JOHN D. M., S.S., J.C.D., A Comparative Study of the Third Plenary Council of Baltimore and the Code, IX-221 pp., 1932.
84. CARBERRY, REV. JOHN J., PH.D., S.T.B., J.C.D., The Juridical Form of Marriage, X-177 pp., 1934.
85. DOLAN, REV. JOHN L., A.B., J.C.D., The Defensor Vinculi, XII-157 pp., 1934.
86. HANNAN, REV. JEROME D., A.M., S.T.D., LL.B., J.C.D., The Canon Law of Wills, IX-517 pp., 1934.
87. LEMIEUX, REV. DELISE A., A.M., J.C.D., The Sentence in Ecclesiastical Procedure, IX-131 pp., 1934.
88. O'ROURKE, REV. JAMES J., A.B., J.C.D., Parish Registers, VII-109 pp., 1934.
89. TIMLIN, REV. BARTHOLOMEW, O.F.M., A.M., J.C.D., Conditional Matrimonial Consent, X-381 pp., 1934.
90. WAHL, REV. FRANCIS X., A.B., J.C.D., The Matrimonial Impediments of Consanguinity and Affinity, VI-125 pp., 1934.
91. WHITE, REV. ROBERT J., A.B., LL.B., S.T.B., J.C,D,, Canonical Ante-Nuptial Promises and the Civil Law, VI-152 pp.,, 1934.
92. HERRERA, REV. ANTONIO PARRA, O.C.D., J.C.D., Legislacion Eclesiastica sobra el Ayuno y la Abstinencia, XI-191 pp., 1935.
93. KENNEDY, REV. EDWIN J., J.C.D., The Special Matrimonial Process in Cases of Evident Nullity, X-165 pp., 1935.
94. MANNING, REV. JOHN J., A.B., J.C.D., Presumption of Law in Matrimonial Procedure, XI-111 pp., 1935.
95. MOEDER, REV. JOHN M., J.C.D., The Proper Bishop for Ordination and Dimissorial Letters, VII-135 pp., 1935.
96. O'MARA, REV. WILLIAM A., A.B., J.C.D., Canonical Causes for Matrimonial Dispensations, IX-155 pp., 1935.
97. REILLY, REV., PETER, J.C.D., Residence of Pastors, IX-81 pp., 1935.
98. SMITH, REV. MARINER T., O.P., S.T.Lr., J.C.D., The Penal Law for Religious, VIII-169 pp., 1935.
99. WHALEN, REV. DONALD W., A.M., J.C.D., The Value of Testimonial Evidence in Matrimonial Procedure, XIII-297 pp., 1935.
100. CLEARY, REV. JOSEPH F., J.C.D., Canonical Limitations on the Alienation of Church Property, VIII-141 pp., 1936.
101. GLYNN, REV. JOHN C., J.C.D., The Promoter of Justice, XX-337 pp., 1936.
102. BRENNAN, REV. JAMES H., S.S., M.A., S.T.B., J.C.D., The Simple Convalidation of Marriage, VI-135 pp., 1937.
103. BRUNINI, REV. JOSEPH BERNARD, J.C.D., The Clerical Obligations of Canons 139 and 142, X-121 pp., 137.
104. CONNOR, REV. MAURICE, A.B., J.C.D., The Administrative Removal of Pastors, VIII-159 pp., 1937.

105. Guilfoyle, Rev. Merlin Joseph, J.C.D., Custom, XI-144 pp., 1937.
106. Hughes, Rev. James Austin, A.B., A.M., J.C.D., Witnesses in Criminal Trials of Clerics, IX-140 pp., 1937.
107. Jansen, Rev. Raymond J., S.T.L., J.C.D., Canonical Provisions for Catechetical Instruction, VII-153 pp., 1937.
108. Kealy, Rev. John James, A.B., J.C.D., The Introductory Libellus in Church Court Procedure, XI-121 pp., 1937.
109. McManus, Rev. James Edward, C.SS.R., J.C.D., The Administration of Temporal Goods in Religious Institutes XVI-196 pp., 1937
110. Moriarty, Rev. Eugene James, J.C.D., Oaths in Ecclesiastical Courts, X-115 pp., 1937.
111. Rainer, Rev. Eligius George, C.SS.R., J.C.D., Suspension of Clerics, XVII-249 pp., 1937.
112. Reilly, Rev. Thomas F., C.SS.R., J.C.D., Visitation of Religious, VI-195 pp., 1938.
113. Moriarty, Rev. Francis E., C.SS.R., J.C.D., The Extraordinary Absolution from Censures, XV-334 pp., 1938.
114. Connolly, Rev. Nicholas P., J.C.D., The Canonical Erection of Parishes, X-132 pp., 1938.
115. Donovan, Rev. James Joseph, J.C.D., The Pastor's Obligation in Pre-nuptial Investigation, XII-322 pp., 1938.
116. Harrigan, Rev. Robert J., M.A., S.T.B., J.C.D., The Radical Sanation of Invalid Marriages, VIII-208 pp., 1938.
117. Boffa, Rev. Conrad Humbert, J.C.D., Canonical Provisions for Catholic Schools, VII-211 pp., 1939.
118. Parsons, Rev. Anscar John, O.M.Cap., J.C.D., Canonical Elections, XII-236 pp., 1939.
119. Reilly, Rev. Edward Michael, A.B., J.C.D., The General Norms of Dispensation, XII-156 pp., 1939.
120. Ryan, Rev. Gerald Aloysius, A.B., J.C.D., Principles of Episcopal Jurisdiction, XII-172 pp., 1939.
121. Burton, Rev. Francis James, C.S.C., A.B., J.C.D., A Commentary on Canon 1125, X-222 pp., 1940
122. Miaskiewicz, Rev. Francis Sigismund, J.C.D., Supplied Jurisdiction According to Canon 209, XII-340 pp., 1940.
123. Rice, Rev. Patrick William, A.B., J.C.D., Proof of Death in Pre-nuptial Investigation, VIII-156 pp., 1940.
124. Anglin, Rev. Thomas Francis, M.S., J.C.D., The Eucharistic Fast, VIII-183 pp., 1941.
125. Coleman, Rev. John Jerome, J.C.D., The Minister of Confirmation, VI-153 pp., 1941.
126. Downs, Rev. Joseph Emmanuel, A.B., J.C.D., The Concept of Clerical Immunity, XI-163 pp., 1941.

127. Esswein, Rev. Anthony Albert, J.C.D., Extrajudicial Penal Powers of Ecclesiastical Superiors, X-144 pp., 1941.
128. Farrell, Rev. Benjamin Francis, M.A., S.T.L., J.C.D., The Rights and Duties of the Local Ordinary Regarding Congregations of Women Religious of Pontifical Approval, V-195 pp., 1941.
129. Feeney, Rev. Thomas John, A.B., S.T.L., J.C.D., Restitutio in Integrum, VI-169 pp., 1941.
130. Findlay, Rev. Stephen William, O.S.B., A.B., J.C.D., Canonical Norms Governing the Deposition and Degradation of Clerics, XVII-279 pp., 1941.
131. Goodwine, Rev. John, A.B., S.T.L., J.C.D., The Right of the Church to Acquire Property, VIII-119 pp., 1941.
132. Heston, Rev. Edward Louis, C.S.C., Ph.D., S.T.D., J.C.D., The Alienation of Church Property in the United States, XII-222 pp., 1941.
133. Hogan, Rev. James John, A.B., S.T.L., J.C.D., Judicial Advocates and Procurators, XIII-200 pp., 1941.
134. Kealy, Rev. Thomas M., A.B., Litt.B., J.C.D., Dowry of Women Religious, IX-152 pp., 1941.
135. Keene, Rev. Michael James, O.S.B., J.C.D., Religious Ordinaries and Canon 198, V-164 pp., 1942.
136. Kerin, Rev. Charles A., S.S., M.A., S.T.B., J.C.D., The Privation of Christian Burial, XVI-279 pp., 1941.
137. Louis, Rev. William Francis, M.A., J.C.D., Diocesan Archives, X-101 pp., 1941.
138. McDevitt, Rev. Gilbert Joseph, A.B., J.C.D., Legitimacy and Legitimation, X-247 pp., 1941.
139. McDonough, Rev. Thomas Joseph, A.B., J.C.D., Apostolic Administrators, X-217 pp., 1941.
140. Meier, Rev. Carl Anthony, A.B., J.C.D., Penal Administrative Procedure Against Negligent Pastors, XI-240 pp., 1941.
141. Schmidt, Rev. John Rogg, A.B., J.C.D., The Principles of Authentic Interpretation in Canon 17 of the Code of Canon Law, XII-331 pp., 1941.
142. Slafkosky, Rev. Andrew Leonard, A.B., J.C.D., The Canonical Episcopal Visitation of the Diocese, X-197 pp., 1941.
143. Swoboda, Rev. Innocent Robert, O.F.M., J.C.D., Ignorance in Relation to the Imputability of Delects, IX-271 pp., 1941.
144. Dube, Rev. Arthur Joseph, A.B., J.C.D., The General Principles for the Reckoning of Time in Canon Law, VIII-299 pp., 1941.
145. McBride, Rev. James T., A.B., J.C.D., Incardination and Excardination of Seculars, XX-585 ppp., 1941.
146. Krol, Rev. John T., J.C.D., The Defendant in Ecclesiastical Trials, XII-207 pp., 1942.

147. COMYNS, REV. JOSEPH J., C.SS.R., A.B., J.C.D., Papal and Episcopal Administration of Church Propeprty, XIV-155 pp., 1942.
148. BARRY, REV. GARRETT FRANCIS, O.M.I., J.C.D., Violation of the Cloister, XII-260 pp., 1942.
149. BOLDUC, REV. GATIEN, C.S.V., A.B., S.T.L., J.C.D., Les Etudes dans les Religions Clericales, VIII-155 pp., 1942.
150. BOYLE, REV. DAVID JOHN, M.A., J.C.D., The Juridic Effects of Moral Certitude on Pre-Nuptial Guarantees, XII-188 pp., 1942.
151. CANAVAN, REV. WALTER JOSEPH, M.A., Litt.D., J.C.D., The Profession of Faith, XII-143 pp., 1942.
152. DESROCHERS, REV. BRUNO, A.B., PH.L., S.T.B., J.C.D., Le Premier Concile Plenier de Quebec et le Code de Droit Canonique, XIV-186 pp., 1942.
153. DILLON, REV. ROBERT EDWARD, A.B., J.C.D., Common Law Marriage, X-148 pp., 1942.
154. DOWELL, REV. EDWARD JOHN, PH.D., S.T.B., J.C.D., The Time and Place for the Celebration of Marriage, X-156 pp., 1942.
155. DONNELLAN, REV. THOMAS ANDREW, A.B., J.C.D., The Obligation of the Missa pro Populo, VII-131 pp., 1942.
156. ELTZ, REV. LOUIS ANTHONY, A.B., J.C.L., Cooperation in Crime.
157. GASS, REV. SYLVESTER FRANCIS, M.A., J.C.D., Ecclesiastical Pensions, XI-206 pp., 1942.
158. GUINIVEN, REV. JOHN JOSEPH, C.SS.R., J.C.D., The Precept of Hearing Mass, XIV-188 pp., 1942.
159. GULCZYNSKI, REV. JOHN THEOPHILUS, J.C.D., The Desecration and Violation of Churches, X-126 pp., 1942.
160. HAMMILL, REV. JOHN LEO, M.A., J.C.D., The Obligations of the Traveler According to Canon 14, VIII-204 pp., 1942.
161. HAYDT, REV. JOHN JOSEPH, A.B., J.C.D., Reserved Benefices, XI-148 pp,. 1942.
162. HUSER, REV. ROGER JOHN, O.F.M., A.B., J.C.D., The Crime of Abortion in Canon Law, XII-187 pp., 1942.
163. KEARNEY, REV. FRANCIS PATRICK, A.B., S.T.L., J.C.L., The Principles of Canon 1127.
164. LINAHEN, REV. LEO JAMES, S.T.L., J.C.D., De Absolutione Complicis In Peccato Turpi, 114 pp., 1942.
165. MCCLOSKEY, REV. JOSEPH ALOYSIUS, A.B., J.C.D., The Subject of Ecclesiastical Law According to Canon 12, XVII-246 pp., 1942.
166. O'NEILL, REV. FRANCIS JOSEPH, C.SS.R., J.C.D., The Dismissal of Religious in Temporary Vows, XIII-220 pp., 1942.
167. PRINCE, REV. JOHN EDWARD, A.B., S.T.B., J.C.D., The Diocesan Chancellor, X-136 pp., 1942.
168. RIESNER, REV. ALBERT JOSEPH, C.SS.R., J.C.D., Apostates and Fugitives from Religious Institutes, IX-168 pp., 1942.

169. Stenger, Rev. Joseph Bernard, J.C.D., The Mortgaging of Church Property, 186 pp., 1942.
170. Waldron, Rev. Joseph Francis, A.B., J.C.D., The Minister of Baptism, XII-197 pp., 1942.
171. Willett, Rev. Robert Albert, J.C.D., The Probative Value of Documents in Ecclesiastical Trials, X-124 pp., 1942.
172. Woeber, Rev. Edward Martin, M.A., J.C.D., The Interpellations, XII-161 pp., 1942.
173. Benko, Rev. Matthew Aloysius, O.S.B., M.A., J.C.L., The Abbot *Nullius.*
174. Christ, Rev. Joseph James, M.A., S.T.L., J.C.L., Dispensation from Vindicative Penalties.
175. Clancy, Rev. Patrick M. J., O.P., A.B., S.T.Lr., J.C.D. The Local Religious Superior, X-229 pp., 1943.
176. Clarke, Rev. Thomas James, J.C.D., Parish Societies, XII-147 pp., 1943.
177. Connolly, Rev. John Patrick, S.T.L., J.C.D., Synodal Examiners and Parish Priest Consultors, X-223 pp., 1943.
178. Drumm, Rev. William Martin, A.B., J.C.L., Hospital Chaplains.
179. Flanagan, Rev. Bernard Joseph, A.B., S.T.L., J.C.D., The Canonical Erection of Religious Houses, X-147 pp., 1943.
180. Kelleher, Rev. Stephen Joseph, A.B., S.T.B., J.C.D., Discussions with non-Catholics: Canonical Legislation, X-93 pp., 1943.
181. Lewis, Rev. Gordian, C.P., J.C.D., Chapters in Religious Institutes, XII-169 pp., 1943.
182. Marx, Rev. Adolph, J.C.D., The Declaration of Nullity of Marriages Contracted Outside the Church, X-151 pp., 1943.
183. Matulenas, Rev. Raymond Anthony, O.S.B., A.B., J.C.L., Communication, a Source of Privileges.
184. O'Leary, Rev. Charles Gerard, C.SS.R., Religious Dismissed After Perpetual Profession.
185. Power, Rev. Cornelius Michael, J.C.L., The Blessing of Cemeteries.
186. Shuhler, Rev. Ralph Vincent, O.S.A., J.C.D., Privileges of Regulars to Absolve and Dispense, XII-195 pp., 1943.
187. Ziolkowski, Rev. Thaddeus Stanislaus, A.B., J.C.D., The Consecration and Blessing of Churches, XII-151 pp., 1943.
188. Henneghen, Rev. John Joseph, S.T.D., J.C.L., The Marriages of Unworthy Catholics: Canons 1065 and 1066.
189. Carroll, Rev. Coleman Francis, M.A., S.T.L., J.C.L., Charitable Institutions.
190. Ciesluk, Rev. Joseph Edward, Ph.D., S.T.L., J.C.L., National Parishes in the United States.
191. Coburn, Rev. Vincent Paul, A.B., J.C.L., Marriages of Conscience.

192. Connors, Rev. Charles Paul, C.S.Sp., A.B., J.C.L., Extra-Judicial Procurators in the Code of Canon Law.
193. Coyle, Rev. Paul Raymond, A.B., J.C.L., Judicial Exceptions.
194. Fair, Rev. Bartholomew Francis, A.B., S.T.L., J.C.L., The Impediment of Abduction.
195. Gallagher, Rev. Thomas Raphael, O.P., A.B., S.T.Lr., J.C.L., The Examination of the Qualities of the Ordinand.
196. Gannon, Rev. John Mark, S.T.L., J.C.L., The Interstices Required for the Promotion to Orders.
197. Goldsmith, Rev. J. William, B.C.S., S.T.L., J.C.L., The Competence of Church and State over Marriages — Disputed Points.
198. Goodwine, Rev. Joseph Gerard, A.B., S.T.B., J.C.L., The Reception of Converts.
199. Kowalski, Rev. Romuald Eugene, O.F.M., A.B., J.C.L., Sustenance of Religious Houses of Regulars.
200. McCoy, Rev. Alan Edward, O.F.M., J.C.L., Force and Fear in Relation to Delictual Imputability and Penal Responsibility.
201. McDevitt, Rev. Vincent John, Ph.D., S.T.L., J.C.L., Perjury.
202. Martin, Rev. Thomas Owen, Ph.D., S.T.D., J.C.L., Adverse Possession, Prescription and Limitation of Actions: The Canonical "Praescriptio."
203. Miklosovic, Rev. Paul John, A.B., J.C.L., Attempted Marriages and their Consequent Juridic Effects.
204. Mundy, Rev. Thomas Maurice, A.B., S.T.L., J.C.L., The Union of Parishes.
205. O'Dea, Rev. John Coyle, A.B., J.C.L., The Matrimonial Impediment of Nonage.
206. Olalia, Rev. Alexander Ayson, S.T.L., J.C.L., A Comparative Study of the Christian Constitution of States and the Constitution of the Philippine Commonwealth.
207. Poisson, Rev. Pierre-Marie, C.S.C., A.B., Ph.L., Th.L., J.C.L., Droits Patrimoniaux des Maisons et des Eglises Religieuses.
208. Stadalnikas, Rev. Casimir Joseph, M.I.C., J.C.L., Reservation of Censures.
209. Sullivan, Rev. Eugene Henry, S.T.L., J.C.L., Proof of the Reception of the Sacraments.
210. Vaughan, Rev. William Edward, J.C.L., Constitutions for Diocesan Courts.
211. Lyons, Rev. Joseph Henry, J.C.L., The Joinder of Issue in Canonical Trials.

www.ingramcontent.com/pod-product-compliance
Lightning Source LLC
LaVergne TN
LVHW050242080826
844660LV00012B/578